Stephen F. Kelly was educated at Ruskin College, Oxford, and the London School of Economics, and he was for many years a political correspondent with *Tribune*. In 1978, he joined Granada Television, working on programmes such as *World in Action* and *What the Papers Say*. Now a freelance writer and television producer, he devotes most of his time to writing about football and labour history. He is a regular contributor to many newspapers and magazines, and is also Fellow in Media at the University of Huddersfield.

The author of highly acclaimed biographies of Kenny Dalglish, Graeme Souness and Bill Shankly, as well as *Back Page United*, he lives in Manchester with his wife and two children.

Also by Stephen F. Kelly

Idle Hands, Clenched Fists
The Official Illustrated History of Liverpool FC
Forever Everton
Back Page Football
Back Page United
Victorian Lakeland Photographers
A Game of Two Halves
Liverpool in Europe
The Kop
Graeme Souness: A Soccer Revolutionary
Not Just a Game
The Pick of the Season
Bill Shankly: It's Much More Important Than That
Dalglish

Fergie

*The Biography of
Alex Ferguson*

Stephen F. Kelly

HEADLINE

First published in 1997
by HEADLINE BOOK PUBLISHING

First published in paperback in 1998
by HEADLINE BOOK PUBLISHING

10 9 8 7 6 5 4 3 2

ISBN 0 7472 5632 2

Typeset by Avon Dataset Ltd, Bidford-on-Avon, Warks

Printed in England by
Mackays of Chatham plc, Chatham, Kent

HEADLINE BOOK PUBLISHING
A division of Hodder Headline PLC
338 Euston Road
London NW1 3BH

For Judith, Nicholas
and Emma,

as ever

Contents

Acknowledgements

It goes almost without saying that this book could never have been compiled without the kind assistance and good patience of many people, but there are some who deserve a special mention for the help which they have given me and to whom I owe an especial gratitude.

These include Queen's Park Football Club, Bob Crampsey, Jimmy Reid, John Byrne, St Mirren Football Club, Renfrew District Libraries, Manchester Central Library, Manchester Chorlton Library, the University of Huddersfield, Ayr United Football Club, St Johnstone Football Club, Dunfermline Football Club, Keith Bradley MP, Graham Hobbs, Malcolm Mackay, Bill Campbell and Judy Diamond of Mainstream, the Amalgamated Engineering Union, Cliff Butler, Denis Mooney, Sandy Ross, Ian Williamson, Leon Swerling, Duncan Simpson, Willie Cunningham, Duncan Carmichael, John Murphy, Callum Mackay, Gus Macdonald, Stewart Duff, Alastair Blair, Bobby Brown, Doug Newlands, the Professional Footballers' Association, Tony Higgins and the Scottish Professional Footballers' Association, the Scottish Football Association, Wilf McGuinness, Falkirk Football Club, the *Manchester Evening News*, Rangers Football Club, Ray Spiller and the Association of Football Statisticians, Brian Labone, East Stirlingshire Football Club, *Goal* magazine,

Queen of the South Football Club, Drew Herbertson, David Thomson and the Scottish Football League, Manchester United Football Club, Industrial Tribunals Office, Glasgow, Aberdeen Football Club, Andrew Thomas, Robert McElroy, Michael White, Alex Totten, Willie Todd, Stan Park, Bob Greaves and finally the *Paisley Express*.

Unfortunately Alex Ferguson chose, as is his right, not to co-operate in the writing of this book. Although this presented some difficulties there were, nevertheless, many who agreed to talk to me on the basis that they remained anonymous. These were principally people currently involved with Manchester United Football Club. I fully understand their reasons for not wishing to have their names disclosed but would at least like to place my gratitude on record.

An especial thanks is also due to Tim Bamford, Clive Leatherdale and Cliff Butler who all read the manuscript in order to try and iron out any errors. Needless to say, any mistakes, and undoubtedly there will be some, which remain in this book are mine and mine alone.

As ever I am indebted to Ian Marshall at Headline for whom I hope this project has been a labour of love, my editor at Headline, Lindsay Symons, and my copy-editor, Sarah MacLeod. My appreciation is also due to my agent John Pawsey who remains as supportive as ever.

Finally, my deepest thanks to my family, to my mother Mary Kelly for her long-suffering support over the years and periodic bouts of baby-sitting, and to my parents-in-law Tony and Marjorie Rowe Jones, equally for their child-minding assistance and newspaper cuttings. But especially my appreciation must go to my wife Judith Jones, and to Nicholas, already a diehard United supporter, and Emma, a United supporter in the making. Without their support this book could never have been completed.

Stephen F. Kelly
Manchester, June 1997

CHAPTER ONE

'Fergie Out!'

As Alex Ferguson jumped into his car and sped away from Old Trafford into the dimness of the night he might have wondered if his days as manager of Manchester United were numbered. Saturday 9 December 1989 was turning into a nightmare, a day he would want to forget. It had rained most of the day, a typical dirty Manchester day. The weather matched his mood. That afternoon had marked the lowest point in his managerial career at Old Trafford. It was the moment he peered down the barrel of a gun with any number of people ready to pull the trigger. It was a silent drive home down the Chester Road through the busy evening traffic. The windscreen wipers flapped incessantly as the rain continued to pour out of the Manchester skies. His son Darren sat beside him, equally numbed by what had happened.

Earlier in the week United had lost at Arsenal in what was the beginning of their winter slump. They could almost rationalise that result. At least Arsenal were the reigning champions. But worse had now followed. That afternoon they had faced Crystal Palace at home. One point off bottom spot, Palace had been thrashed 9–0 at Anfield a few weeks earlier. On paper it had looked a comparatively easy fixture, but United had lost 2–1. What's more, Ferguson had added to everyone's misery by taking the deeply unpopular decision to leave Mark Hughes out of the line-up and put him on the bench. It had not gone down well, particularly on the terraces, where the ever-popular Sparky could do little wrong. In the end Ferguson had been forced to eat humble pie and respond to the crowd's demands by bringing Hughes on. It made little difference. United crashed to their seventh defeat of the season, bringing them down into the lower half of the table. That match more than any other symbolised their malaise. Any dreams of the championship were fast disappearing over the horizon – and the knives were being sharpened for Ferguson.

That evening as he drove home through the gloomily lit streets, immersed in a sea of worries, further trouble was about to be heaped on his shoulders. The draw for the third round of the FA Cup was about to be made. United had already been knocked out of the League Cup back in October, beaten 3–0 by Tottenham at Old Trafford; a result that seemed to sum up everything that was wrong at the time. With United's prospects in the league now disappearing well out of sight, the FA Cup was all they had to play for. Ferguson crossed his fingers as he switched on the television. What United needed more than anything was a comfortable home draw, preferably a third or fourth division side – a nice gentle game to give them time to sort themselves out and instil a little confidence in everyone. But as the balls were plucked out of the bag Ferguson started in horror. Not only were United drawn away, they were up against Brian Clough's Nottingham Forest, one of the best cup-fighting teams in the country. Only Liverpool at Anfield could have been more daunting. It could not have come at a worse moment. 'Pass me the rope,' was the way he later described it. He began to wonder if he was really cursed. Could things get any worse? The answer was yes.

The manager expected no favours from the press the following morning, nor did he get any. The back pages were already beginning to speculate wildly about his future at Old Trafford. He could cope with that, but more importantly his decision to drop Hughes had lost him vital support among the fans. That *did* concern him. He believed in the fans – they were his lifeline. If he lost their support he was finished. That week he even sought out Matt Busby for some advice. 'Don't read the paper,' suggested the United godfather. It was good advice (Prime Minister Clem Attlee would have approved), but Busby probably omitted to tell him not to read the local fanzine.

'Fergie Out!' raged *Red Issue* as it tore viciously into the manager. 'Three years into the reign of Alex Ferguson, it is patently obvious that United are certainly in no better condition than the day he took over . . . in many respects it could be said that we are in much poorer shape.'

Apart from a couple of wins over Liverpool, it went on, it had been 'a grim period' in United's history. 'We have spent more money than any club in the history of British football and yet we have little apart from an expensive collection of misfits to show for it.' Ferguson must have cringed when he read that.

One fan, Ian Williamson, remembered the Palace match vividly, though not just because it was his first-ever visit to Old Trafford. 'We were all coming through the tunnel at the back of the South stand after the game. It's one of those favourite spots where people like to chant because of the echoing sound. Suddenly this chant started up, "Fergie, Fergie, Fergie. Out, Out, Out!" My first-ever visit to United and here were their fans calling for the manager's head. It was astonishing, all these United supporters denigrating their manager.'

A week later in the *United Review* Ferguson openly admitted that he had been deeply hurt by the fans' response. 'I have got to say,' he wrote, 'that the reaction of the crowd was the worst experience of that nature of my career.' He tried to explain the reasoning behind his decision to leave

Hughes on the bench: 'It was not a snub to the player, but something which had to be done,' adding that it in no way meant that Hughes was being discarded. But it didn't stop the 'Fergie Out' banners from appearing on the terraces.

It was to be a difficult couple of weeks. Ferguson was convinced that he was working along the right lines. He had embarked on a complete overhaul of the club from youth level to senior level. New players had been drafted in and the management team was being steadily rebuilt. His team selection, training and preparation were all good. There was no problem with motivation, and his handling of the press was okay. And yet United had gone eight matches without a win. Ferguson was so depressed he had even stopped going out at night. Brian Kidd and Archie Knox tried – and failed – to persuade him to go out and have a bit of fun. 'I was doing a bit of trench-digging,' was the way he later described it.

Yet Ferguson had spent the close season making some brave decisions. 'The midfield cracked up last season,' he admitted in the *United Review*, 'and it was necessary to do something drastic.' By the summer break his patience had also run out with Paul McGrath. He could no longer tolerate McGrath's drinking, which he believed was having a bad effect on others in the squad. Now the stories had started to appear in the tabloids, and Ferguson decided to call it a day. In August McGrath was sold to Aston Villa for £450,000. Ferguson knew that they might miss his combative presence on the field (though injuries had restricted his appearances) but his absence in the dressing room could only be beneficial. It would break up the drinking clique and serve as an example to others.

It was the same with Norman Whiteside, McGrath's main drinking partner. His persistence would be missed, but injuries had taken their toll – Whiteside had made only six appearances that season. The United manager felt that he could no longer rely on him, even on the field, and

Whiteside was offloaded to Everton for £750,000. But the decision to sell McGrath and Whiteside was something else that had not gone down well with the Old Trafford faithful, and there were rumblings in the local press and fanzines.

Ferguson tried to appease the fans by dipping into the transfer market to make a number of important signings. They were badly needed recruits. One man he had been eyeing up for some time was the Middlesbrough defender Gary Pallister. But with little enthusiasm from his scouting staff, Ferguson hesitated, then turned his attentions elsewhere, in particular to Glenn Hysen, the stylish Swedish central defender.

Hysen was out of contract at his Italian club Fiorentina, and United quickly agreed a fee and brought the 30-year-old over to look around Old Trafford. It all seemed tied up – until Fiorentina began to up the fee from £300,000 to £500,000 and Liverpool began to get a sniff of what was going on. Ferguson and chairman Martin Edwards flew to Italy convinced that they had a deal with the club only to bump into a delegation from Liverpool. Ferguson quickly realised that an auction was about to take place even though they had already shaken on a deal. The fee had now risen to £600,000 with Hysen's personal terms also increasing. Ferguson was furious but was not prepared to go any higher. At 30 years old, Hysen was at his peak. No manager would get more than a couple of seasons out of him at best. United pulled out of the deal, only to discover that Hysen had in fact already signed for Liverpool.

Like any manager, Ferguson also found other possibilities falling by the wayside. Trevor Steven, the England and Everton full back, came to look over Old Trafford but showed little interest in joining the club. Ferguson did not want that kind of player; he was only interested in those who were genuinely committed to playing for United. Instead Steven went to Rangers for a huge fee.

With Hysen lost to Liverpool and Steven to Rangers,

Ferguson was forced to readjust his sights. A few weeks into the new season he went back to the idea of Gary Pallister. Eventually he decided to take the gamble, although in doing so he was forced to stump up considerably more than Hysen would have cost, paying Middlesbrough a British record fee of £2.3 million. Ferguson had initially been prepared to offer only £1.3 million but Middlesbrough stuck to their demand, and finally United capitulated. In the end Pallister turned out to be a far better investment than Hysen. It may have taken Pallister a few years to mature into a United player, while Hysen quickly picked up honours in a rejuvenated Liverpool side, but eight years later, Pallister would still be plunging the knife into Liverpool's heart, whereas two years after Hysen joined Liverpool he was gone, discarded by new manager Graeme Souness on a free transfer.

Gary Pallister was not the only big name to be enlisted. Perhaps the most exciting was that of Neil Webb, the Nottingham Forest midfielder. A cultured, intelligent ball player, Webb was signed earlier to instil invention and pace into the United midfield and provide a long-term replacement for Bryan Robson. Ferguson had approached Forest with the intention of making an offer for Stuart Pearce, who was also out of contract, but Pearce eventually decided to stay put. Ferguson had tried on several previous occasions to sign Neil Webb but each time had been rebutted by the cantankerous Brian Clough. This time, with Webb out of contract and keen on a move, especially to Old Trafford, a deal was quickly tied up. At £1.5 million he looked an inspired signing, almost a bargain – even scoring on his debut as United trounced Arsenal 4–1 – but sadly a ruptured Achilles tendon early on in the season while he was on duty with England was eventually to lead to premature retirement. Webb came back from the injury but he was never the same player; short of pace, hesitant and visibly aware of his past injury. With a dynamic Webb operating in the midfield alongside Bryan Robson, United might well have flourished sooner than they did. Luck can play such a major role in football, and Ferguson was desperately unlucky to lose Webb through injury. It would have repercussions over the next couple of seasons.

Also signed during the close season, in fact on the same day as Neil Webb, was Mike Phelan of Norwich City. Phelan, a defensive midfielder who could play just as comfortably at the back, cost United £750,000. A couple of weeks into the season, after United had lost three games in succession, Ferguson jumped into the transfer market again, this time adding Paul Ince to his squad. Ince was a tough, versatile youngster who did not come cheap; United had to pay West Ham £2.4 million. The signing of Ince had partly been necessitated by the horrific injury to Webb. Like Pallister, Ince would take time to settle, looking far from the pedigree player his high fee suggested, but eventually Ince and Pallister would prove to be among the most significant signings Ferguson was to make for United.

Yet not all Ferguson's signings during the close season were so successful. Danny Wallace was recruited from Southampton for £1.2 million, and although he brought the occasional buzz to Old Trafford, he was often out of his depth. On his day he could be electric but more often than not he was a damp squib and was soon overshadowed by Giggs, Sharpe and Kanchelskis.

Despite splashing out almost £7 million, United hardly looked like a team eager to challenge for league honours. Instead they seemed to be going backwards. In his first full season Ferguson had taken United to within a whisker of the title; now, three years later, they were struggling nearer the foot of the table. Injuries had taken their toll with Webb, Robson, Wallace, Donaghy, Ince and Sharpe all missing vital games that season, many of them during the autumn and winter months. And still the shadow of Liverpool hung over him. 'We just cannot accept the domination of Liverpool,'

Ferguson told the fans at the start of the season. 'Hear, hear!' they replied.

As the season kicked off there had also been a sensational twist to the United story. An unnecessary, energy-sapping pre-season jaunt to Japan and Thailand to satisfy the sponsors had hardly helped morale, but then the day before the season began Old Trafford was rocked by the news that United had been sold for £20 million. Chairman Martin Edwards had decided to sell his controlling interest in United to a 37-year-old unknown businessman, Michael Knighton.

Edwards, the son of Louis Edwards, the dominant boardroom figure of the sixties and seventies, had surprisingly decided to hand over control, claiming that United needed a massive cash injection. He was certainly set to get one himself, with the takeover guaranteed to net the Edwards family a £10 million fortune. Ground improvements were essential, with the Stretford End scheduled for redevelopment, but the £7.5 million cost had meant that plans had already had to be postponed. The fact was that United, although not quite broke, were in deep financial crisis. They did not have a bottomless treasure chest as everyone seemed to imagine. Ground developments and Ferguson's forays into the transfer market had left them short. Knighton was promising an immediate £10 million cash injection. 'The deal,' insisted Edwards, 'was too good to turn down.' Maybe, but it was intolerably unsettling for both manager and players.

Yet the season kicked off hopefully enough with a 4–1 win over league champions Arsenal, perhaps inspired by an impromptu performance in front of the Stretford End by Michael Knighton, who gave a ball-juggling exhibition that left everyone convinced that here was a man who knew something about football as well as money. Ferguson had tried to persuade Knighton against putting on a United strip for his ball-juggling antics, fearing that it would detract from the business in hand. Predictably, it was Knighton who adorned the front pages the next morning. Some months later the whole deal would fall through, although the protracted negotiations and newspaper investigations left more than a few scars. However, something positive did emerge from the projected takeover: it focused sharply the thoughts of the accountants at Old Trafford. United had to get their finances straight, and with Lord Justice Taylor's report after Hillsborough set to recommend all-seater stadiums, United would need even more cash. Out of Knighton was born the idea of floating the club on the stock market. Years later an even richer Martin Edwards would look back at his narrow escape.

It was impossible for Ferguson to ignore the brouhaha going on upstairs. Everyone was talking about it. It was splashed all over the back pages as well as the financial papers, and with each day came a further revelation into the financial machinations of the new chairman. Ferguson had always claimed that the essential working relationship in any club was that between manager and chairman. He took the sensible option and welcomed Knighton on board when it had seemed he would be joining, insisting that they could work well together.

After their splendid opening victory over the league champions, United then drew their next match away at Crystal Palace and followed that with three successive defeats. After just five games they were struggling in 16th spot. But the following week their fortunes brightened as they thrashed Millwall 5–1.

Seven days later they crossed the city to Maine Road and were hammered 5–1. It was one of the blackest days in Ferguson's Old Trafford career. Not only was it their heaviest defeat so far, but it was at the hands of their closest rivals. Ferguson took to his bed. He went straight home after the game, crept upstairs and buried his head in a pillow. He couldn't believe it; nor could his wife when she returned home. Ferguson remained in his bed the whole night, turning over in his mind every move, every goal.

'It's been the longest ten days of my life,' he later confessed, 'an eternity in which I must have gone over that game a thousand times . . . it's been a nightmare.' City fans would do their best to remind him of the nightmare all season. It was the worst beating he had taken as a manager. 'I was as close to putting my head in the oven as I have ever been,' he said (and there would have been plenty of volunteers to turn on the gas). The compilers of the next home programme conveniently forgot to put in the league tables.

Ferguson suffered as much as any United fan. 'You feel you have to sneak around corners, feel as if you are some kind of criminal,' he confessed. He was as emotionally involved as the average supporter. Throughout the season he took their line. He recognised that as long as he could keep them on his side he had a chance. Dave Sexton, with his detached approach, had lost favour with the fans long before his eventual dismissal; Ferguson was not going to fall into that trap.

In his programme notes he was unusually critical of the team. Week after week they were given a public dressing-down. Individuals were never singled out but there was a rare frankness in what he said about the team collectively. 'We really have to cut out this idiotic, silly stuff,' was typical. The side were 'edgy, nervous, frustrating, lack the cutting edge'. But the fans, for all their vagaries, never came in for one iota of criticism. Busby, Shankly and Stein would have been proud of his attitude.

The defeat by Crystal Palace in early December was to be the start of another horrifying sequence of second-rate results. They also lost their next game, at home, to Tottenham. The following week they travelled to Anfield with Ferguson expecting the worst. But, as always seemed to happen against Liverpool, United conjured up some passion and performed with gritty determination to sneak away with a goalless draw that left Kenny Dalglish looking more the manager at the wrong end of the table. If only United could play with that kind of commitment every game, mused the manager. Unfortunately they did not seem able to do so: they lost 3–0 at Aston Villa a few days later. By the turn of the year United had lost nine league matches and won only six. They were in 15th place and just a couple of points off the relegation zone. It was an alarming situation. Patience was continuing to wear thin on the terraces.

Serious questions were being asked about Ferguson's star-name, fat-fee signings. Pallister looked naive, awkward and unsure. Ince had not settled and hardly looked the little tough man he was alleged to be. Mike Phelan also appeared erratic, while Webb was injured and would not reappear until the latter stages of the season. There was little to cheer about around Old Trafford.

The searching questions came not just from the press, but also from former players and managers. Tommy Docherty, Pat Crerand and Willie Morgan all waded in, and all were openly critical of him. 'I'm staggered at the non-stop sniping I am getting from them,' complained Ferguson bitterly, adding that 'they should have a better under-standing of the problems, and I would have thought that they would have had more respect for the club they are supposed to care for than to undermine our work.'

But Ferguson was far from despondent. He had bounced back from his earlier depression and was optimistic that the foundations he was laying would eventually bear fruit. As the 1990s broke he promised the supporters 'a decade of success', admitting that 'the eighties have not ended on a very happy note and we all owe the supporters a great deal. I honestly believe we have a great future. We have a lot of good young players and I think we have now set things up to ensure that there will always be a flow of quality into

Old Trafford and that never again will we have to spend fortunes very quickly in an effort to arrive at the standard we all want to see from Manchester United.' Few beyond the Old Trafford staff shared his optimism.

United would not notch up their seventh league win until late February when they beat lowly Millwall at the Den. It was their first win since mid-November, three months earlier. During that time they had lost six matches and drawn five. Apart from the catalogue of injuries, Ferguson recognised that too many players were trying to settle at the same time. If he had made any mistake it was to conduct so much business in the transfer market in so short a time. Half of them were still living out of suitcases in hotels. All that Ferguson could do was to trust in his own instincts. The English scene might have been foreign to him but judging players was still the same. 'In hindsight I was perhaps a manager in too much of a hurry and over-ambitious,' he later admitted.

The third round Cup tie against Forest could not have come at a worse moment. Things had been bad enough when the draw was made back in December. Now, a month later, Ferguson was reflecting on a further heap of poor results. The odds were stacked against United. It was a nervous party that made the short journey to the City ground that bitterly cold January morning, pale, bewildered faces peering out of the coach's windows at the frost on the hills.

The papers hadn't helped, either; some suggesting that Ferguson's job was on the line if they didn't win this one. Others had simply written off United's chances altogether. There were whispers that the United board would not tolerate another season without a trophy. But the whispers were far from the truth. In fact Martin Edwards had already had the foresight to call the manager into his office to have a word about it.

'I thought you should know that you have the full

support of the board and myself,' insisted Edwards. 'You have nothing to fear, I can promise you. This club will be standing by you, even if we lose to Forest. We believe in you.' Ferguson was grateful but knew that plenty of other managers had been given a similar vote of confidence by the chairman only to be sacked 24 hours later. He couldn't help but be worried. Even he knew that no matter how much support he had from the board, there would come a time when they would be swayed by the back pages and their own supporters. Defeat at Nottingham would have the terraces baying for his blood. That was another reason for keeping the supporters on his side. Things had to start improving soon.

'We knew how hard Alex Ferguson was working,' says Martin Edwards, looking back at that dramatic moment. 'We knew the tremendous effort he was putting in, not only with the first team but with the A and B teams and at youth level, and felt that eventually he would be able to turn it around.' It was easy to say in hindsight.

Fortunately the players and the fans seemed to sense the drama of the occasion. The United bus stole through the back streets of Nottingham with none of the usual bluster and laughter. And although there was quiet for much of the journey, there was also a steely determination not to lose this last opportunity to win something that season. Ferguson decided to stick with Mark Hughes and Mark Robins, who was enjoying an encouraging run in the first team. Young Robins had emerged from the United youth system; a graduate of the Lilleshall School of Excellence. The persistent little striker brought a refreshing commitment to the front line, and that afternoon at Nottingham he proved to be United's saviour. As far as the FA Cup was concerned, he was the answer to Ferguson's prayers as he netted United's winner. Ferguson would be forever grateful. In many respects United had been lucky; Forest even had a late equaliser disallowed. Within minutes of the final whistle, the draw for the fourth round was made. United had been drawn away, but this time it was to lowly Hereford.

Ferguson sensed that maybe his luck was finally beginning to turn. There would be other problems in the years ahead, but in time the pundits and fans alike would look back and realise that victory over Forest had been a defining moment in the history of United and the career of Alex Ferguson.

CHAPTER TWO

Fergie In

The year 1941 had been a disheartening one for the war effort. The Nazis had betrayed their pact with the Soviet Union and invaded Russia, tightening their noose around the old city of Leningrad, while the nightly raids on London had left the nation dispirited. Even the women had been called up into the armed services. But then in December came a ray of hope. The US Pacific Fleet lying in its home base of Pearl Harbor in Hawaii had been destroyed by Japanese bombers. That in itself may not have been an event to celebrate, but its consequences were extensive. Out of tragedy emerged expectation. Japan had declared war on the United States and, like it or not, the Americans had now been dragged into the growing conflict. It was an historic moment. On New Year's Eve prime minister Churchill confidently told the Canadian parliament that 'the tide is turning'. Alex Ferguson was born that same day, New Year's Eve 1941. Within the month American troops would be crossing the Atlantic on their way to Europe, while the Nazis were about to become bogged down on their Eastern Front by the most appalling winter the Soviet Union had ever known. The fight back had begun.

It was little wonder Hitler had sent his bombers to Glasgow with the simple message: destroy the city. Glasgow

15

was a vital cog in the production of wartime equipment. Its shipyards, which had lain almost idle in the 1930s, were now generating ships at the rate of almost one a week. The steelworks at Motherwell and elsewhere on the Clyde were equally busy, churning out the materials to forge tanks, guns, planes and ships. It was a frightening time, leaving an indelible memory on those who experienced the raids and their aftermath. At daybreak, thousands would pour out of their air-raid shelters, often inadequate in themselves, to survey the damage. As they blinked and stepped out into the daylight it was to face the devastating truth. Streets would be destroyed; homes where children and families had played and laughed would be little more than a heap of rubble. For today's generation it is almost impossible to imagine the terror of not knowing if your house is still standing. Glasgow did not suffer as much as other cities – Coventry and the East End of London were the principal targets – but Clydebank and Govan had their fair share of bombs.

Alex Ferguson was only three and a half years old when the war ended in 1945. He would remember little of it. His most formative years would be confined to the era of peace. Post-war Britain fairly glowed with optimism. There were no substantial levels of unemployment as there are today; no drugs or graffiti. And even in Glasgow there was little crime. Freed from six long years of tortuous war, there was a nervous gaiety.

A new Labour government, elected in the euphoria of victory, had swept to power and was beginning the mammoth task of reconstruction. Prime minister Clement Attlee with his briar pipe and his chirpy style was leading the fight back. Aneurin Bevan was constructing a new National Health Service, while the chancellor Stafford Cripps was struggling with a wrecked economy. New housing estates were springing up where before only the rubble of bombed buildings had lain. In the shops forgotten items were creeping across the counter once more. There was still rationing, but at least you could get hold of sugar, bacon and butter easily enough, which was an improvement on wartime shopping. And in the High Street, the mannequins in the classy shop windows were dressed in suits, furs and silk dresses. They may not have been affordable to most folks but they were there, and their very presence brought a swirl of optimism to the shopper.

There were also jobs. Britain needed to rebuild, and as the post-war years progressed, employment was plentiful. That Britain was able to demob so many men from the services and provide jobs was an astonishing achievement in itself. Mainly they worked in the construction industry, but also in the docks, the shipyards, the coal mines and the steelworks.

Of course, it wasn't all so simple and it would be wrong to paint too romantic a picture. There was still poverty, though it was not as socially divisive as the poverty of the 1990s. Anything was better than war. Nobody had much money but they coped, often helping each other where they could. The poverty was communal. There was little greed. Plenty of people were homeless but they were rarely left to sleep on the streets or on park benches.

At the centre of the reconstruction, in Scotland at least, stood Glasgow, still a major port, a leading shipbuilder and a supplier of steel to the world. It had been bloodied by the war but it was not down and out. Glasgow remained a vital cog in the rebuilding of the nation, as well as much of the Empire. Yet even in the early fifties it still carried the painful scars of war damage, with large areas of the city little more than rubble.

After the war the politicians and planners finished off the work of the German bombers, demolishing many of the slums. It was done in good faith. In their place new high-rise blocks shot up, or huge dormitory housing schemes. There was little or no attempt to preserve the communities of old; Billy Connolly once described them as 'deserts wi' windaes'.

In the late forties Govan could still claim to be the centre of world shipbuilding with the Upper Clyde boasting three major yards – Fairfields, Alexander Stephens and Harlands. Further down on the Lower Clyde was John Brown's, perhaps the most famous of all the yards, where the two mighty Queens had been built.

It was in this background, this mixture of optimism and occasional despair, that the young Alex Ferguson spent his childhood. There was adversity. Life in the tenement blocks immediately after the war was far from easy. There was no television, and not everyone had a radio. A visit to the cinema was not a regular outing but a treat. But it was a community, with the shipyards as its focal point. The climate and the environment shaped people's lives and character. 'Everything dovetailed around the yards,' remembered Ferguson on one occasion. 'You got your sense of identity from what was happening in them. Coming from that kind of background brought out the determination in you.'

Today, Govan is mainly an area of high-rise council flats, sweeping highways and roads designed for little more than fast-moving traffic. But in the shadow of the daunting tower blocks you can still see old Glasgow with its traditional tenements, cobbled streets and imposing red sandstone buildings. There's almost a grandness about the place that belongs to a bygone era. In other parts of Glasgow that stateliness has been refined as the old buildings have been swankily repaired and cleaned. They're proud of Glasgow again, but in Govan there's still not too much pride about their history except when it comes to celebrating a battle that took place 300 years ago.

Religion is, even today, a pressing influence in this area. Forty years ago it was more so. Govan was at the centre of Protestant Glasgow. Here, every July, the flutes and drums echo out as aproned men with their sashes and umbrellas march jauntily through the main streets, cheered on by partying crowds. This is Protestantism in its meanest, most flamboyant style. And as the mace is tossed high into the Glasgow sky, Protestants celebrate the battle of the Boyne in 1690, when King William of Orange defeated James II. Three hundred years, and they still haven't forgotten in this part of the land.

In the 1950s your religion was crucial. It dictated where you lived, which school you went to and often where you were employed. On the docks, in those days of casual labour, there were Protestant work gangs and Catholic gangs. It was no good expecting work from the Protestant boss if you were a known Catholic. What's more, there was no hiding your religion here. Your school history revealed all.

They were communities, yet the one divisive element was the religious bigotry of the street, 'the Billy and Dan mentality', as Jimmy Reid once described it. 'Some days coming home from school, boys would stop you in the street and ask, "Are you a Billy or a Dan?" You did a quick calculation and hoped you guessed their religion right before answering. If you got it wrong you got battered,' he remembers.

It was not a healthy situation. In families the bigotry was passed on down the line. Protestant kids rarely mixed with Catholic kids and inter-religious marriages were a rarity. You stuck with your own kind. Glasgow was a mainland version of Belfast. For anyone living in Glasgow it was impossible to escape the pervading influence of religion.

The uncompromising Calvinism of John Knox may have been complete, with only a handful of Catholics surviving the purges of the 17th and 18th centuries, but it was to be challenged in the 19th century by the mass influx of Catholics escaping the dire poverty and hunger of Ireland. In 1790 it was said that there were only 39 practising

Catholics in Glasgow, with no more than 40,000 in the whole of Scotland. But then the potato famine of the 1840s struck in Ireland and the demography of Scotland was set to alter radically. For the Irish there was only one escape – emigration. In their thousands they boarded rickety ships for the mainland in the hope of finding immediate salvation or a passage further afield to the Americas. They made initially for the major mainland ports of Liverpool, Manchester and Glasgow. From there, some took a passage to Boston, New York or even Australia, but most stayed, unable to find the money to take them across the Atlantic, and settled in the ports where they had first disembarked.

By the end of the century the Catholic population of Scotland had reached a staggering 400,000. Although many of them looked beyond Glasgow for employment and housing, most stayed in the city, where work was easier to find. In the Clyde Valley they found jobs in the steel and coal industries; later they found work in the shipyards and in heavy engineering. In Greenock alone the Catholic population at one point stood at 31 per cent while in Clydebank it was 24 per cent. In Coatbridge it was even higher, with almost one in every two a practising Catholic. Inevitably there would be conflict. When times were hard, when jobs were few, the Scottish Protestants looked for scapegoats. They were all too obvious. The lack of jobs, the changing culture was all blamed on the influx of Catholics who with their different ways of worship and belief seemed to pose a threat to traditional Scottish culture. The Catholics became ghettoised in their jobs and their homes.

Even football was to take on the religious mantle. Rangers had been formed in 1872 by a bunch of lads from Gareloch. Initially religion played no part in the game but with the formation of a Catholic club, Celtic, in 1887, the rivalry between the increasingly successful Rangers and Celtic forced Rangers to become a more overtly Protestant club. It added a little more spice to the rivalry and was good for business. Rangers would never look back. Housed in the centre of Protestant working-class Govan, it was a natural and public focus for people's Protestantism, and so the club donned the clothes of Protestantism. Fixtures between the two clubs soon took on new proportions, with the rivalry regularly spilling off the field and on to the terraces. At times the football seemed almost incidental in a war of the religions. Even today it is just as bad. Celtic may have shed the armour of religion, but at Ibrox, you still have to wonder about their gestures. Go to any Old Firm game and you will still see and hear the same hatred, the same sectarianism in their songs and chants.

If religion was central to the culture of Glasgow, so too was drink. But this was not just social drinking, it was serious drinking. No popping in to the local for a pint on the way home from work; it would be a two- or three-hour session, maybe a whole evening before the breadearner rolled home. On a Saturday the bars of Glasgow would be awash with fans, before and after the games. There were Celtic bars and Rangers bars. Indeed, there are still are, and there is much the same drinking culture as there always has been.

Alex Ferguson was born in a small terraced house in Govan. A year later brother Martin arrived. The house is still there, with its neat door and bright windows, but later they moved a short distance away to Govan Road, in the shadow of the giant Ibrox stand, where he and his brother were brought up. This house no longer exists, having been torn down to be replaced by a fire station.

His father worked in the yards for almost 40 years, most of his working life spent as a boilermaker at Fairfields. In the evening a sea of bonnets would make their way up Govan Road from the yard. Alex would be watching out for one bonnet in particular. His father was a strict disciplinarian, the kind of man who was never late for work or an appointment of any kind. It was something that was to rub off on his son. He was also the kind of man who believed in an honest day's work for an honest day's pay. You didn't shirk, you did your best; you never skipped work and rarely stayed off ill. His father also taught him never to give in. 'Give in once and you give in twice,' he told him. But he also made his son keep his feet on the ground, telling him not to get high ideas and always to remember his background. They were values that were to prove crucial.

Although many of Alex's father's characteristics were to rub off on him, he took after his mother more. She was the determined person in the household, the one with ambition for her sons. Alex inherited her edge, her determination and will to win. Martin was more placid.

Like most other kids from Govan, Alex was football daft, always dribbling a small ball around, and there were plenty of bomb sites to set up a pitch. A few coats would be thrown on to the ground to form goalposts and they would be off, lost in the magical world of Glasgow and Scotland football. A favourite spot was known as 'The Works' where on a Sunday you even had to queue up to get a game. Hours later they would traipse back home, with muddy knees in need of a good wash and a few cuts and bruises, but always re-living the day's goals. Even then he hated losing.

At school it was the same – out in the playground at every opportunity, a small ball appearing mysteriously out of someone's pocket and the coats shaping the pitch. He went to Govan Parish School, a typical Victorian red-brick building in the heart of Govan. In the high-ceilinged classrooms, the emphasis was on the three Rs. There were the usual fights and he was never far off, though he wasn't too proud or stubborn to run when the going got a bit too tough. Today the letters IRA have been provocatively painted on the walls.

After Govan Junior, it was Govan High, and much the same pattern. He hated science. By then Ferguson's football was shaping up; there was no denying his talent. He was soon playing for the school team, then it was Glasgow Schools. His brother was similarly talented, and often they played together in the same side – when they were not squabbling. They both progressed to play for Harmony Row and then Drumchapel Amateurs, one of the best-known amateur sides in the area. Alex was a centre forward, a plunderer, a scorer of goals, forged in the spirit of men like Mason, Steel or Reilly. Martin was a passer of the ball.

Like all the kids from Govan, Alex's obsession was Rangers. They all hero-worshipped players like George Young and Sammy Cox as well as the three Willies – Waddell, Woodburn and Thornton. George Young was the epitome of a Rangers player, a Rob Roy if ever there was one – muscular, committed, a warrior to frighten anyone – while Cox was said by one commentator to have 'a tackle like a trap snapping'. Yet it wasn't just the Rangers players who were his heroes. There were others such as Third Larnark's Jimmy Mason, Billy Steel of Derby County and later of Dundee, and Laurie Reilly, the young Hibernian centre forward. All three had scored for the Scottish side that had tortured England 3–1 at Wembley in 1949 in a performance likened by Bernard Joy to that of the Wembley Wizards. After the game, goalkeeper Jimmy Cowan had been carried shoulder-high from the field as Scotland celebrated, clinching the British championship. But it was the goal scorers Mason, Steel and Reilly who would live in the hearts of Scotland's youngsters. And then there was the Hibernian side of the late forties boasting one of the finest forward lines ever to have graced a Scottish field – Smith, Johnstone, Reilly, Turnbull and Ormond.

Ibrox today is a very different proposition from the ground of Alex Ferguson's youth. Today it's a swanky, modern stadium, one of the finest in the land, with seats for almost 50,000. There are executive boxes, dining rooms, television areas, and even offices available for outside companies. It smacks of money and success. When Alex

Ferguson stood on its terraces as a young lad, it was in a swaying, baying crowd of madness, rather like one of those Hieronymus Bosch paintings. Early in 1939 just over 118,000 stood here to watch an Old Firm battle, and even after the war attendances regularly topped the 100,000 mark as the Glasgow giants clashed in the gladiatorial arena. Ferguson would stand in the vast crowd with his mates most Saturdays, supporting the team he loved.

Like many kids, Ferguson would collect sets of photos of these stars, even sending away for glossy prints. Celtic's flame-haired Bobby Evans was a favourite of just about everyone except the most bigoted Rangers supporters. Evans, known as the 'Pride of Parkhead', was a half back in the style of Alex Forbes of Arsenal. Then there was Willie Redpath of Motherwell, a right half and exhibition footballer whose sideline was ball juggling at boys' clubs. Redpath would come on to the pitch at home games flicking the ball from foot to head, watched enviously by hordes of youngsters who would race home after the game to practise their own circus skills.

The war had not dented Rangers' claim to be Scotland's number one club but an era was drawing to a close. Other clubs were challenging their superiority: Hibernian in Edinburgh won two successive titles, and even Celtic and Aberdeen picked up the championship. Between the mid-fifties and sixties, however, Rangers returned to their winning ways, though not before they had been thrashed 7–1 at Hampden by Celtic in the League Cup final, a game rumoured to have been extinguished from the official records of Rangers Football Club. Yet despite their humiliation at the hands of their most loathed enemy, Rangers were set to become the dominant force in Scottish football once more. They picked up half a dozen championships and even more cups. If you wanted to watch title-chasing football, Ibrox was the place to be, not Parkhead. It was a glorious period in the club's history that would come to an abrupt end with the emergence of Jock Stein's Celtic in the mid-sixties. This was the Rangers of Jim Baxter, Ralph Brand, Willie Henderson, Ian McMillan – one of the finest Rangers sides of all time. They were a joy to watch, though once, after humiliating Celtic 3–0 in the 1963 Scottish Cup final, the Rangers manager Scot Symon berated his men for torturing the Celtic players. He meant it as well – they were that good. And there were 120,000 spectators to testify to it. By then Ferguson was in his early twenties and ready to join his heroes.

Ferguson's loyalty to Rangers had never wavered. Most home games the young Alex would be trying to get into Ibrox one way or another. He couldn't always afford it and by his own admission 'skipped' in once or twice. He had a route carefully worked out but on one occasion slipped from a wall and fell into a pool of water. Within seconds a steward was standing over him, threatening to tell his father. He never did, but it gave Alex a few anxious hours as he waited for the knock on the door.

Coming from Glasgow also made it easier for the young Ferguson to relate to the national side. All internationals were played at Hampden, just down the road, and it wasn't difficult to get in. 'I can remember dodging school to go to the league match in 1950,' he once recalled. 'Scotland won 1–0. They played Inter-League games at Ibrox and full internationals at Hampden.' There were 72,000 crammed into Ibrox that November day to watch their Scottish heroes beat an English League side that boasted the likes of Johnny Aston, Billy Wright, Henry Cockburn, Johnny Hancocks, Stan Mortensen, Nat Lofthouse and Tom Finney. Alex was just a month off nine.

It wasn't until four years later, when he was 12, that he witnessed his first full international, a World Cup qualifier, when he saw England take their revenge on Scotland with a 4–2 win at Hampden in front of 134,000. 'It was pouring with rain,' he recalls. 'I was lifted over the barrier next to the invalid cars. I stood there and watched the game.' He went home with the magical names ringing in his ears – Sammy Cox of Rangers, Bobby Johnstone of Hibs, debutant Willie Ormond and wee Bobby Evans of Celtic.

In the mid-fifties when Alex Ferguson left school there were jobs aplenty. Even the shipyards had job vacancy adverts hanging from the doors. Anyone leaving school, even without qualifications, could be sure of three or four job offers. Employers were queuing to sign up youngsters for apprenticeships. Usually an apprenticeship lasted five years before you became a journeyman and started earning top pay.

When Ferguson left school, he was taken on at the Remington Rand typewriter and shaver factory in Hillington as a toolmaker. He was set to work in the typewriter factory, along with all the other apprentices. The shaver factory was next door. Toolmaking was a good solid trade for a young lad in those days. There would always be jobs for toolmakers – or so the thinking went.

The factory was only a short distance from Govan, just past the King George V docks, on one of those typically large industrial estates, full of Art Nouveau but functional buildings. Rolls-Royce was on the same estate. Today it's very different. Most of the large employers have disappeared, along with Britain's manufacturing industry. Now it's just a series of small factories, shopping outlets and fast food restaurants.

Ferguson was enrolled on a five-year apprenticeship, with one day a week at Technical College where he studied engineering. All the apprentices worked in the toolroom, and Ferguson was well liked. One old chum remembers how he used to do tricks. 'He'd put a penny on his foot and flick it up into the air, catching it on his head or the back of his neck.'

Ferguson's football of course made him popular at the factory. He was combining football with work, first playing with the famous amateur club Queen's Park, then with St Johnstone. It was hard going, putting in a long day at the factory before training in the evening or even playing a mid-week game, and then perhaps another match on the Saturday. It didn't leave time for much else. And on top of that there was the travel.

Callum Mackay, the convenor of the shop stewards' committee at Remington's, remembers going to see him play football once or twice. 'I particularly remember one occasion,' he says. 'He'd been playing against Rangers and I think he scored a couple of goals. Well anyhow, we had a manageress in the canteen who was a real blue nose. She was furious on the Monday. When Alex walked into the canteen she let fly, giving him a good cuff around the ears. He had to get out of the place as quickly as he could.' Everyone knew him and liked him, but one person in particular took a fancy to him, although first impressions weren't too favourable.

At the Glasgow Locarno one Saturday evening, he had asked a young woman to dance with him. These were the rock and roll years of Elvis, Jerry Lee Lewis and Little Richard. She wasn't particularly impressed by his appearance, let alone his ability on the dance floor. He was sporting two black eyes and a broken nose, the result of a clash in some game. She thought he looked a bit of a thug. She had no idea he was a footballer. It turned out that the young woman, Cathy, also worked at Remington's. They had a point of contact. It wasn't long before they found themselves chatting to each other at work, and they began to see more of each other. Then the strike began. She had no money, like most of those on strike. Ferguson himself was lucky; he was earning money from his football. He was a good bet; she agreed to go out with him. 'It wasn't love at first sight,' she once admitted, but his style clearly grew on her. They married when he was 24 years old.

Ferguson was soon recruited into the Engineering Union,

the AEU, and before long found himself representing the apprentices in the toolroom on the shop committee. Remington's was a solid union company, one of the strongest in the whole of the Glasgow area. It was well organised and had a reputation as a good payer in the area. 'We always encouraged the young lads,' remembers Callum Mackay. 'We'd try and get them involved in the union and such things. Alex used to come to meetings. He was on the shop stewards' committee and was also on the District Committee of Junior Workers. They'd meet every Saturday morning at the AEU headquarters in Renfrew Road. He was nearly always there, always involved, even though it was difficult for him with his football. But he was a committed trade unionist. I wouldn't say he was a leader, but he was well liked.'

Even if Mackay didn't spot any leadership potential, it was certainly on show a few years later when Ferguson led the apprentices out on strike. The strike of engineering apprentices had begun in the Glasgow shipyards over pay and conditions. Apprentices were forbidden to go on strike; it was written into their indentures as a condition of employment. Go out on strike and you had broken your agreement, which meant the sack. Instead, the apprentices had to rely on their seniors in the union and the goodwill of their employers for any improvements to their working conditions. The journeymen did not always have too much sympathy with the lads and usually had enough of their own battles to fight without taking on any other causes. It was also a tradition that apprentices were not well paid. They were supposed to be learning the trade and were paid far less than the journeymen, even though they were often doing the same job as their seniors.

The strike began among the apprentices at the Alexander Stephens shipyard in Govan and slowly spread among the shipyards of the Upper and Lower Clyde. Gus Macdonald, now chairman of Scottish Television, was a young apprentice in the Stephens shipyard at the time and was instrumental in bringing Ferguson and Remington's out on strike. A passionately involved political activist and trade unionist, he was one of the ring leaders in the dispute. 'We used to go marching to each of the yards trying to get them to come out and support the fight,' he recalls. 'I remember that we also went up to Remington Rand's at Hillington and put our case to them. Alex Ferguson was the shop steward of the apprentices at the time and he came out in support of us.'

In the end there were about 100,000 of them out on strike. Macdonald and others were being sent around the country to bring out more apprentices. Macdonald himself was sent down to London with the simple instruction, 'Bring London out!' The strike lasted about a month, though in the end it proved more difficult to get some of the lads back to work than it had been to get them out. Jimmy Reid, at that time a leading light in the Young Communist League, was heavily involved in the dispute. So too was Billy Connolly, who worked at Alexander Stephens alongside Gus Macdonald.

In the end the apprentices claimed victory as the engineering employers backed down and they were given a handsome 30 per cent increase. For many young lads it was an education, their first involvement in political action. It was a lesson Alex Ferguson would not forget.

CHAPTER THREE

Elbows and Knees

It wasn't long before the young Alex Ferguson had been spotted by the league clubs. Queen's Park was one of the oldest and most distinguished clubs in the whole of Scotland, if not Britain. The Glasgow club had seen him playing with one of the boys' clubs and decided to give him a try.

Founded in 1867, they were a strictly amateur club, based at Hampden Park, Glasgow. Such was their adherence to amateurism that they did not even boast a manager, just a coach. The club's glory days had been in the last century, when they won ten Scottish Cups in less than 20 years. Since then there had been little to shout about. The season before Ferguson joined them, 1957–58, they had finished bottom of the First Division, with just nine points. They had lost a staggering 29 games.

On 15 November 1958 Ferguson made his debut in Scottish League football, playing for Queen's Park at Stranraer. Queen's Park lost 2–1 but Ferguson was on the scoresheet. It wasn't long before the 16-year-old was a regular in the first team, playing each week at Hampden Park, in those days capable of holding 130,000 but probably only attracting a thousand or so when Queen's Park played. During his first season, 1958–59, Ferguson made eight appearances and scored a total of four goals, playing three of his games at inside right and five at inside left.

He also made an impression on the watching selectors for the Scotland youth side. He was invited for a trial and then chosen to play for Scotland against Ireland. Unfortunately he had to cry off through illness but a short while later, on 28 February 1959, he won his first youth cap, making his international debut for Scotland against England at Muirton Park, Perth. They drew 1–1 but in the following game against Wales at Stark's Park, Kirkcaldy, on 18 April he scored as Scotland won 3–1.

He was soon winning rave notices in the local papers. Willie Waddell was one of the first to spot his talents. 'The leggy Ferguson was a finer type, who excelled in his ball skill and passing. At times he was well out of his position because of his urge to go forward,' wrote Waddell in one of the Glasgow papers.

'He moved around the Paisley goal area with the merciless menace of a spider stalking his prey,' commented another local newspaper. But it wasn't enough to stop the rot. Queen's Park ended up next to bottom of the Second Division. They had tumbled from the bottom of one division to the bottom of another in just one season. It had been a fairly dramatic collapse in their fortunes.

His second season with Queen's Park was more successful as he made 23 appearances, scoring 11 goals. The side also finished in mid-table, a dramatic improvement on the previous season. 'He was a battling centre forward,' remembers club director Malcolm Mackay, 'a bit like a Mark Hughes rather than a Gary Lineker, always a handful in the penalty area.' Mackay also uses one or two other choice adjectives. Bob Crampsey, then a young supporter of the club, remembers him as 'a peripheral player', though he adds that 'you could always see that he had ability. He was full of energy and it was obvious that he would not stay at Queen's Park very long.'

And did he show leadership qualities at that stage? 'He didn't have to,' says Mackay, 'he was still a young lad, though even as a youngster he was having to fight his own corner. That took character. He was playing for a side in the Scottish League, at a much higher level than he had ever played in before, and he had to battle to claim and then keep his place. He didn't like losing. He had a competitive edge to him, desperately wanting to win.'

Bob Crampsey also recalls him as a 'great encourager on the field, always shouting and mouthing off'. Crampsey vividly recollects seeing him score against Falkirk. 'Falkirk were by far the better side that afternoon and had had most of the possession when suddenly Ferguson broke away, ran the length of the field and scored.'

Queen's Park was sometimes regarded as a cut above the rest, elitist and snobby. 'Many of our players had been to good schools, even public schools,' says Mackay, 'but Alex had been born and brought up in Govan. He had no airs or graces about him. He was down to earth. In particular he was a principled lad, full of opinion even then. But there was no bullshit about him.'

Queen's Park was an amateur club in the finest traditions of amateurism. Nobody was paid a penny, although there were always rumours about boot money. None of the rumours was true, but at a recent Queen's Park dinner, guest of honour Alex Ferguson began his speech by taking off his shoe and pulling out – lo and behold – a £10 note.

It wasn't long before the professional clubs spotted him. 'We didn't want to lose him,' says Mackay, but St Johnstone moved in and in the summer of 1960 snapped him up. 'When we played St Johnstone the next season all our players were kicking the hell out of him for leaving us,' Mackay remembers with a smile.

It was a former Queen's Park player who was to give Ferguson his first break in professional football. Bobby Brown had been their goalkeeper just before the war, later going on to play with Rangers and Scotland. At the time, Brown was manager of St Johnstone, then a Second Division side. They played Queen's Park regularly and Brown always kept in close touch with his old club. 'They gave a player a good grounding,' he says. 'It wasn't like a professional club where if you had one bad game you were dropped. At Queen's Park they'd stick by you.'

Brown himself had made his debut with Queen's Park in 1939 as a 16-year-old playing against Celtic. The club's scouting system was renowned and they were forever picking up good lads missed by Rangers and Celtic. They would then give them their opportunity and stand by them. As Brown says, 'You could always sign a prospect or two from Queen's Park.'

Brown was also forced into buying cheap. St Johnstone had a huge overdraft, so large that in the early sixties they were a part-time club. Even Brown was not a full-time manager, combining his footballing duties with being a schoolmaster. He knew that in signing players from Queen's Park he wouldn't even have to pay a transfer fee as they were an amateur club. Back in the 1930s the Perth side had been one of the top six clubs in the country, but as Scottish football was reorganised after the war, for some reason or another they had been dumped into the Second Division. Now, instead of lucrative fixtures against the likes of Rangers, Celtic, Hibs and Hearts, it was Forfar, Arbroath and Berwick. Over the years Brown had continued to keep in close contact with the Hampden club and it hadn't been long before Ferguson had been brought to his attention. St Johnstone had just been promoted to the Scottish First Division and were on the lookout for a goal scorer to help keep them in the top league. Ferguson seemed the ideal man.

He made his debut on 3 September 1960, and over the next four years went on to play 45 games for the club, scoring a creditable 22 goals. But as the club's historian

Alastair Blair puts it, 'He was really only a bit player.'

Ferguson's first season did not hold too much promise. He had just four outings, scoring one goal. They finished up fourth from bottom but at least managed to avoid relegation. They were duly rewarded with a week's holiday in Blackpool. Unfortunately most of the lads were unable to get time off work and couldn't make the trip, but Ferguson managed to get a week off and along with Doug Newlands, Bobby Gilfillan and Ron McKinven went off to the Lancashire seaside resort, accompanied by Bobby Brown and trainer John Mathers. Newlands, who was the club's outside right and first full-time professional, remembers Ferguson as 'a nice wee lad'.

'He was enthusiastic and always asking for advice,' says Newlands, who was also the man instrumental in persuading Ferguson to turn full-time professional. 'He came to see me at my house one evening. He'd been offered a full-time contract with the club and wanted to know if he should take it and if it was enough money. Well, we talked it over and I told him to go for it but to ask for more money. I guessed that the club would split the difference, which in fact they did. I suppose we were only talking about £300 or £400 a year extra but that was a lot of money in those days. I also told him to talk it over with his dad.'

It had been a hard routine for Ferguson being part-time. He was still working at Remington's during the day and then in the evening would usually make the 60-mile trip to Perth for training, going by train with three or four of the other Glasgow-based lads. Some evenings they'd work out in Glasgow, with Johnny Mathers coming down to oversee them. 'He was good at training,' says Doug Newlands, 'always keen, never one to shirk or try to skive off.'

But it wasn't an ideal situation. He wasn't getting the games and the travelling was a slog. In September 1962 he approached the manager and asked for a transfer. Brown reported it to the board but it was decided that he could not go. The word may or may not have filtered out but coincidentally, a couple of months later, in November, Hamilton Academical made an approach for him, offering St Johnstone the princely sum of £250. The Saints said no.

Whether his asking for a transfer had any influence on events that season remains in doubt but it certainly earned him a few more call-ups to the first team. In all he played 13 games. Unfortunately his five goals did not help St Johnstone escape the big drop, their appalling goal average the crucial factor as three clubs ended up on the same number of points. St Johnstone had scored just 35 goals all season.

However, it didn't take long for Bobby Brown to sort them out. A year later they topped the Second Division, six points ahead of East Stirlingshire, and were duly promoted. Ferguson scored nine times, his best season at Muirton Park as he made 15 appearances.

'He was a useful player,' says Brown, who, like Ferguson himself, would later go on to manage Scotland. 'He was good around the penalty area. Anything loose in the box and he had an eye for it. He wasn't a silky player but he did have an eye for goal.' Yet he wasn't a tall man, just 5 feet 10 inches and weighing in at around 10½ stones.

St Johnstone director Stuart Duff remembers him as 'a lazy player. He wasn't a footballing centre forward. He was a good old-fashioned poacher. And his strike rate of one goal every other game looks even better today.' Alastair Blair says much the same thing. 'Everyone I've ever spoken to about his days here at St Johnstone says the same thing. He played football with his elbows and knees.'

Among those playing with Ferguson at Muirton Park was Jimmy Gauld, who had earlier played First Division football in England with Charlton Athletic and Everton. After St Johnstone Gauld would go on to play for Mansfield and became mixed up in the sensational football bribes scandal of the sixties.

Although memories of the footballing Ferguson are few at St Johnstone, one stands head and shoulders above all others. It was his famous hat trick against Rangers at Ibrox as the Saints beat Rangers 3–2 on 23 December 1963. Even today Ferguson is the only St Johnstone player ever to have scored a hat trick against Rangers. The occasion moved one budding poet to compose some doggerel in memory of the great victory.

> *Sadly they tolled each bell in the steeple,*
> *Proud banners lay crumpled and mute were 'The*
>   *People'.*
> *Stilled was their laughter and graven their mirth,*
> *For Rangers had fallen to the wee Saints of Perth.*
> *The Gers v Saints – 'twas a foregone conclusion,*
> *They'll rattle them in – at least half a dozen.*
> *And when at half-time one-nil was the score,*
> *They smugly sat back and waited for more.*
> *Alas and alack – 'twas vain wishful thinking,*
> *Saints equalised in less than a twinkling.*
> *Then salted the wound by taking the lead,*
> *While bold Jimmy Millar was 'losing the heid'.*
> *Till sharp as a lance the ref's whistle blew,*
> *From penalty spot, the score was 2–2.*
> *The faithful relaxed and chanted eas-ee,*
> *And that's when young Fergie scored goal No. 3.*
> *Three–two was the score, young Alex scored all,*
> *The mighty have fallen, how great was their fall.*
> *And when super leagues come to encircle the earth,*
> *Remember Great Rangers and the Wee Saints from*
>   *Perth!*

Most people will tell you that Ferguson did not appear to enjoy himself at Muirton Park. Bobby Brown remembers him vividly as the 'spokesman' of the dressing room. 'He was the shop steward. He always had plenty to say and was not backwards in coming forward. When the wages were being discussed he was there. He wanted to know what everyone was earning and would let you know if he thought it was enough or not, even though most of them were all part-timers.' The minutes of the board also reveal that Ferguson was always ready to complain about some injustice. Shop steward Ferguson seemed to be carrying on where he had left off at Remington's.

St Johnstone finished the 1963–64 season in 13th place, well clear of relegation, but only three points ahead of Third Lanark, who finished third from bottom. Ferguson had played 13 games, scoring seven goals.

His goal-scoring average of a goal every other game had brought him to the attention of the big clubs, and in June 1964 Dunfermline swooped and in a straight player exchange brought him to East End Park, with Dunfermline's Dan McLindon travelling in the opposite direction. It was only two months since Jock Stein had left the managerial post at Dunfermline to take over at Celtic. It was Willie Cunningham, the new manager, who had previously been Stein's number two at Dunfermline, who landed Ferguson.

'He was a true professional, a good goal scorer; he was just what I needed,' says Cunningham. In his four years at East End Park, Stein had created a minor miracle, transforming Dunfermline into one of the most attractive sides in the Scottish First Division. Under Cunningham the seeds that Stein had sown would flourish.

In his first season at the club Ferguson would be virtually ever present, scoring 15 goals in 27 league appearances. In all he found the net 23 times during the season as Dunfermline enjoyed one of their most successful seasons ever. Up until a week before the season ended they looked to be heading for a Scottish league and cup double, but then in that final week they drew a crucial league fixture against St Johnstone and eventually finished in third place, just one point behind champions Kilmarnock. With that draw Dunfermline's hopes of the title were dashed. Sandwiched in between that game and the final game of the season was the Scottish FA Cup final and the biggest disappointment in Ferguson's career to date. He was looking forward to the 1965 final, although towards the end of the season he had lost his place in the league side to John 'Chick' McLaughlin.

At 2.20 p.m. Willie Cunningham walked into the Hampden Park dressing room and announced his team for the final. There was no place for Ferguson; everyone looked aghast. Up until then he had played in all Dunfermline's Cup matches. Now he was out and McLaughlin was in. Nobody had forecast it and there had been no hint of it in any of the papers. Ferguson was distraught and stormed off to the stands to watch from a distance.

'It was one of those decisions I had to make,' says Cunningham. 'McLaughlin was playing well and even scored for us that day and yes, I'd make the same decision again.'

But if Cunningham had reckoned his tactics would win him the match, he was to be disappointed. Dunfermline lost 3–2. Stein had put one over on his former club. Celtic had not won a trophy for eight years but this was to be the start of the most glorious era in their history. Two seasons later they would be European champions. 'It all started there,' said Stein once. 'Had we lost that game we might never have got started.' Sitting up in the stands, Ferguson had played his part in Celtic winning the European Cup! But he might also have been cursing as he watched the Celtic defenders mixing it on the park. Dunfermline's best 'mixer' was not on the pitch. He would have revelled in it.

'He didn't take the decision particularly well,' remembers his former manager. 'But then that was only natural. He was very disappointed.' A few days later they faced Celtic at East End Park in the final league match of the season. This time Ferguson was restored to the line-up and Dunfermline won 5–1, with Ferguson scoring one and making another. It made you think.

Ferguson also made his debut in Europe that season, ironically in Gothenburg, as Dunfermline took on Orgryte IS in the UEFA Cup. Twenty years later he would return to Gothenburg to win a European trophy. Dunfermline beat the Swedes and in the next round had another impressive victory, this time over VfB Stuttgart. That win put them into the quarter-finals, where they faced Atletico Bilbao. They won the first game 1–0, then lost by the same score in Spain and in the replay finally went down 2–1.

The following season was perhaps Ferguson's finest as a player. He struck 31 league goals in 31 games to end the season as the top Scottish goal scorer. Even today it remains a record for Dunfermline in the top division. 'What is particularly impressive,' claims Dunfermline historian Duncan Simpson, 'is that there were some outstanding strikers around at the time with other clubs, particularly at Rangers and Celtic. Ferguson topped them all.'

They ended the season in fourth place, though well behind champions Celtic. And in the Scottish Cup they reached the semi-finals before losing 2–0 to Celtic. In Europe they again reached the quarter-finals of the UEFA Cup, beating Copenhagen and Zbrojovka Brno before losing to the eventual finalists Real Zaragoza. In all, Ferguson had scored 45 goals in a total of 52 games. It was a remarkable record. One newspaper called him 'an elusive menacing forager'.

'He was essentially a poacher and in some respects a bit like Gerd Muller,' remembers Duncan Simpson. 'He had tremendous pace over the first five yards. He could get into the box so quickly. And once there he was an awkward customer.'

The following season, 1966–67, was to be his final one with Dunfermline, although it would not be quite as successful as their previous campaign. They finished eighth and could only reach the quarter-finals of the Scottish Cup. But Ferguson was still knocking them in, scoring 20 league goals with a season's overall total of 29.

That year Ferguson was also chosen to represent the Scottish League against the Football League at Hampden Park. The Scots, despite boasting the likes of Billy McNeill, John Greig, Peter Cormack, Steve Chalmer, Dave Smith and Willie Henderson, lost 3–0 to the English, who had included Bobby Moore, Jimmy Greaves, Peter Thompson and Ian Callaghan in their side. It was only nine months since England had won the World Cup. Brian Labone, the former Everton centre half who played in that match, has only vague memories of Ferguson. 'He didn't give me much trouble on the night,' he recalls. 'He was hardly in the game.'

At the end of the season Ferguson's goal scoring talents were finally recognised by his country when he was chosen to go on Scotland's summer world tour. He scored on his debut as Scotland beat Israel 2–1. In the next game he struck twice as they defeated Hong Kong 4–1. Three days later he hit the only goal of the game in a 1–0 win over Australia in Sydney. In a second game against the Australians in Adelaide he failed to score, but in Melbourne in the final game against them he hit both Scotland's goals. He missed out on the match against New Zealand Under-23s, because he was too old, but on 8 June in Auckland he struck a hat trick as Scotland defeated an Auckland Provincial XI 4–1. His next game, against Vancouver All-Stars in Canada, was to be his final appearance on the tour but he still managed to get on the scoresheet as Scotland won 4–1.

There's no doubt that it was very much a second-rate Scottish squad with few of the nation's household names on view. There was no Law, Baxter, Bremner, Gemmell or Lennox. McCalliog and Ure were the only well-known players. Sadly no caps were presented for the tour and Ferguson's seven appearances and ten goals went without any lasting recognition. But try telling him that he never played for Scotland!

He had acquitted himself well and it was little wonder that when he returned home he was to find himself at the centre of a major transfer deal. Rangers, his boyhood club, had been tracking him and came in with a £65,000 offer. Dunfermline did not want to lose him but they could hardly say no to that kind of money. It was the biggest deal ever between Scottish football clubs. Ferguson was suddenly the most expensive player in Scotland.

In all he had scored 97 goals for Dunfermline in 145 appearances. Sixty-six of those goals had come in the league in just 88 outings. He had scored eight hat tricks for his club. 'He had a real appetite for the game,' remembers Willie Cunningham. 'He was a true professional. Even then I could sense that he was going to make a manager. He had opinions.' It would not be the last time that their paths would cross.

And so in the summer of 1967 it was back to Govan, to Ibrox, home of his boyhood dreams. But it had not been the best of years for Rangers. Celtic had just lifted the European Cup, beating Inter Milan in Lisbon to become the first British side to win the trophy. They had also pipped Rangers to the title and beaten them in the Scottish FA Cup final. For the next few seasons Rangers would always be second best to Celtic.

Ferguson, the most costly player in Scotland, had been brought in by new manager Davy White to turn things around. Expectations were high. But in truth Rangers' problems were far too complex for Ferguson to solve. Yet in his first season he went some way to justifying his huge price tag. In 29 league appearances he scored 19 goals and added a further seven in 22 other games. It was an impressive strike rate but was still not enough to bring any silverware back to Ibrox. They finished second in the league, two points behind Celtic, having taken the title race to the final game of the season when a defeat at home by Aberdeen cost them the championship. Celtic also won the Scottish Cup.

In September 1967, following his successful summer trip with Scotland to Australia, Ferguson was given another chance to play at a higher level when he was again chosen to play for the Scottish League side, this time against the Irish League at Windsor Park. The Scottish League won 2–0, with Ferguson and John Greig the two scorers.

The following season turned out to be equally frustrating. Colin Stein had been signed from Hibs to partner Ferguson and give the attack some much needed flair, but it didn't seem to work out, and instead Ferguson's own prospects took a dive. He played just 12 league games, scoring six goals, and managed another six in other competitions as Rangers again finished runners-up, this time trailing Celtic by five points.

Colin Stein remembers that Ferguson was something of a handful to play against: 'He was a fiery character. We were both sent off for fighting when I played against him for Hibs. He wasnae quiet in the dressing room either. I always thought he'd become a manager.'

Lifelong Rangers supporter Robert McElroy has a similar memory: 'He could put himself about a bit. He was a rumbustious, uncompromising type of player. But in fact he was never heavily built. He was light, only about ten and a half stones. Maybe that was why he had to be more fired up.'

The highlight of the season turned out to be the Scottish Cup final against Celtic in 1969. Ferguson had not played in any of the earlier rounds but shortly before the final Colin Stein was injured and Ferguson was given the nod by manager Davy White. In the dressing room before kick-off the manager's instructions were clear. 'If there are any corners to Celtic, your job is to come back and mark Billy McNeill,' he told Ferguson. The towering McNeill was a threat in the area and was well known for his sudden appearances in the penalty box at corners. In the first minute Celtic were awarded a corner. Bobby Lennox raced across to take the kick. McNeill strolled upfield unmarked towards the area, with Ferguson nowhere to be seen. The inevitable happened. McNeill headed Celtic into the lead.

'To say something went wrong with our marking is an understatement,' says John Greig. 'Alex Ferguson told me later something had distracted him in the penalty area. Whatever it was, Billy McNeill rose up with an almost free header and stuck it past Norrie Martin. If you lose a goal like that early on, all the tactical preparation for the rest of the game counts for nothing.' Rangers lost 4-0.

After the game there was bedlam in the dressing room as Davy White tore into Ferguson. He had been given a specific job and in the first minute he had let them all down. It had been impossible to recover after that. Rangers had been humiliated in front of 132,000. And it was all Ferguson's fault.

To make matters worse, Rangers had come back at Celtic with Ferguson being offered a golden opportunity to level the score. A John Greig shot had been parried away by the suspect Celtic keeper John Fallon and the ball fell tantalisingly at Ferguson's feet, but instead of firing it into the back of the net he fell over it. 'It looked easier to score,' remembers Archie Macpherson. A couple of minutes before half-time Celtic added two more and were in an unassailable lead.

Ferguson would never play for Rangers again; Davy White did not want to know him any more. He even left him out of the squad for the Rangers tour of North America that summer. Ferguson was furious and went off to ask for a transfer. In October 1969 he was sold to Falkirk for £20,000. Rangers had taken a loss of £45,000 on their man, a not inconsiderable amount of money in those days. A month after Ferguson had left White was sacked. Into his shoes stepped Willie Waddell, a known admirer of Ferguson and a man Ferguson would almost certainly have thrived under. But it was not to be.

'He was never really popular with the Rangers fans,' reckons Robert McElroy. 'That goal in the 1969 Cup final coloured their opinion of him. But even before that he never really fired them up, although his strike rate looks good in hindsight.' McElroy also remembers his being sent off playing for Falkirk against Rangers not long after he had left Ibrox. 'That didn't win him any fans either,' he says, 'especially as it was John Greig on the receiving end.'

Ferguson's footballing career was to be peppered with dismissals – something that in later life as a manager would come in useful as he had to commiserate with his own charges. But his record does not make for bedtime reading. He was first sent off in May 1964 for kicking an opponent. Then in January 1966 he was dismissed again for fighting. The following year he took another early bath, this time for 'striking an opponent'. The opponent was Colin Stein, who a short time later was to become his partner up front at Ibrox, but at this stage was playing for Hibs against Rangers.

In September 1970 Ferguson was dismissed for the fourth time when he again 'deliberately kicked an opponent'. On this occasion the man on the receiving end was none other than his old Rangers mate John Greig. Ferguson was now playing for Falkirk against Rangers. His fifth dismissal came in February 1972 for kicking yet again, and his final dismissal was in February 1973 for, yes, 'deliberately kicking an opponent'. In addition he was also cautioned on 15 occasions, though it is not uncommon these days for a player to be cautioned that many times in a season. However, his regular dismissals do suggest that he was something of a 'hard player', not averse to landing a kick or two on opponents. That said, six sendings-off in a career that stretched over 16 seasons doesn't exactly make him a demon. Ferguson could be hot-headed but was hardly a danger to women and children.

In all Ferguson had played a grand total of 73 games for the Gers, scoring a creditable 39 goals. By the autumn of 1969 he had been relegated to the reserves and at times was even playing with the third team. It was time to get away from Ibrox.

When Falkirk bought Ferguson that October for £20,000 he was their most expensive player, and the man who signed him was none other than Willie Cunningham – the man who had sold him to Rangers. 'We needed a goal scorer,' says Cunningham, 'and I knew Alex could score goals.'

Ferguson made his debut for the Brockville club on 25 November in a Dewar Shield game against Dundee, scoring what one observer described as 'a tremendous goal'. Falkirk won 5–2 and Ferguson was the toast of the town, although he was somewhat upstaged by his new striking partner Andy Roxburgh, who hit a splendid hat trick. A short time later he made his league debut at Berwick, again scoring in a 3–1 win for Falkirk. Ferguson turned out to be an inspired investment for Falkirk that season as the club went on to top the league and win promotion to the Scottish First Division. Ferguson had more than played his part, contributing 14 goals in 21 appearances.

He had formed an effective partnership up front with Andy Roxburgh, and the following season he was still knocking them in as Falkirk ended the season in a creditable seventh place. He had hit another 14 goals in 28 outings, but it was really to mark the end of his goal-scoring days. He was now 30 years old and in the 1971–72 season he struck just nine goals despite playing 28 games. The following season he did not even manage one goal in 17 appearances.

Ferguson and Roxburgh formed another partnership around that time in a Falkirk Football Club quiz side.

Falkirk supporter Michael White recalls going to Birmingham to watch the quiz team compete against Millwall on BBC Television's *Quizball*. 'I remember it was neck and neck when Roxburgh was asked a simple question. He got it wrong and Ferguson hit the roof. He couldn't believe that Roxburgh had not known the answer. He was calling him all names after the show. He was so annoyed at losing.'

On the football pitch Ferguson also teamed up again with Alex Totten, who had previously played with him at Dunfermline. Totten remembers how good he was with the boys when he was appointed coach. 'He'd spend hours with them, helping them and just talking to them. You could sense even then that he had something. But he didn't suffer fools gladly.'

Ferguson's appointment as coach was a mark of manager Willie Cunningham's respect for his ability. The more Cunningham saw of him the more he was impressed by his off-the-field attitude. 'He was so professional,' he says, 'and I began to see something there for the future. He was a leader and knew the game inside out.'

During his final season at Brockville, Ferguson was to find himself involved in a spot of conflict with the man who had signed him and made him coach. After a 6–1 thrashing at St Johnstone, Cunningham hit the roof. He was furious at their performance and in a fit of rage told the players that he was withdrawing all travel and subsistence expenses for training. A huge row erupted. The players reacted by walking out, led by union rep Alex Ferguson. With a match scheduled to be played against Montrose in a few days' time there was a real threat that it would not take place.

A spokesman for the players, probably Ferguson, was quoted in the *Falkirk Herald* saying that 'this action has not been taken lightly. We realise we are professional footballers with contracts to honour, but when men are treated like children, it's high time something was done about it.' Willie Cunningham, however, was not to be budged.

Tension was rising around Brockville and a board meeting was quickly convened by chairman Willie Palmer. Unfortunately the earliest time they could meet was on the Saturday lunchtime before the game, but at the meeting Cunningham would still not relent. He'd made a stand and he was sticking by it. It was a question of who was running things at Brockville – the players, the directors or the manager. Outside the club's offices journalists and television crews waited to hear if the game was going ahead.

It was a tricky lunchtime for the board, enough to give them indigestion. The incident had grown totally out of proportion. Cunningham's initial action might have been over the top but the players' walkout had hardly been a restrained response. If the board backed the manager then the players would carry out their threatened strike, the club would no doubt be docked points and might even be faced with a string of transfer requests. On the other hand, if they climbed down, it was tantamount to snubbing the manager. The board finally decided that they could cope with the latter and went off to meet Ferguson and the players in a local hotel. At 2 p.m., with just an hour to kick-off, an agreement was finally hammered out. There was little doubt who had won.

The game went ahead with Falkirk beating Montrose 3–0, but it wasn't the manager who had chosen the team. Cunningham was still angry, convinced that he had been let down by the board who had gone over his head in coming to some sort of a settlement. It was also clear that Cunningham had been reprimanded by the board for his action. 'I didn't want to climb down,' he says today. 'I was winning, but the directors decided to back down.'

Cunningham remembers Ferguson as a tough negotiator:

'He was determined to win and wasn't going to back down. It had to be his way or nothing.'

In the end Ferguson and the players had won, but for some months there were bad feelings around Brockville. Perhaps Cunningham felt let down by his coach. Whatever the reason, Ferguson was frequently left to train on his own. It was an intolerable situation. He decided he simply could not go on that way, and a move was inevitable. Today Cunningham, although as much of an admirer of Ferguson as he ever was, points out that Ferguson 'might have found out a different perspective since he became a manager'.

There is no doubt about what Ferguson's perspective was as a player. Throughout his playing career, he was actively involved with the Scottish Professional Footballers' Association, the footballers' trade union. In the early 1970s he was elected chairman and years later went on to receive the Association's merit award for service. Tony Higgins, the Scottish PFA's current full-time secretary, was recruited by Ferguson. 'I used to see him regularly on the train when I was playing for Hibs,' Higgins explains. 'He'd talk to me about various things going on in the union and he got me involved. Over the years, Ferguson was heavily involved in the union, always fighting for the rights of players. He's been a great spokesman for us.'

Ferguson ended his playing days at Somerset Park as a part-timer with First Division Ayr United. He joined the club on a free transfer, signed by Ayr manager Ally MacLeod, on 3 September 1973, and stayed just one season. By then he was 31, pushing 32, and his days as a brisk striker were behind him. What he lacked in pace he more than made up for in muscle. He did not make a great impact at Somerset Park and is barely remembered at the club as a player. He notched up just 18 league appearances and scored nine goals, with a tenth scored in the Scottish Cup. Up front Ferguson was teamed with George McLean, the former Rangers man, commonly known as Dandy. The fans dubbed them Fergie and Dandy.

Towards the end of the season Ferguson lost his place. He regained it briefly but played his final game in football on 13 April 1974 as Ayr drew 1–1 at Falkirk. Despite Ferguson's lack of impact, it had not been a bad season for Ayr. They finished in seventh place on the same number of points as sixth-placed Hearts and reached the quarter-finals of the Scottish Cup. Ferguson had played 349 games in Scottish football. His final goal, his 181st in all, came in the 5–0 hammering of Cowdenbeath in the Scottish Cup on 27 January 1974.

As Ferguson left the club to take over as manager at East Stirlingshire, the *Ayr Advertiser* quoted him as saying, 'I feel sure that I have had enough playing experience to have a shot at being a manager.' Team-mate John Murphy, who later became a scout for him at Aberdeen, remembered that even then he showed every sign of becoming a manager. 'He was always thinking about the game, always encouraging others. It was clear that he would go into management and become a very good manager.'

CHAPTER FOUR

A King in Paisley

When Willie Muirhead, chairman of East Stirlingshire Football Club, sat down at his desk to pick up the telephone, little did he know that the incoming call was about to launch the career of a man who would in time become one of the most successful managers in British football.

It had not been the best of seasons for East Stirlingshire, the tiny Falkirk club. They had ended the 1973–74 season in 16th place in the old Scottish Second Division. The manager had been taking some stick for continually playing his son-in-law and at the end of the season the club directors decided a new face was needed. The directors had gone off to Munich for the World Cup finals, not in search of a new manager but in the hope of some fun and the fulfilment of dreams with the Scottish side. The chairman Willie Muirhead was left at home to find a new manager.

It wasn't an easy task. Who would want to manage a club without resources, fans or ambition? Gates had fallen to below 500, the club was without a goalkeeper and there were only eight outfield players, including the famous son-in-law and a bunch of untried youngsters.

Then one morning while Muirhead was sorting out the mail the telephonist rang through to say that one of the other directors was on the phone from Munich. 'He wanted to know if I had managed to find a new manager,' says Muirhead. ' "No," I replied. He then said that he had been talking to Ally MacLeod in Germany, who at the time was managing at Ayr United. MacLeod had told him that he had a reserve team player who was keen to become a manager. He was called Alex Ferguson.' Muirhead vaguely remembered him as a player with Falkirk. 'He used to flap his elbows like chicken wings. He was a good player but definitely not great,' he recalls.

Given the lack of options, Muirhead decided at least to give Ferguson a call and sound him out. He liked what he heard, but Ferguson told him that he was also in the running for a coaching job at Queen's Park. Nevertheless, they agreed to meet, along with their wives, at a hotel in Falkirk.

Muirhead was immediately impressed. 'He was a family man, a trustworthy person,' he says. 'I knew straightaway I had got myself a manager far superior to anyone I had interviewed.' Muirhead immediately offered him the job. There was no contract, just a shake of hands. It was 27 June 1974.

'I have got a big job on my hands,' admitted Ferguson to the local paper a few days later. 'Shire have been in the doldrums for a long time and it will be a long and gradual process to change the image of the team.' But he was confident: 'I think I have enough experience as a player to have a go at being a manager.'

Yet what he found at Firs Park was frightening. It was little wonder the club was in the doldrums. They had been rooted to the lower half of the Second Division for years. There was no money, no youth training scheme. It was a friendly place but it was also a shambles. You couldn't really blame the directors. They did their best but there was no support and never would be. Ferguson's first priority was to buy new players. He went to see the board. As a gesture of goodwill they agreed to let him have £2,000. Muirhead remembers going away on holiday and coming home to discover that Ferguson had spent the lot on one player, Billy Hulston. He couldn't believe it, though quite how many players the board expected to get for £2,000 is questionable. Ferguson was in trouble. The chairman looked at him. 'And who else have you got?' he wanted to know. Ferguson told him. He had signed, as Muirhead later put it, 'a bunch of cast-offs from other clubs'. It wasn't a harmonious start and was hardly helped by results. The pre-season games were a farce. Six games without a win, 17 goals conceded.

If nothing else, Ferguson at least had enthusiasm, buckets of it, and he set about his first managerial job with some vigour. Two weeks into the season, his famed disciplinarianism was taking shape. Star striker Jim Meakin had accepted a wedding invitation on match day. Ferguson told him he couldn't go; Meakin went. Ferguson went spare and Meakin was promptly suspended. The board backed Ferguson all the way. But they didn't always see eye to eye. On one occasion Ferguson had spent £40 on hiring a minibus to bring some schoolboy players in from Glasgow. He was looking to try to develop a youth scheme and wanted to tap the rich vein of footballing talent in Glasgow, but at the monthly board meeting he was berated for spending the money without permission. Fuming at the board's petty-mindedness, he promptly stood up, put his hand in his back pocket, pulled out £40 in notes and tossed them on the table, then he quietly walked out. Later that evening Willie Muirhead was forced to call him at home and smooth out their differences.

Yet despite the 'cast-offs', the youngsters and the son-in-law, East Stirlingshire began to put together a useful set of results and even climbed into the top six, giddy heights for the little club. Crowds had doubled to average 1,200 and more money was coming in through the turnstiles. When they beat local rivals Falkirk, it was like winning the Cup and VE Day together.

Ferguson was the toast of Firs Park. Prior to the game he

had taken his players for their pre-match lunch to the same hotel as the Falkirk team. It was deliberate, a game of psychology. Ferguson's players laughed and joked their way through lunch, showing no signs of pre-match nerves or worries. It worked; they won 2–0. It was Ferguson's first success with a little bit of psychology. It would not be the last.

Already his managerial style was taking shape. Other clubs were beginning to sit up and take notice, chief among them St Mirren. They had been alerted by their former manager, Willie Cunningham, who had signed the young Ferguson from St Johnstone and then when he was with Falkirk had signed him again, this time from Rangers. Cunningham knew him well and had spotted his leadership abilities. Willie Todd, the then chairman of St Mirren, called Cunningham to ask his advice about a replacement. Cunningham had no hesitation in recommending Ferguson. 'I simply told them he was the man for the job,' he claims. Todd was impressed by Cunningham's confidence in the young man and it wasn't long before an offer to manage the Paisley club was forthcoming. Ferguson had been at East Stirlingshire just over three months and initially turned down the offer, but St Mirren were persistent.

Ferguson wasn't sure it was worth his while to move. St Mirren had finished the previous season just a few places above them in the league, and there was virtually no difference between the clubs now. He asked Jock Stein for his opinion.

'Go to the highest point of St Mirren's ground at Love Street and look down on it. Then do the same at Firs Park,' Stein told him. 'See the difference. St Mirren has so much more potential.' The capacity at St Mirren was more than twice that of East Stirlingshire. St Mirren had won trophies; East Stirlingshire had won nothing other than the Second Division championship in 1932. There was no comparison; Ferguson decided to go. Willie Muirhead wasn't too pleased but had guessed that he would accept the offer. 'I'll say now what I said then about him leaving,' he recalls. 'It was a bloody tragedy for East Stirlingshire. He was the best thing that ever happened to the club.'

Ferguson was reluctant to part company, feeling that he owed East Stirlingshire some loyalty. After all, they had given him his first break. But in life you sometimes get only once chance and you either take it or you don't. Ferguson decided to take it. He had been at Firs Park just four months. East Stirlingshire's loss was to be St Mirren's gain.

When Ferguson arrived at Love Street he found a club in despair. Jock Stein might have told him about the view and the potential but there wasn't much else in evidence. Gates were low, averaging between 1,000 and 1,500 each week, and the club was languishing at the foot of the old Scottish Second Division. They had ended the previous campaign in 11th spot, and with a new Premier League and two other divisions about to be introduced the St Mirren directors were desperate to stop the club crashing into the lowest division. Even so, there was little money in the coffers and certainly not much to be spent in the transfer market.

It left Ferguson with little choice but to concentrate on home-grown talent. It would in time prove to be the most valuable lesson he ever learnt in football. He quickly instituted links with the community and local schools. John Byrne, then a headteacher in Paisley, remembers being invited by Ferguson along to the club to discuss schools football. Byrne ran the local school team and Ferguson was keen to tap any potential players in the area. 'We were all invited along. He asked to meet teachers and all those involved with football in the local schools. He was only young at the time but he took the trouble to talk to us. He wanted to know what good young players we might have and wanted to encourage a relationship with the schools.'

Ferguson quickly developed a young side. They were

nearly all inexperienced players, but a couple of older hands were signed up to give some weight and experience. He also set up a network of scouts whose job was to spot good young players. 'We didn't have any money to buy players,' says former chairman Willie Todd. 'There was no alternative. We had to get them for nothing.' Ferguson established four youth teams of different age levels. The first was for 12-year-olds, the next for 13-year-olds, while the other two were for 15- and 16-year-olds. 'The youngsters knew that they would have a much better chance of playing reserve team and first team football with us than they would ever have done had they gone to Parkhead or Ibrox,' says Todd.

Ferguson's youth policy was to pay rich dividends. Frank McGarvey was signed from Kilsyth Rangers as a 17-year-old while Billy Stark came from another juvenile team at the same age. Both players would go on to give distinguished service to the club, Stark eventually following Ferguson to Aberdeen while McGarvey went to Liverpool. 'He really used to wind the kids up,' remembers the former chairman. 'He used to tell them they were a bunch of layabouts, but it got them going.'

One of the older players brought in to help was Jackie Copland from Dundee United. He was one of Ferguson's biggest signings, costing £17,000. To raise the cash Ferguson went to the Supporters' Club. In his first season he released 18 of the 32 players on the club's books. He began by calling them into his office one by one and telling each of them that they were being placed on the transfer list. It was a distressing job, and after a while he began to think that he would be there all night, so he decided to call eight in all together. 'It was a disaster,' he later confessed. 'They were all young lads.' He realised that the very least he owed them was his time and an explanation. It was another vital lesson in man-management.

At the end of his first season in charge St Mirren had

finished in sixth spot and duly went into the newly created Scottish First Division. It was a decent achievement considering their starting point, but better was to come. The following year against much tougher opposition they again finished sixth. Then in 1977 they finished in top spot, four points ahead of Clydebank, and were promoted to the Premier Division. They had lost just two games all season. 'We played our best football of the last 20 years that season,' remembers one supporter.

Ferguson was now in the Scottish big time. Instead of visits to St Johnstone, Arbroath and Hamilton, it was a case of taking on Celtic, Rangers and Hibs. It was a formidable task but he approached it in a calculated way. By the end of the 1977–78 season St Mirren had just hung on to their place in the big time, finishing second from bottom. They had also reached the quarter-finals of the Scottish League Cup, before losing over two legs to Celtic.

Yet it was also to be Ferguson's final season with the Paisley club. Allegations had been made about the way he had handled some of the club's money – there was never any suggestion that any of it had gone into his own pocket, but that he had used it to pay trialists. They were said to have been given expenses and so forth. None of this was illegal but the club felt he had overstepped the mark, paying out this money. They were only small amounts of cash, and the wonder is that St Mirren should have been so concerned. Certainly the supporters weren't. They reckoned Ferguson was merely doing his best to encourage players to join the club. But the club had little money and frowned upon his expenditure, and he was sacked.

Ferguson took the club to an Industrial Tribunal in a case of unfair dismissal. The dispute rumbled on for some time, long after he had left Love Street, and was to cause considerable disruption in his early months at Aberdeen. Unfortunately he lost, and it all left a bitter taste. There were those at the time who tried to persuade Ferguson against going to a Tribunal as it would only raise unnecessary issues. But Ferguson insisted that there was a principle at stake.

Even today the whole episode is still shrouded in mystery. It is also further confused by some suggestions from disappointed fans that Ferguson had been 'tapped' beforehand by Aberdeen. Certainly within days of leaving Love Street he was on his way to Pittodrie. Today, St Mirren are somewhat embarrassed by the episode, preferring to forget that it ever happened.

Perhaps it was just as well that there was a parting of the ways. The truth was that Ferguson had gone as far as he could with St Mirren. They would never be able to match the top shots in the Premier League.

'He will always be remembered in Paisley for the way he publicised the team,' claims the club's unofficial historian and lifelong supporter John Byrne. 'He had the knack of creating enormous interest in the club. I remember we were drawn against Dundee United in the Cup. They were in the Premier League and had been in the top three. We were only in the First Division. Alex claimed we could beat them.' St Mirren did, winning 4–1. They then faced Motherwell in the next round and such was the interest generated by Ferguson that a crowd of over 26,000 turned up at Motherwell, the biggest crowd they had known in years – so big that the kick-off had to be delayed in order to get everyone into the ground. Unfortunately they lost 2–1.

Local journalist Stan Park remembers how Ferguson used to tour the town in a loudspeaker van on a Saturday morning. 'He'd be urging people to come to the game that afternoon. He would go around the town centre and then up to the housing estates.' Suddenly women and children started coming to matches, something which was unusual in those times. 'He made the town feel alive again,' says Park. 'He was a king in Paisley.' His departure, its abruptness and the manner of his sacking, saddened many people.

Paisley would now have to learn to live without him.

'It wasn't a good time for Paisley,' Park remembers. 'Jobs were disappearing and the town was becoming an industrial wilderness. But he gave people something to cheer about, they could forget what was happening during the week. He made life a little more worthwhile.'

CHAPTER FIVE

A Far Cry

Fish and agriculture were a far cry from the bleak landscape
and heavy engineering of Strathclyde. Prior to 1970
Aberdeen was known for little else. A thriving port on the
north-east coast of Scotland, it had long been the base for
Scotland's eastern fishing fleet. The smell of fish pervaded
the entire city, especially at dawn as the industrious fish
market opened its doors for business. For the remainder of
the morning you could smell little else in the city. Seagulls
would mewl and swoop above the harbour, clustering
around the rigging of the fishing vessels before wheeling in
on the easterly breezes to scoop up some fishy breakfast.
Then they would perch on the refrigerator lorries for a well-
earned rest.

Aberdeen is popularly known as the granite city, many
of its buildings carved out of the dark granite rock that
used to be one of its chief exports. Today, the city still has a
sombre air, not helped by the Gothic architecture of its
colleges and churches. There are buildings with wedding
cake spires, a university that looks as a university should,
and a castle that resembles a royal residence even though it
was actually built by the Salvation Army. Walk down the
main thoroughfare, Union Street, said to be precisely a mile
long, and you might imagine that you are in the centre of

some small but not humble capital, one with a certain style and character. And on the hill overlooking the harbour are the homes of the bourgeoisie, Victorian mansions, proud and spacious. Of course Aberdeen has changed since the mid-seventies, but even today you can still feel the Victorian presence. The humour of the city was rumoured to match its grim appearance.

Before 1970, Aberdeen did not attract too much attention. There was a steady flow of tourists, primarily to Balmoral on Royal-spotting trips, and also to the sandy but wind-swept beaches that stretch northwards. But a 150-mile journey from Edinburgh hardly made it the most accessible of cities, and the weather didn't help, with gales lashing in from the east and a bitterly cold wind swirling around the harbour. Even on a warm summer's day Aberdeen could be inhospitable. Industry was light, with most activity centred around the busy harbour, its fishing fleet, agriculture and a large Michelin factory. Unemployment had never exceeded 3 per cent of the working population since the war. But it was a comfortable place to live, even if it was miles from anywhere, with the quality of life said to be among the best in the country.

But then in the early 1970s came a discovery that was to change Aberdeen beyond recognition: black gold. Off the coast of Aberdeen, in the wild North Sea, American drilling rigs located oil. Initially, only a handful of people realised the implications. Extracting the oil was still a complication, but once engineering minds had tackled the problem the landscape of Aberdeen would never be the same.

It was boom time. In the harbour the fishing smacks sat alongside a new fleet of vessels, servicing the mighty oil industry. There were jobs galore. The Texans rolled in. Offices, transport, small engineering companies, diving facilitators, heliports, service industries, hotels, all sprang up or developed as the multi-million-dollar oil business hit the Grampians. The industry was going to make Aberdeen and the British economy rich, predicted the experts. And so it did, although there was always a keen argument as to how long the oil would last. In the early seventies they predicted just 20 years' supply of oil. By the 1980s it looked likely to last beyond the millennium. Aberdeen was like some Yukon outpost, attracting a rush of prospectors as they heard the news of gold, all desperate to make a quick buck. And there was money to be made. The economic focus of Scotland suddenly shifted from the heavy industrial belt of central Scotland to the north-east coast. And in football the Old Firm was set to be replaced by the New Firm.

By the time Alex Ferguson arrived in Aberdeen in 1978, the oil boom was well under way. Aberdeen had been transformed from a sleepy royal Scottish borough into the centre of a mega-rich industry with a buzzing international community. Texan hats, cowboy boots and string ties might have been clichés but you could occasionally spot them in the hotel lobbies. Mostly they kept themselves to themselves, living in their closely knit communities or gathering at the Petroleum Club, an American-style country club where they could meet and talk their own language, and drink beyond the statutory ten o'clock limit. There was even an American school. *Newsweek* dubbed Aberdeen 'Sin City' but in truth there was little evidence of prostitutes, gambling and lavish spending.

The one thing few people visited Aberdeen for was the football. Aberdeen Football Club might have been founded in the early years of the century, but they had been short on honours during their 70 years of existence. They'd claimed the Scottish League in 1955 and had won a couple of cups, but in the pecking order of the Scottish game they came a long way behind the Glasgow and Edinburgh clubs. The city had produced a few footballing gems, most notably Denis Law, but had not had the nous to spot him, something which seems astonishing in such a small city. Instead, Law disappeared over the horizon to Huddersfield Town.

Aberdeen was out on a limb. The nearest city was Dundee, over 70 miles away, with Peterhead the nearest population centre of any size. And even that was an hour's journey. Edinburgh and Glasgow were 150 miles away, a good three hours' slog by road. The Aberdeen stadium was within a stone's throw of the coast, lashed by gales, bitter winds and the salt spray. On match days they reckoned you could still hear the groaning east winds loud above the stoical silence of the Grampian crowd.

Inevitably Aberdeen's isolation meant that they had only small support. Gates didn't always top the 10,000 mark, and only a visit from the Glasgow giants ever filled Pittodrie to capacity.

And yet by 1978 there were signs that Aberdeen were on the brink of something. Ally MacLeod had become manager in November 1975 and had almost taken the club into the lower division in his first season. Relegation would have guaranteed him the sack, but gradually things improved. In his first full season in charge the Dons had finished third in the table behind the Glasgow giants and had won the League Cup, beating Celtic 2–1 in the final. MacLeod had then been tempted away to manage the national squad and had been replaced by Billy McNeill, the former Celtic skipper. In McNeill's first season in charge they finished second, just two points behind champions Rangers, and were also losing finalists in the Scottish Cup. The Dons had not known such giddy success since the fifties. But then McNeill too was off, leaving Aberdeen managerless for the third time in three years.

The Dons had mulled over the prospect of Alex Ferguson a year earlier but had decided instead to opt for McNeill. After all, McNeill was a household name, the fulcrum of the famous Celtic side that had lifted the European Cup in 1967, the kind of man players and fans respect. But now, with Jock Stein standing down at Parkhead, McNeill was returning to the scene of his former glory. He was the obvious successor and nobody could quibble. But his departure left Aberdeen stranded.

By coincidence, Alex Ferguson was now without a job. Aberdeen chairman Dick Donald knew that Ferguson was the man to go for. They could make a quick appointment and would not have to go through the complications that appointing a current manager would involve. It was neat and tempting.

But although the board was easily persuaded, the fans were not so convinced for Ferguson had a reputation as a hothead. He'd been sent off once too often in his career and, as the papers pointed out, it wasn't exactly that much of a career either. He was also young, only 35, and still largely inexperienced as a manager. What the fans wanted was a big name to replace McNeill, one of the biggest names in Scottish football.

It was a risk, but Ferguson came recommended. A year earlier departing manager Ally MacLeod had put a word in to chairman Dick Donald. MacLeod knew Ferguson from his days as manager at Ayr United when Ferguson briefly played under him, and he assured Donald that Ferguson would do a good job for them. The chairman put his trust in MacLeod's judgement and appointed Ferguson.

In many ways Ferguson was lucky. He was stepping into a club ripe for success. There would still be much to do but the foundations had already been laid. Yet his first season in charge was to prove something of a disappointment. By Ferguson's own admission, he was largely responsible for this himself. His father was seriously ill and Ferguson spent a considerable amount of time commuting between Glasgow and Aberdeen, wanting to spend what time remained with him. It was a significant, though understandable, distraction. He was under emotional strain, his mind was not always on the job and the hours spent travelling took him away from other vital work. Fighting his case of unfair dismissal against St Mirren at the

Industrial Tribunal would prove another distraction during that first season.

The tongues were soon wagging around Aberdeen. Rumour had it that the players were not especially impressed by their new boss. More than anything, Ferguson just wanted to get through his first season, take a break, and then regather his thoughts, but the flak was flying. The local paper didn't help either, giving over space to the views of disgruntled supporters, and reporting on the unease of some of the players. It may have seemed harmless but what it was doing was to give credence to the rumours. It all added to the pressure. Nonetheless, chairman Dick Donald remained supportive. He understood the difficulties Ferguson was going through and simply told him to hang on.

After the previous season's promise, Ferguson's opening salvo seemed a damp squib to many supporters. They were hoping to make that final leap to the top of the table but they never really challenged and never had the look of prospective champions. At one point they went three months without a league win. And yet there was much to be pleased about. They still finished a creditable fourth in the league, trailing champions Celtic by just eight points, and also managed to reach the League Cup final, where they were unlucky to lose to Rangers.

Like Billy McNeill, and MacLeod before him, he had taken the club to a League Cup final in his first season. Aberdeen were desperately unlucky, with Steve Archibald injured in the first minute by a Derek Johnstone tackle. Limping though he was, Archibald still managed to open the scoring for Aberdeen early in the second half. But then there was further bad luck as goalkeeper Bobby Clark, Aberdeen's most capped international player, crashed to the ground injured and, with Aberdeen half waiting for the physio to come on, Rangers carried on attacking and scored. Even then the ball took a deflection off an Aberdeen defender. Clark could do nothing. Then came even worse luck as Doug Rougvie was sent off after a clash with Derek Johnstone. To this day the arguments still rage about what precisely happened, but the outcome was that Johnstone was poleaxed, with the trainer on the field for more than five minutes giving him attention. Rougvie, who had already been booked, claimed that he had simply pushed him aside. It was debatable, and Rougvie had his marching orders. The Dons were doomed. From 1–0 up and in virtual control they were now down to eight fit men and two passengers. A Rangers winner was inevitable. It came six minutes into injury time.

Ferguson was incensed after the match. Initially he was furious with Rougvie for getting himself sent off. But when Rougvie pleaded his innocence and was backed by the players, who insisted that Johnstone had conned the referee with his antics, Ferguson's wrath was redirected towards the Rangers man. Rougvie was in tears and Ferguson was soon warning people to keep him away from Johnstone before any further damage was done. It had not been the most savoury of finals and the Rougvie/Johnstone incident would sour relations between the two clubs for some considerable time.

Ferguson's first season at Pittodrie threw up its difficulties, not least with the players. He didn't have to read the local press to sense the unease in the dressing room. The attitude was wrong and needed changing. Eventually a confrontation blew up between Ferguson and captain Willie Miller, which could have ended with one of them being shown the door. Instead it finished with both men learning a little more respect for one another and helped ease the festering tensions between manager and players. 'From that time on Willie Miller and I have formed one of the best relationships a manager and a captain could ever have. I now have nothing but admiration for him,' wrote Ferguson many years later. It had been a defining moment.

Many other managers would have backed down.

As ever there was also the question of drink, and after a 3–0 defeat in Germany by Fortuna, another lesson was to be learnt. Instead of returning to their hotel and heading for bed, one bunch of players opted for a spot of nightclubbing. Ferguson was not amused when he discovered their absence, especially with a crucial league game coming up. A few days later they lost to Hearts at home, and Ferguson blamed the nightclubbing. Some of the culprits would soon be on their way, discarded by Ferguson as having the wrong attitude.

One player saw the incident as a turning point. 'There was a hell of a row afterwards,' he said. 'We were told that we could either knuckle down and learn to be professionals or go elsewhere. The gaffer wasn't going to have second best. He wanted to be a winner and if that meant no drinking and early to bed, then so be it.' It was a lesson he would carry over to Old Trafford.

Essentially there was an *attitude* problem. This was in evidence when, after a draw with one of the Old Firm, Ferguson walked into the dressing room to discover his players celebrating. It was as if they had won the cup. He could scarcely believe it. It seemed that drawing was good enough for them, when what they should have been chasing was a victory. He was furious. 'I had to change that. They had the wrong attitude,' he confessed.

The problem showed itself in other ways. One player who turned up for training with a perm was promptly sent home and told not to return until he had washed it out and looked more presentable. It was the no-fancy-stuff, go-to-work-smart, Bill Struth Govan background coming out in Ferguson. Football was as much about attitude as it was about ability. One journalist remembers interviewing Ferguson after he'd lost a semi-final. 'Semi-finals are no good to us,' he snarled. All he was interested in was a final and winning.

Alex McLeish, who was to become a cornerstone of the successful 1980s side, remembers his management style vividly. 'It was a combination of bullying and joking. He has the ruthlessness of a man who must have success, no matter whose toes he stands on to achieve it. In a way we all benefited from his temper. It made you realise what the game could mean to someone.'

Mark McGhee also spotted how Ferguson wanted to have control over everything. 'At Pittodrie he'd know how many toilet rolls we used in a week. Like Mrs Thatcher he had total belief in his own ideas.' Ferguson might agree but would not thank him for the comparison with the former Tory leader.

Had anybody fancied a wager on Aberdeen to win the Scottish championship back in November 1979, they could probably have found odds of around 50–1 if they searched hard enough. By then the Dons had already lost five league fixtures and been knocked out of Europe at the first hurdle. The omens were not good.

They even lost their opening game of the season at Partick Thistle. Back in the dressing room Ferguson didn't appear too bothered. 'Don't laugh,' he is reputed to have told the players, 'but I've got a scent about the way things are going to turn out this season.' Whether or not he was just saying it for effect, to boost the already sagging morale of his troops, will never be admitted. Such bravura could easily have led to his own downfall, but by the end of the season he would be proudly reminding anyone who cared to listen of his famous prediction. Ferguson and Aberdeen were about to come of age.

Ferguson's team was largely the same as that inherited by Billy McNeill. A handful of players had left in his first season, bringing in much-needed money. Most of it had been spent on buying Mark McGhee from Newcastle for £70,000. There would be even less activity in his second season. The biggest deal seemed to be the signing of Dougie Bell, who came on a free transfer from St Mirren. One or two more players left, including Don Sullivan and Ian Fleming, both of whom Ferguson was prepared to let go. It was rich in talent and shrewd buying, boasting characters such as Steve Archibald, Jim Leighton, Gordon Strachan, Willie Miller, Joe Harper, Doug Rougvie and Alex McLeish.

Despite their poor form in the league, Aberdeen were again making giant strides in the League Cup, beating both Rangers and Celtic, home and away, as they progressed towards the final. It was the first time any Aberdeen side had ever dished out four successive cup defeats to the Old Firm. Ferguson might be a Govan man but he still delighted in defeating his old favourites. One year in Aberdeen had already been enough to instil a sense of annoyance at the Old Firm's domination of Scottish football both on and off the field.

The League Cup final turned out to be another case of so near yet so far for the Dons. Having eliminated the Glasgow giants, Aberdeen must have fancied their chances against Dundee United. Although they dominated the Hampden final, there was a distinct absence of luck, and after extra time the game petered out into a goalless draw. Ferguson intended to change things around for the replay at Dens Park but in the end kept the same team, whereas Dundee United made a few vital changes to their line-up. The result was a 3–0 win for United. It taught Ferguson to be more ruthless, more unshakeable in his own beliefs.

Ferguson's tenure at Pittodrie was becoming increasingly uncertain. The trouble was that expectations had been raised and he had 'lost' yet another final, his second, and his club's fourth, in as many years. It was enough to turn any fan. Ferguson was beginning to feel the pressure. He recalls 'feeling worse than I have ever felt in my life' after losing that replay. That night he lay awake, half expecting the phone to ring, half expecting someone to suggest calling it a day. He was on the verge of quitting. The season had promised so much but now seemed to be lying in tatters around him. In the league they were hovering well behind the leaders, in sixth spot, and didn't look likely to fare much better.

But rather than quit, he decided to go on the offensive. The following morning, tired and still depressed, he was striding through the front doors at Pittodrie well ahead of anyone else. He changed into his kit and was back at the entrance twenty minutes later to greet each player personally and to thank them for their efforts in the replay. It was a cunning piece of man-management. The players, just as depressed themselves, were given a vital lift by his enthusiasm, just when they needed it most. Had he launched into an inquest it might have made everything worse. It was to prove a crucial turning point.

The problem was that they were far too inconsistent. There were flashes of inspiration in the Cup, and they had turned the Old Firm over, but when it came to the league and the need for consistent performances, Aberdeen seemed to be unsure. But it would only be a matter of time. Ferguson had already taken the crucial steps earlier in the season when he moved Gordon Strachan out of the central midfield and on to the right. It would take him time to adapt to his new role but once he did, consistency would begin to flourish.

The weather was also to wreak havoc with Scottish football that winter. Game after game was postponed as the nation struggled with the atrocious weather conditions. Celtic went two whole months without a league game as the fixtures piled up. With so many postponements, games in hand and so forth, it was difficult to make head or tail of the league. As late as mid-March, snow was still covering Pittodrie. At one stage, Aberdeen trailed Celtic by ten points. Admittedly they had three games in hand, but they had only collected 20 points from 18 games. However, as the teams emerged from the grip of winter the gap began to narrow. Soon it was down to nine points but they now had five games in hand.

The lengthening backlog of fixtures had not helped either Rangers or Celtic, both of whom were going through a transitional period as they developed new sides. It was impossible for them to inject any consistency into their game. This was all to Aberdeen's advantage. Yet to win the title the Dons needed to start winning themselves, while Celtic needed to lose a few games. Astonishingly, Celtic suddenly started throwing points away like confetti at a wedding, while Aberdeen went on a 15-match run without defeat. Celtic were thrashed 5–1 at Dundee and then were beaten twice at Parkhead by the Dons. Rangers also lost five games, and over a period of three weeks, the league table was turned upside down. There were just four games to play, three of them away from home, but the Dons were at the top of the table. In their next game Aberdeen beat Ferguson's old club St Mirren but then drew at Dundee United. This left them one point behind Celtic but with a game in hand.

The season reached its climax the following weekend as Celtic travelled to St Mirren for their final match while Aberdeen went to Hibs. Easter Road was something of a bogey ground for Aberdeen, but in the warm sunshine the Dons put superstitions behind them and polished off their opponents 5–0. Meanwhile, at Love Street, Celtic could manage only a draw. Aberdeen with their superior goal difference clambered over Celtic and claimed the title, and they still had one game to play. Ferguson, like most of the fans, was being given regular updates on the scoreline from Love Street. As soon as the final whistle sounded and confirmation of the Celtic score came in, he was racing on to the pitch. It was his first championship and the beginning of a new era for Scottish football. Ferguson was on his way.

CHAPTER SIX

Celebrate Your Victories and Mourn Your Defeats

Aberdeen had claimed their first championship in 25 years and only the second in their entire history. Suddenly Ferguson was the toast, not just of the Grampians, but of Scotland itself. But who was this man? For the first time in years somebody had stolen a march on the all-powerful Glasgow Giants, yet nobody seemed to know much about the man at the helm of Scotland's premier club. There were plenty of doubters on hand to question his ability. Rangers and Celtic, they claimed, were nothing like as powerful as they had once been. Both sides were said to be going through transitional stages. Aberdeen's reign wouldn't last; it was a fluke. And as for Ferguson, well, he had inherited his team from Ally MacLeod and Billy McNeill. Furthermore, Ferguson had lifted the championship crown with the lowest number of points anyone could remember. One paper rated them the poorest champions Scotland had ever known.

There was an element of truth to all these arguments. It was undoubtedly true that both Celtic and Rangers were in transitional phases. The great Celtic side of the sixties and seventies had long gone, and Kenny Dalglish, the focus of the Celtic side that had clinched further titles, had also

disappeared, going off to Liverpool to weave his magic.
And Rangers, although they had won trophies in the
seventies, were hardly a team to compare with the masters
of the fifties, the sides that Ferguson himself had watched
and adored every week at Ibrox. It was also true that
Ferguson had inherited the efforts of McNeill, although
McNeill's side, while commendable, was nothing special.

But all that would be to simplify matters. There was no
doubt that Ferguson had brought order and ambition to
Aberdeen. He had given the players that extra edge and
crucial belief in themselves and had not been afraid to take
unpopular decisions. To have beaten the Old Firm with all
their resources was still quite an achievement. 'What
he did was to harness the hardest, meanest defence in
Scotland with an attack that had flair,' says journalist Clive
Leatherdale, who lived in Aberdeen throughout the
Ferguson era. He would do much the same years later at
Old Trafford.

But Aberdeen's success had its down side. Steve
Archibald, whose 22 goals that season had been so critical
to the side's ambitions, had become a target for several big
clubs south of the border. For months there had been talk of
Archibald going. It was no longer a matter of *if*, but *when*
and which club. In the end it was Tottenham who in May,
days after the end of the season, signed him up for £700,000.
There was little Ferguson could do about it. It was a record
deal between English and Scottish clubs and Dick Donald
could hardly turn his nose up at that kind of money.

Joe Harper had also reached the end of the road and
suddenly Aberdeen were left short of firepower. But in truth
Harper, at 32, had contributed little to the championship
season. He had been injured most of the time, which at least
saved him the indignity of being dropped. Ferguson was
not a Harper fan. The little Scot was never a team player
and although he might have his moments in front of goal,
for far too long he would drift in and out of games.

Ferguson wanted grafters, players with spirit, and Harper never fitted into that category. 'I don't think we would have won the league championship with Joe in our side,' confessed Ferguson in his book *The Light In The North*. He was probably right.

Ferguson's assistant Pat Stanton also decided to move on, to take up the manager's job at Hibernian. Eventually Ferguson would bring in Archie Knox from Forfar as his replacement. It would be a long and fruitful partnership that would have many twists and turns in the Ferguson story. The Archibald money was partly spent in recruiting new players, but the Aberdeen manager still had much to learn about the market. Few of the new signings made much impression and in time they would be moved on. The lesson was that he shouldn't sell a player until he had a suitable replacement lined up.

But while Ferguson was not having much success in the transfer market, some of the youngsters he was drafting into the side were showing considerable promise. He'd signed most of them during his first season at the club and now they were maturing into first team players, proving to be sound investments. It was a policy that would prove crucial to the Ferguson story in the coming years. 'Aberdeen had long had a good youth policy but Ferguson made it better,' says John Murphy, one of his scouts. 'And as the club became more successful, so we could attract youngsters from all over Scotland.'

Among those earning their spurs in the coming season would be Ian Angus, Neale Cooper, Steve Cowan and Neil Simpson. Only a handful of them were from Aberdeen; most were from the Glasgow area. It was remarkable that Aberdeen was able to recruit youngsters from under the very noses of Rangers and Celtic. It also says much that those youngsters wanted to sign for Aberdeen, rather than hoping for the Glasgow giants to spot them. At Parkhead or Ibrox they might have waited years for their chance, but at Pittodrie they were soon thrown a shirt and told to get out there. And once they were out there, Ferguson put his faith in them. Clive Leatherdale remembers a young Neale Cooper having a 'stinker of a game'. But Ferguson pointedly refused to substitute him, despite the crowd's noisy demands. At the press conference after the match Ferguson was asked why he didn't take Cooper off. 'The boy needed the game,' replied Ferguson. 'I wasn't going to pull him off. It would have destroyed his confidence.' It was an example of Ferguson's skilful man-management.

John Murphy, whom he'd known as a player at Ayr United, was the man who was assigned to recruit youngsters from the Ayrshire area. 'He told me to look for three things,' says Murphy. 'Pace, attitude and skill. If you had those three things he reckoned you were half-way there to being a player. But above all he wanted pace.

'He was terrific with the young lads,' he remembers, 'there was nobody better. He could get the best out of them. He might have been a grumpy, bad-tempered old bugger at times, but he could get 150 per cent out of you, whether it was playing football or just making the tea.'

Archibald's absence would soon be felt. Mark McGhee was now the lone man up front. Ferguson experimented but nobody else seemed ideal. The players he brought in simply were not up to the job. And yet Aberdeen made an encouraging start to the season that had them racing three points ahead of Rangers at the top of the table by December. But it wouldn't last, and the principal cause of their downfall was to be a club that in the years ahead would be a thorn in Ferguson's side – Liverpool.

Aberdeen were now among the big boys, the championship giving the club its first stab at the European Cup. When they had last won the title back in 1955, the idea for the competition was still brewing in the mind of Gabriel Hanot, of the French sports daily, L'Equipe. Aberdeen should rightfully have been the first Scottish participants then, but

Hibernian had taken up that honour in their place as they had responded favourably to the idea.

From being sacked from St Mirren two years earlier, Ferguson was about to pit his footballing wits against the finest in Europe, and in particular against the former European champions themselves – Liverpool, the team who would by the end of that 1980–81 season be crowned Kings of Europe again.

In the opening round of the tournament Aberdeen faced Austria Memphis and in front of 20,000 at Pittodrie won 1–0. One goal seemed barely enough to edge them into the next round. However, in Austria they played a taut, tactical game and managed a goalless draw. But then came mixed blessings as they were drawn against the English champions and twice winners of the European Cup, Liverpool. There was huge excitement in Scotland and especially in Aberdeen. It was a Scotland against England showdown.

'But in the short term it was nothing less than a night-mare,' admitted Ferguson in hindsight. Once the draw had been made it was impossible for anyone at Pittodrie to concentrate on the domestic programme. The Liverpool game simply dominated and interrupted everything. It was like a giant shadow hanging over them. Immediately prior to the Liverpool match, Aberdeen were knocked out of the League Cup and began to look jittery in the league.

For the visit of Liverpool Ferguson had drawn up a careful tactical plan, but as with so many well-laid plans, it was in rags within five minutes as Terry McDermott chipped Leighton to put the English side in the driving seat. They never looked back and held on to win 1–0. Injuries robbed Aberdeen of a full-strength side for the second leg at Anfield, but it would probably have made little differ-ence. Liverpool were a class apart. They strolled to a 4–0 win. 'I was never so glad to get a game out of the way in my whole life,' remembered a disconsolate Ferguson.

That defeat left Aberdeen with a giant hangover, which

would eventually take its toll in league form. The slide began in November with a scrambled draw at Kilmarnock, followed by defeat at Morton and then a rash of draws over Christmas and the New Year. As January drew to a close they lost at Ibrox and at home to Morton. Another draw followed and another defeat. Suddenly the Dons were out of it. There were injuries galore: the loss of McMaster and Strachan had left the midfield bereft of any culture. All that Aberdeen could do was finish second, seven points behind Celtic. A couple of years earlier Ferguson would have been delighted, but after winning the title, his ambitions had taken on new dimensions. It was all about success, not about coming second. They fared no better outside the league. In the Scottish Cup, they were unfortunate to come across Morton, their bogey side, and lost yet again. It seemed to sum up their season.

But for injuries and the clash with Liverpool, Aberdeen might have successfully defended their title. As it was, strains and fractures had left Ferguson desperately short on experienced players when he most needed them. He still had a small squad, and although the youngsters had performed beyond all expectation, they lacked vital experience with only a couple of dozen games between them.

In the close season Ferguson wisely decided to invest the residue of the Archibald money in a few new players. If they were going to compete with the Old Firm they had to spend. Chairman Dick Donald agreed and Ferguson was given his blessing to recruit. Top of the list was St Mirren's winger Peter Weir, whom Ferguson had signed for St Mirren when he was manager. In the end Weir cost Aberdeen £200,000, with the popular Ian Scanlon going in the opposite direction. Losing Scanlon was a disappointment to the fans, but with St Mirren reluctant to part with Weir it was the only card Ferguson could play if he was to secure his man. He was an inspirational buy.

Aberdeen kicked off the season in appalling style,

receiving a 4–1 hiding at Dundee United, having trailed hopelessly 3–0 at half-time. Then in their second game, this time at Pittodrie, they lost 3–1 to Celtic. It was the first time they had lost their first two opening fixtures since the 1959–60 season. Things began to improve with their next game, but then came a UEFA Cup clash with Bobby Robson's Ipswich Town, holders of the trophy, and the current league leaders in England. This was surely a game to test Aberdeen's progress, especially after the previous season's humiliation by Liverpool. They came through their test with flying colours, drawing 1–1 at Portman Road, and then winning 3–1 in front of 24,000 at Pittodrie. New signing Peter Weir was the man who inflicted most of the damage, scoring two goals and giving a performance that won him new admirers at Pittodrie. Ipswich manager Bobby Robson was suitably impressed, and the loss of Ian Scanlon was quickly forgotten. 'You'll win the trophy,' Robson assured Ferguson.

In the next round Aberdeen were drawn against the largely unknown Romanian side Arges Pitesti, with a 3–0 lead from the home leg enough to put them into the next round, but only just. In Romania Aberdeen were in for a rude awakening as their opponents began to dig uncomfortably into the Aberdeen midfield and soon found themselves a couple of goals ahead.

Then came an incident that was to become legendary. At half-time Ferguson was fuming, letting fly at Gordon Strachan after the wee Scot had dared to question him. In his temper the Aberdeen manager lashed out at a tea urn, not realising that being East European it was far more solid than the variety found in most Scottish dressing rooms. It was not made of aluminium but of some far heavier metal. Ferguson felt the full force of it, almost breaking his hand. The tea urn shot up into the air, sending tea everywhere: dripping off the ceiling, running down the walls and slopping over Archie Knox. There was a deafening silence.

Nobody dared say anything, let alone laugh. Fortunately nobody bar Ferguson was hurt but it was enough to gee Strachan up for the second half. He responded by striking a penalty inside of ten minutes of the resumption as Aberdeen began a fight back that would eventually level the game and put the Dons into the next round.

That win presented Aberdeen with a plum tie against Franz Beckenbauer's Hamburg. Aberdeen had already passed a stiff test against Ipswich Town, but playing a German side was a very different proposition. The styles were dissimilar, the tactics less certain, and then there was the travel factor, as well as playing in a different kind of stadium. Ferguson warned the team that it would not be easy, especially with the first game at home. Yet all seemed to be going well as Aberdeen strode arrogantly into a 3–1 lead. It could have been more – Gordon Strachan had squandered a penalty, an opportunity that would have made them unassailable, and Black had headed against the post. But with three minutes remaining, Doug Rougvie crashed to the ground injured. He was clearly in some pain and unable to continue but instead of someone having the sense to kick the ball into touch Aberdeen played on. Suddenly Horst Hrubesch found himself unmarked in the area and didn't need a second chance to snap up the goal. It was a strike that turned the tie. From a comfortable lead, Aberdeen had now given Hamburg two precious away goals. In Germany, Beckenbauer's class would be the deciding influence as Aberdeen consistently gave the ball away. Ferguson would remind them later, 'If you give the ball away in Europe, you're dead.' The Dons lost 3–1.

There wasn't much comfort in the league either. The early season defeats had left them dispirited and with a mountain to climb almost before they had started. The pattern continued. In truth, the rot had set in just before the Hamburg game when Celtic beat them 2–1 at Parkhead. Shortly after came an appalling run as they drew two, then lost to Morton and Celtic again before drawing a couple more games. They had gone three months without a win and were languishing in sixth place. Celtic led the table from start to finish, though in the spring Aberdeen began a spirited challenge that might have robbed the Glasgow side of the title. In their final 16 games Aberdeen won 15 and lost just one, scoring 43 goals and conceding a mere ten. The defeat came at Morton, in injury time, as a ball deflected off the referee and into the path of Morton's Rooney. Such was their luck with Morton. A win there and they might have caught Celtic, who pipped them to the title by two points. But at least Aberdeen took the title to the wire with the championship still at stake until the final game of the season. Aberdeen needed to beat Rangers by five clear goals and hope that Celtic might lose at home to St Mirren. It was mission impossible, but at half-time with Aberdeen leading 4–0 and Celtic drawing 0–0 you might have thought a miracle was about to happen. In the end Celtic scored deep into the second half while Aberdeen could not add to their four goals.

Really there were no excuses. The title had been thrown away before Christmas. There weren't even that many injuries for Ferguson to use as an explanation, as he had legitimately in previous seasons. Aberdeen had simply blown it over the winter months. The harsh winter weather might have contributed a touch, with so many games cancelled and continuity suffering, but on the Richter excuse table it rated about two.

But there was some consolation as their fine spring form took them all the way to the Scottish Cup final and a win over Rangers. After beating Motherwell in the first round they then faced Celtic at Pittodrie, where the Glasgow side had twice come from behind to win in the league already. But not this time. Ferguson reshuffled his pack and Aberdeen ran out 1–0 winners. It marked a change in their fortunes. In the quarter-finals they faced First Division

Kilmarnock, who had the audacity to steal a first-minute lead and even after Aberdeen had equalised still found enough to take the lead again. But a couple of Gordon Strachan penalties reasserted the superiority of the Premier League side. The semi-final brought Aberdeen face to face with St Mirren, and after a 1–1 draw at Hampden, Peter Weir hit the winner in the replay at Dens Park.

And so, back to Hampden where inevitably their opponents turned out to be Rangers. But with the Falklands War dominating everyone's thoughts there wasn't quite the usual fervour you might have expected for a Scottish Cup final. In the league Aberdeen had got the better of Rangers, but the question was whether they had the attitude to beat them in a Cup final. Peter Weir was missing, but equally Rangers had their problems with Derek Johnstone and Ian Redford absent, while many of their side were pushing the wrong side of 30. Yet Rangers began well, opening the scoring and giving Aberdeen enough trouble to make them wonder if they weren't jinxed when it came to Cup finals. But then Alex McLeish curled in a delightful shot from the corner of the area and the scores were level. Yet still Aberdeen looked nervous, daunted by their opponents and the occasion.

In the interval Ferguson gave them a roasting. Did they really want to win the Cup, or did they always want to be a provincial side? It was make or break; lose today and they finished the season with nothing. It worked. After the resumption Aberdeen began to pick up their normal game and take control. They dominated the second half – yet still they seemed incapable of turning territorial advantage into goals. Extra time came and with it total domination by Aberdeen as they lashed in three goals to win the Cup 4–1. They had proved that they weren't just one-championship wonders as some of the press had dubbed them. They had now established foundations from which they could grow further.

The youngsters Ferguson had introduced to the side had settled to become regulars, while goalkeeper Jim Leighton, Gordon Strachan, Alex McLeish and Willie Miller had been selected for Scotland's World Cup campaign in Spain. It was an honour, not just for the club, but for Ferguson himself – his tuition had doubtless helped improve all four. None of them would let him down, proving that they were well capable of playing at a far higher level than the Scottish Premiership offered. And by the end of the 1982–83 season they would have proved their pedigree to everyone in Europe as Aberdeen clinched one of the major European trophies.

CHAPTER SEVEN

European Glory

Ferguson's only worry since winning the Scottish Cup had been Rangers' attempt to prise the indomitable Willie Miller from his grasp. Ferguson needed and respected Miller; his strong presence was as reassuring in the dressing room as it was on the pitch. In the end Miller decided to give his manager and his club a vote of confidence and stay put at Pittodrie. To have lost such a key man would have been a devastating blow, but to have him remain on board was an enormous boost for everyone at Aberdeen.

The Dons opened their campaign in the European Cup-Winners' Cup against the Swiss club Sion and in the home leg gave them something of a football lesson as they romped to a 7–0 victory. It was a portent of things to come. In Switzerland they added another four to the aggregate scoreline to run out 11–1 winners. Yet in the league they kicked off with another miserable start, losing 2–0 at Dundee United before drawing their third game and then losing their fourth at home to Rangers. It was the first time Rangers had beaten them at Pittodrie in years, but it would be Aberdeen's last defeat for some time.

Back in Europe they faced the unknown Albanians Dinamo Tirana and were hopelessly unprepared for what was to come. The Albanians had earlier refused visas to the club with the result that nobody from Aberdeen had been able to go out and watch their opponents. They were playing a side they had never heard of, never seen and knew nothing about. In the event Aberdeen controlled the first leg at Pittodrie from start to finish, yet at the end of 90 minutes had little to show for their efforts but the slenderest one-goal advantage. Aberdeen were treading dangerous waters, especially with such a potentially difficult visit to a country that had in the past proved inhospitable and unfriendly to visitors. As it was, Aberdeen's trip passed without incident and even their match ended in a goalless draw. The sweltering temperature in the nineties hardly helped as both sides sat back, intent on conserving as much energy as possible. It made for a classic stalemate but at least Aberdeen had overcome a tricky hurdle.

Next in line were another Eastern European side, the better-known Lech Poznan of Poland. Aberdeen took a two-goal advantage to Poland, though in truth it should have been more after both Black and Strachan had rattled the woodwork. But two goals proved enough, and once Dougie Bell had headed them in front in Poland, the Poles were never going to overturn Aberdeen's three goal lead. The Dons were into the quarter-finals of a European tournament for the first time in 15 years. But when they drew Bayern Munich, no one was quite sure whether to cry or leap with excitement. At least they had until the spring to decide!

If ever there was a moment, a match, an incident that transformed Aberdeen from a sleepy backwoods Scottish club into a major European force, it was their tie against the mighty Bayern Munich, three times winners of the European Cup, countless times winners of the Bundesliga, and the side who had just knocked Tottenham Hotspur out of the competition. It was to be a turning point in Alex Ferguson's career.

Aberdeen had one significant advantage: the first leg was

away. On the debit side Gordon Strachan was unfit. Ferguson drummed into them the importance of holding the ball and not committing suicide as they had against Hamburg. 'Don't give it away,' he emphasised time and again. 'If you do, you'll be punished.'

Fortunately most of them had learned the lesson, and in front of 35,000 in Munich's Olympic Stadium they went on to blunt the ambitions of some of the most revered footballers in all of Europe. Breitner, Rummenigge, Hoeness, Augenthaler and Dremmler were all stifled by an inspired performance from Aberdeen, led by the uncompromising Willie Miller. It ended goalless; a few months previously Tottenham had crumbled 4–1 in the very same stadium. All Aberdeen had to do now was to repeat the performance at Pittodrie and score a goal or two. On paper it seemed simple, but in practice it was far from that.

Strachan was fit for the second leg, a huge bonus for the Dons, as was the capacity crowd of 24,000 inside Aberdeen's all-seater stadium, the first in Britain. It would turn out to be the greatest evening in Pittodrie's history. Yet, after Bayern had taken the lead in the tenth minute, only a few of the most fanatical supporters would have given the Dons much chance against one of the mightiest teams in Europe. It needed a bit of luck, and it came in the 38th minute as Neil Simpson scrambled the ball over the line for Aberdeen's equaliser. A minute later Eric Black struck the bar and Aberdeen's confidence was restored.

Yet after the interval Aberdeen looked to be down again as Pfluger's sizzling 20-yard volley edged the Germans ahead once more. Aberdeen had it all to do again. Ferguson was convinced his side were finished. Bayern looked comfortable on the ball and were passing with all the swagger of a European side bred on arrogance. Ferguson had to gamble if he was to get anything from the tie. He decided on a controversial move by substituting full back Stuart Kennedy, who was being given a hard time by Bayern's Pfluger. The defence was moved around, with John McMaster coming on to take over from Neale Cooper, who was shifted to left back. Doug Rougvie switched sides into Kennedy's berth. Taking Kennedy off was not a popular decision, but sometimes hopeless situations demand drastic action. Managers stand or die by such moments. McMaster made an immediate impact but still the goals failed to materialise. A second substitution was called for. This time Ferguson introduced teenager John Hewitt and pulled another youngster, Neil Simpson, off. 'It was a mad gamble,' he admitted years later, 'but if you want to win games, you have to be brave.' The gamble was to pay off.

Moments later Aberdeen were awarded a free kick on the edge of the box. The crowd fell silent. Strachan and McMaster stood hovering over the ball deciding who would take the kick. It was a well-rehearsed Aberdeen trick. Then suddenly the ball was whipped into the box and McLeish glided in to head an equaliser. Pittodrie erupted; Ferguson was off his seat. A minute later Aberdeen were ahead as Eric Black headed on a cross from John McMaster. The Bayern goalkeeper could only get a hand to it and the ball fell delightfully for John Hewitt to stroke into the net. It had been an astonishing turnaround. Pittodrie and the whole of Aberdeen were ecstatic. The final ten minutes were not for the faint-hearted. It was a nail-biting time as Aberdeen clung on. Ferguson screamed his orders, urging his midfielders to hold the ball, play it back if necessary but not to give it away. When the final whistle sounded the ground erupted. Aberdeen were into the semi-finals. Ferguson sent his players back on to the pitch to acknowledge the delirious cheers of the Pittodrie faithful. Aberdeen had truly come of age.

It was the kind of result that made the whole of Europe sit up and take notice. If they hadn't heard of Aberdeen Football Club before, they certainly had now as football fans around Europe digested the result: Aberdeen 3, Bayern Munich 2.

But while the Dons were marching majestically towards a European final, their domestic form was inevitably suffering. After their poor opening to the season they had gone ten games before losing again. Then came another run of eleven games without defeat. By mid-March they had lost only three league fixtures and looked odds-on favourites to take the title. But with the spring came Europe, tired legs, distractions, and a successful run in the Scottish Cup that was also a focus for their attentions. The first disaster came against title-chasing Dundee United, who came to Pittodrie just three days after Bayern had been humiliated and showed the Germans how it should be done, winning 2–1. In hindsight it was to be the most significant result in the Premiership that season. United would go on to win the title while Aberdeen would finish in third spot, just one point behind them. Aberdeen managed to pull themselves together enough to win their next match, even though it was against their bogey team, Morton, but that was followed by two successive defeats. The first was at home to St Mirren, the next at Ibrox. Aberdeen's league dreams had been turned upside down. Although they would not lose again that season – in fact they would win five of the remaining six fixtures, scoring sixteen goals and conceding none – it was too late.

When Ferguson came to look at the papers following the Bayern match, he saw some topsy-turvy results in the Cup-Winners' Cup. All the favourites had surprisingly been beaten: out had gone Bayern, Barcelona, Inter Milan and Paris St Germain. Suddenly the route to the final looked considerably easier, with only Real Madrid threatening. Fortunately in the draw for the semi-finals a few days later, Aberdeen avoided the Spanish giants and found themselves pitted against the Belgian side Waterschei. It couldn't have been better; the only snag was that the first leg was in Aberdeen.

Ferguson decided that they should put the Belgians under pressure from the start but even he could never have guessed that things would go so well. Within two minutes they were ahead as Eric Black turned Dougie Bell's cross into the net. Two minutes later it was 2–0 thanks to Neil Simpson. The Belgians now had little choice but to gamble and press forward; inevitably it left gaping holes in their defence. In the second half Aberdeen ran amok, firing in three more goals to eventually win 5–1. Nobody had any doubt that Aberdeen were through to the final. And yes, the formalities were completed a fortnight later in Belgium, even though they lost 1–0. But Ferguson was barely distraught at losing. The job had been settled in the first leg and it was hardly surprising that his players were not psyched up for the return. The only concern was an injury to Stuart Kennedy, which turned out to be far more serious than anyone imagined at the time. He had played his last game for Aberdeen.

Ferguson had no fears about Real Madrid. He'd watched them once and had seen nothing about them to worry him. 'We can beat them,' he told his staff. 'I really believe it. Don't be frightened by the name. Remember Bayern Munich. There's no need to be overawed.' He decided to play it low-key, as if it was any other European match, and to make sure that none of the staff, even if they were nervous, showed any hint of nerves to the players.

The final was set for Gothenburg, and more than 12,000 Aberdonians made the trek across the North Sea to Sweden, totally outnumbering the Spanish fans, who had been presented with an extraordinarily long and arduous journey. Only a few of them bothered. More than 500 Dons fans travelled by sea from Aberdeen on the sequestered Shetland ferry *St Clair*, with Ferguson waving them off from the quayside. 'I'll be here to welcome you home as well,' he promised them. Indeed he would. And he wouldn't be empty-handed.

* * *

It was 11 May, the most important date in Aberdeen's history. Mrs Thatcher had called a general election two days earlier, but nobody was thinking about politics in a rain-soaked Gothenburg. Aberdeen were off to a flying start, almost scoring in the first minute as Eric Black screwed the ball beyond the goalkeeper only for it to slam against the crossbar. Six minutes later Black, alone in the six-yard box, drove a right-foot shot into the bottom corner of the net to put Aberdeen a goal ahead. However, seven minutes later hearts sank as a back pass from Alex McLeish slowing in the rain left Jim Leighton stranded with little option but to bring down Santillana. In another era he would have been dismissed as well as conceding a penalty, but in 1983 his only punishment was a penalty. That alone was enough as Juanito levelled the score from the spot.

Aberdeen always looked the more likely to score, yet at half-time it remained level, with Real's Stielike a daunting figure in midfield. Ferguson later admitted that they had never taken the Real hardman seriously enough in their team talks. At half-time they had the chance to rectify their error. With Stielike coming under increasing pressure, Real looked less and less likely to score, but equally Aberdeen could not find the net, and at full time the two teams still remained deadlocked. It was much the same in the first period of extra time, but then in the second period, with only eight minutes remaining on the clock before a penalty shoot-out, Aberdeen struck. Ferguson had been dreading a penalty shoot-out. His staff had watched Real at training and had noticed that they had spent a considerable amount of time practising their penalty kicks. It was almost as if they were anticipating a shoot-out.

Ferguson opted for broke and brought on John Hewitt as a final gamble for the injured Eric Black. In the 112th minute the gallant Peter Weir slipped past two defenders on the left and chipped a neat ball on to Mark McGhee, who in turn whipped in a deft cross just beyond the keeper – and there was Hewitt, stealing in to head Aberdeen into the lead. Real were distraught. There was not enough time for them to do anything about it, though they came close in the final minute with a thundering free kick.

Aberdeen had won the European Cup-Winners' Cup, tactically outmatching the Spaniards and their glittering array of international stars. The Real manager, Alfredo Di Stefano, was generous in his praise. 'Aberdeen have what money cannot buy,' he told the press, 'a soul, a team spirit built in a family tradition.' And it was true. Ferguson and his staff had forged a side full of passion and battle. The entire team had cost a mere £400,000, with only Strachan, McGhee and Weir costing any money at all. Six of the side – Leighton, Rougvie, McMaster, McLeish, Miller and Strachan – had been at Pittodrie prior to Ferguson's arrival. It had to be one of the cheapest sides ever to have won a European trophy. And it had all been achieved by the community spirit which Ferguson had engendered.

Ferguson was as delirious as anyone. The celebrations went on long into the night. At the hotel, Ferguson was still partying at six in the morning. By then only three revellers remained. Ferguson deliberately drank little, preferring to keep a clear head and relish the moment rather than let it drift into an alcoholic blur.

Back in Aberdeen they were preparing for a welcome to match the occasion. The entire populace seemed to turn out to greet the returning heroes. Union Street was twenty deep with fans as their open-topped bus paraded the newly won trophy. THE DONS ARE THE GREATEST read a banner on the front of the coach as the players, wearing bobble hats, scarves and team colours, lifted the trophy aloft for the city to see. They even paraded it around Pittodrie.

The following day Ferguson and Mark McGhee were at the dockside to welcome the *St Clair* and the boat people back home. Ferguson stood holding the cup while hundreds of Aberdeen fans leaning over the deck rails of the boat threatened to destabilise the ship. As the fans disembarked Ferguson was at the bottom of the gangway, shaking each one by the hand and thanking them personally for their support. His gesture did not go unappreciated.

Yet a few days later, after all the euphoria of their European triumph, Aberdeen put in a lacklustre performance as they faced Rangers in the Scottish Cup final at Hampden. Aberdeen had reached the final defeating Hibernian, Dundee, Partick Thistle and Celtic. Not surprisingly, Ferguson stuck with his European eleven, but instead of it turning out to be a performance to relish, it was as lethargic and dour an occasion as Hampden had witnessed in years. Eventually Aberdeen won, scoring the game's only goal with four minutes of extra time remaining. It was a double triumph for Aberdeen and their manager.

To have won the Scottish Cup was a massive achievement in itself, yet after their European triumphs Ferguson's sights had been raised. He was embarrassed at Aberdeen's poor showing in the final, disappointed by their lack of endeavour. After the strain of Gothenburg and a long, weary season it was perhaps understandable that at the final hurdle they barely had the strength to run, let alone leap, but Ferguson expected more of them. After the final he publicly lambasted his players. 'We were lucky to win,' he told the press, clearly disgusted by their performance. His comment left everyone agog. It was not his style to criticise his players in public, yet here he was doing just that, after they had won a second cup for him, the same eleven who had battled so bravely in Gothenburg. Maybe the strain had got to him as well; maybe he simply expected too much. When he picked up the papers the following morning he quickly realised his error. A public apology was instantly forthcoming. But it left a slightly sad note at the end of the greatest season in the club's history.

The only other disappointment after their memorable

season was the loss of assistant manager Archie Knox. Ferguson had brought Knox to Pittodrie after his assistant Pat Stanton had quit to become the manager of Hibernian. Knox had previously been manager at Forfar and it was hardly surprising that after Aberdeen's success someone should try to tempt him away with the lure of a number one post elsewhere. The offer finally came from Dundee. Knox had discussed the possibility of moving on a number of occasions with Ferguson. He was keen to take charge of a club again and implement some of the lessons he had learned from Ferguson. Ferguson promised that he would not stand in his way if something tempting turned up. When it did Ferguson could hardly blame him for grabbing his opportunity. They parted amicably, and over the summer Willie Garner was appointed to replace him. History was to repeat itself years later.

The 1982–83 season had put the name of Alex Ferguson up among the most renowned of those who had managed Scottish clubs – Jock Stein, Bill Struth. He wasn't as yet in the same category as some of his fellow Scottish managers like Matt Busby and Bill Shankly, who had managed so successfully at the highest level south of the border, but he was certainly heading in that direction. Six of his players would also create a new record by playing for Scotland against Northern Ireland later that year. It might have been more had the incomparable Willie Miller not been injured. The prestigious French football magazine *France Football* even voted Aberdeen the European team of the year. Now that was some accolade.

CHAPTER EIGHT

The New Firm

In October 1983 John Greig, manager of Rangers Football Club, decided that enough was enough and resigned, although it may well have been a case of jumping before he was pushed. Months earlier Ferguson had been quietly approached by a Rangers director wondering if he might be interested in a sentimental return to Ibrox. Ferguson gave a categorical 'no'. While Greig was still in charge he was not interested. If Greig went then it might be different, but he was not going to be involved in any shenanigans while they still had a manager, and one who just happened to be a good friend of his.

However, once Greig had quit, it didn't take long for more formal approaches to materialise. In football they call it 'tapping'. The call came from John Paton, then vice-chairman at Ibrox. An ex-player with a successful track record, Ferguson was the ideal man for the job, Paton told him. He would be going back to the club he had supported as a boy and had played for as a man. There would be no problem with money.

Yet Ferguson was hesitant. Football journalist Archie Macpherson remembers sitting with him one day in his little cubbyhole at Pittodrie opposite the dressing rooms, hearing him out as he agonised over the prospect of going back to

Govan. The more Ferguson thought about it, the more he rejected the idea. As a supporter and then a player he'd been as fanatical a Rangers man as anyone, but he had changed over the years. He'd grown wiser, escaped the incestuous religious politics of the west coast and particularly of Glasgow. As a manager he'd signed players for their ability, not their religious persuasions. 'How could I go back and not sign Catholics?' he asked Macpherson. 'What would I tell my friends who are Catholics – you lot aren't good enough for us? I just couldn't do that,' he said, shaking his head.

He also had doubts about the politicking inside Ibrox, unsure who was really running the show. Was he the candidate of one group of directors, or was he the unanimous choice of the board? All this uncertainty made him feel uneasy. But there were plenty of others urging him to take the job, not least his former manager Scot Symon, who made a few discreet calls on his behalf to find out exactly what was going on inside the boardroom. Yet although Symon advised him to take the job he also confirmed that there was a struggle going on in the boardroom as directors positioned themselves to become the next chairman. Ferguson's comfortable association with Dick Donald at Pittodrie had convinced him that the relationship between manager and chairman was crucial. It looked as if the next manager at Ibrox would find himself caught up in an unhealthy situation, and the threat of interference was enough to put Ferguson off.

There was also the question of loyalty to Aberdeen. In his book *The Light In The North*, Ferguson speaks highly of the support the club gave him in his early years when he was going through some personal difficulties. His father's illness and the problems which had followed his dismissal from St Mirren clearly interfered with his running of the club, yet Aberdeen had always remained supportive. 'They had seen me through difficult times,' he wrote, 'and had told me that they would have patience in waiting for success.' Ferguson felt that he owed them one.

However, it still wasn't an easy decision. For days he agonised with his wife, often staying up into the early hours, mulling over what would be best for the family. It would be a big step, returning to the hothouse of Glasgow football. For a Govan lad it had its obvious romantic attractions – indeed, he would have been the first Govan man actually to have managed the club. But where there are reservations there should always be hesitation. When something is right, you instinctively know that it is right. Years later Ferguson was able to say that he had no regrets about not going back to Rangers.

There is little question that Ferguson was the favourite, the man earmarked by Rangers for the job. They'd been as impressed as anyone by his work at Pittodrie. But when they put out the feelers the word came back that he could only do the job if things changed at Ibrox – and that meant abandoning their lifelong adherence to Protestantism. In 1983 that was simply not going to happen; the old tribe still ruled. Rangers, of course, came out with the usual platitudes and excuses. They were not a sectarian club, there was nothing to change, they argued. The new manager could sign whoever he wanted, but Ferguson knew otherwise. He'd spent his time at Ibrox and still had enough contacts to know that nothing had changed. The directors might be full of promises, but when it came to carrying them out it would be another story.

Ferguson was never officially offered the job. Nor was another hot favourite, Jim McLean of Dundee United, who also abhorred the sectarian machinations inside Ibrox. Instead Jock Wallace was reappointed. Wallace, then at Motherwell, would have walked across broken glass for the job. It was as clear an indication as you could wish for that nothing had changed.

By the time the old order had been ousted, and David

Murray installed as the club's new owner, Ferguson was already in Manchester and it was left to Graeme Souness to sign Rangers' first official Catholic and bring about a revolution at Ibrox. Rangers had missed their opportunity.

If Ferguson was disappointed he never showed it. No doubt he would have loved the job, but he knew the reality, and the appointment of Wallace only confirmed his suspicions that nothing had changed at Ibrox. Ferguson was carrying out his own revolution, changing the old order. The power of the Glasgow giants had gone; Aberdeen had stolen their youngsters and their glory. It seemed the only way to stop the slide was to offer him a job. Charlie Nicholas, the latest darling of Parkhead, was as perplexed as everyone else. 'We simply didn't know what to do about Aberdeen,' he said. 'They had the Indian sign over us and we just couldn't win.' The whole of Aberdeen smiled when Nicholas wrote that.

Ferguson had instilled a siege mentality into the folk of Aberdeen. He'd built a fortress around Pittodrie that was ready to resist anything Glasgow could throw at it. Not only did he describe Rangers and Celtic as the enemy, but he complained that Scottish football was Glasgow-based, that journalists never ventured to Aberdeen unless one of the Old Firm was visiting, that nobody gave credit where it was due. He'd got up the noses of everybody except the people that mattered – those in Aberdeen. By now he had permanently threatened the monopoly of the Glasgow clubs.

Even if nobody else could fathom out what he was about, his own players understood the logic. 'He gave us a persecution complex about Celtic, Rangers, the Scottish FA and the Glasgow media, the whole west of Scotland thing,' remembers Mark McGhee. 'He reckoned they were all against us; and it worked a treat.' There was method to Ferguson's madness. He had broken the mould and it would prove a good testing ground for when he had to take on Merseyside and the rest of the anti-Manchester United establishment.

Apart from the new face of Willie Garner hovering about the dressing room there was only one other new recruit that summer, Billy Stark from St Mirren. Stark, a beanpole of a midfielder, was being groomed as a replacement for Gordon Strachan, who had served notice that he wished to leave at the end of the 1983–84 season. Strachan had become the focus of attention of a number of English clubs following his battling performances in the 1982 World Cup finals and his inspiring displays at the heart of the Aberdeen midfield. Big money was being mentioned and it was inevitable that both Aberdeen and Strachan would eventually be tempted. But at least they had one more season of the wee man.

Ferguson simply could not understand why anyone should want to leave so successful a side as Aberdeen. They had every challenge they could wish for. It was totally beyond his comprehension, but the fact was that south of the border money was seductive. Chairman Dick Donald ran a tight ship. He always boasted that the club was never in debt, never beholden to anyone, and that the books always balanced. That was why he would never sanction huge transfer fees. Similarly, wages were never as attractive as they were in England. In time Ferguson too would be tempted away from Pittodrie, though it would be for the challenge rather than the money.

Aberdeen had made a steady start to their season, notching up eight goals to win their two opening league fixtures. But after that there was a mixed bag of results. There was a draw with Motherwell, a handsome win at Ibrox that helped plunge the knife deeper into the heart of Rangers manager John Greig, and then defeat at Pittodrie by champions Dundee United. After that came a couple more wins and then a second league defeat, this time by Hibernian.

It was less than satisfactory. Clearly, Ferguson's own uncertainty was unsettling the team, and it didn't help that the papers were inevitably full of speculation. However, once the question mark over Ferguson's future had been removed, the Dons responded with a string of convincing victories that catapulted them to the head of the table. By February they had opened up a six-point gap over their closest rivals, Celtic. They would lose only two more league games that season – the first at Celtic in late April, and the second against St Mirren in the final game of the season, when the title had been well secured and a team of Aberdeen babes were sent on to do battle. It was a remarkable finale, bringing them a record number of Premier League points plus the Premier League's best-ever defensive record. They had conceded just nine goals away from home plus a dozen at Pittodrie, while notching up a total of 78 goals.

Aberdeen's dominance of Scottish football went even further as they picked up the Scottish Cup for the third year in succession, beating Celtic 2–1 in the final. There was really only one disappointment that season, in the European Cup-Winners' Cup, as Aberdeen set about defending their trophy. (It almost went without saying that they failed to achieve anything in the League Cup again, but that was to be expected. It was never high on their list of priorities, an unsatisfactory competition that seemed to change its format every year. It hardly seems to have given Ferguson too many sleepless nights.)

Aberdeen's progress in Europe began in much the same way as their early league form – erratically. They were drawn against Akranes of Iceland in the first round, surely a comfortable enough hop into the next round, especially after they had won 2–1 in Iceland, with the Icelanders squandering a penalty. But much to everyone's surprise, Akranes proved to be sturdier opposition than expected. Back at Pittodrie the Icelanders held out until the 70th minute, then an Aberdeen penalty finally broke the dead-lock and guaranteed their presence in the second round. A last-minute penalty for Akranes gave them some credibility, but it had been an uphill slog for Aberdeen as much as it had for the Icelanders.

Round two found them facing Beveren, top of the Belgian league, and clearly a more sophisticated prospect than the Icelanders. But over in Belgium the determination that had carried Aberdeen to such triumphs the previous season began to reassert itself, earning them a goalless draw. Back at Pittodrie, with Ferguson confirming shortly before kick-off that he was resisting Rangers' temptations, Aberdeen finished off Beveren 4–1 to cruise comfortably into the quarter-finals and relax until the spring. By then Aberdeen were in table-topping form with a 27-game unbeaten run, but it was to come to an end in Hungary as they faced Ujpest Dozsa in Budapest. Aberdeen lost 2–0 and looked to be on their way out of Europe. An angry Ferguson tore a strip off his players, raging at them for squandering at least two golden opportunities that might have levelled affairs. He was as convinced as anyone that Aberdeen's grip on the Cup-Winners' Cup had been prised loose. Back at the hotel he skulked off to his bedroom and was not seen again that night, taking defeat as personally as any of the players.

Aberdeen had never pulled back a two-goal deficit in Europe, but a crowd of over 22,000 turned up at Pittodrie to urge them to new heights. The man who was most inspired by the occasion was Mark McGhee, who opened the scoring in the 37th minute. Yet despite persistent pressure the scoreline remained at 1–0 for a further 50 minutes, with Aberdeen on the verge of elimination and Ferguson cursing those missed chances in Budapest. Then, with just a few minutes left, Mark McGhee struck again, to sidefoot Falconer's cross beyond the keeper. Pittodrie exploded. Aberdeen had escaped, but they had still not won. A further 30 minutes of extra time would now settle who would join Manchester United, Juventus and Porto in the last four. The odds had shifted firmly to the Dons. The Hungarians had come to defend, showing little endeavour up front. They had packed their defence and invited Aberdeen to come at them. But now it was too late for those tactics. They had to come out of their trenches and in doing so looked a confused and scattered army. Within three minutes McGhee had hit his third and the Hungarians were destroyed. Their frustration turned to anger, with goalkeeper Szendrei being shown a red card for butting McLeish.

Aberdeen's opponents in the semi-final were Porto. Ferguson prepared well – better, he claims, than he had ever done for any European tie. The Portuguese were watched, scrutinised then carefully logged. What Ferguson saw was enough to worry him. They were an elegant outfit, their players perhaps a touch on the short side but with enough skills on the ground to compensate for any lack of height. What Ferguson could not legislate for was injury to his own players. Weir was out, while Strachan and McLeish, although they made the side, were returning from injury and far from fit. Perhaps it was the injuries, maybe it was the passionate crowd – more than 65,000 – but Aberdeen looked lethargic and dispirited on the night and lost 1–0. It could have been more, but Ferguson reckoned a one-goal deficit was not too bad to take to Pittodrie. But it was not to be. Porto were a formidable team, and as the mist rolled in off the North Sea to shroud Pittodrie they displayed their abundant ability, winning 1–0.

If Aberdeen had relinquished their hold on one European trophy they did have another to show for their exertions that season – the European Super Cup. It might not have counted for much, being more a friendly contest than anything else, but to have defeated European Cup holders Hamburg in a two-legged match was not to be sniffed at. The first game in Hamburg was goalless, but back at

Pittodrie Aberdeen won 2–0 to take some revenge on their defeat by the German side a few years earlier.

The season might not have held any of the excitement of the previous year, when Aberdeen had won their first ever European trophy and opened eyes across the continent, but they had ended the year with three trophies. Once again they had dominated Scottish football, but perhaps more importantly they had proved that they were not one-minute wonders in Europe. They had won the Super Cup and reached the last four of the Cup-Winners' Cup again. They were a force to be reckoned with.

Aberdeen's success had inevitably placed many of their players in the shop window, and at the front of the window was Alex Ferguson. He'd already turned down a fortune to manage his old club Rangers. Now, in the summer of 1984, came other offers. The Rangers offer had clearly unsettled him. Whether or not he was conscious of it, the fact was that he had put out a signal that he was open to suggestions. Things at Pittodrie would never be quite the same again.

While Ferguson had decided to remain in the Grampians, others did not. The new freedom-of-contract rules for the players were to lead to a mass exodus from Pittodrie. The temptation was always money, something football in England could provide. On every international trip the Scottish players would find themselves comparing wages with the Anglo-Scots. They did not compare well, especially with Aberdeen, who had enough trouble competing with the Glasgow giants.

Gordon Strachan was the first to part company, finally joining Manchester United in August for £600,000 when Cologne imagined he had signed for them. Unbeknown to Aberdeen, Strachan had quietly been talking to Cologne for some weeks, and had even signed a contract with them. In the meantime, Aberdeen had agreed a deal with United. There was total confusion, but fortunately for Strachan the contract he had signed with the German club was not legally watertight. The lawyers reckoned he was free to join United. For once he took Ferguson's advice and opted for the English club. 'It's one of the biggest clubs in the world,' Ferguson told him. It still left a sour taste, and the chaos that Strachan had caused would take some delicate negotiating between Aberdeen, United and Cologne before matters were finally resolved.

Strachan had been a dynamo in the Aberdeen midfield, his relentless energy always an inspiration, and to have so many goals generated by the midfield was always a significant bonus. It was a loss Aberdeen would find difficult to cope with. But Strachan and Ferguson had not been on the best of terms for some time. The manager had decided to drop him back in April in the hope that it might revitalise his season, and Strachan had reacted angrily, criticising the manager's decision in his regular weekly column in the *Daily Express*. It did not go down well with Ferguson, who promptly banned him from writing for the papers any more. The two rowed. After that it was simply a matter of time before Strachan found another club. Strachan's discussions with Cologne also angered Ferguson and he was hardly sad to see the back of him.

Mark McGhee, the scorer of so many vital goals for the Dons, was another loss Aberdeen could ill afford. In the previous season alone McGhee had contributed 24 goals while Strachan had notched up 18. But if the Bundesliga did not claim their prize in Strachan, they certainly did with McGhee, who quit to join Hamburg, the club which had experienced his talents at first hand before.

The surprise man on the move was defender Doug Rougvie, who capitalised on Aberdeen's growing fame by signing for Chelsea. It was another example of a player being tempted by the sound of money and the manoeuvres of mega-rich clubs south of the border. Ferguson was livid. Rougvie had talked privately to Chelsea and then demanded that Aberdeen match their offer. Ferguson was not impressed but at least promised to put it to the Aberdeen board. Rougvie never returned to find out the result of their discussions.

In a matter of weeks Ferguson's team had been ripped apart, all tempted by monstrous money offers and the promise of fame on a wider stage. He'd lost three internationals: a defender, a midfielder and a goalscorer. In June they had boasted eight full Scottish internationals at Pittodrie; now they were down to five.

'It was a shock,' said Ferguson. He still couldn't understand why they would want to leave. Yet you could hardly blame them; they were all reaching that stage in their playing career when a lucrative contract would set them up for middle age. What's more, they had seen their manager tempted and although he had resisted, it had set a train of thought going in other minds.

Their departure presented Ferguson with a colossal problem. How could he replace players of their calibre? Strachan's replacement had already been earmarked with the earlier signing of Billy Stark, who was now tossed the challenge, while into Rougvie's boots stepped young Tommy McQueen, an £80,000 signing from Clyde. Replacing McGhee was trickier, yet Ferguson came up trumps when he enlisted Frank McDougall, the podgy-looking St Mirren striker. His signing surprised everyone, especially as his record suggested an attitude problem, but under his new mentor McDougall was to enjoy a fresh lease of life. At £100,000 he turned out to be a bargain. It was good training for Ferguson, who years later would sign another player said to have a serious attitude problem.

Losing the backbone of his championship-winning side was hardly the way for Ferguson to start defending that title, and an appalling list of injuries didn't help. John McMaster had been an absentee for most of the previous season with a serious injury and now as the new season kicked off a further injury threatened to take him out for the whole of the 1984–85 season. Peter Weir was also suffering and would only make 15 league appearances that season. It meant Aberdeen kicking off with a new-look formation. Little wonder they took time to settle. Ferguson even admits to having wondered at the time if maybe he should have accepted one of the job offers that had come his way. But he hadn't, and he simply had to get on with it.

In the League Cup, now known as the Skol Cup, they took an immediate exit, knocked out on a sticky night by Ally MacLeod's Airdrie. Seven seasons at Pittodrie and still no League Cup for Alex Ferguson – but then the competition had never been a priority for him. His sights were set firmly on Europe, and as Scottish champions Aberdeen went into the draw for the European Cup, the trophy Ferguson wanted more than any other. But, with a team barely on nodding terms with one another, their prospects did not look good. Ferguson feared the worst. Maybe if they could just get beyond the early stages then the side might bed down and become a more cohesive unit, but it was a big maybe.

The opening round came in mid-September against East Germany's Dynamo Berlin, not a known quality side but a difficult one to beat nonetheless. And with new striker Frank McDougall banned from Europe it was always going to be a struggle. Yet they won the first leg at Pittodrie 2–1. Ferguson, cursing the Germans' late away goal, guessed it might not be enough. And so it proved on an unfriendly autumn night in East Berlin. There was no denying that the Dons battled, and with a little more luck they should have gone into the draw for the next round – but whatever luck was floating around Berlin that night was not going in their direction. They eventually lost 2–1 in extra time and then faced a penalty shoot-out. They lost 5–4 and were out of two cups. October had only just begun.

And yet despite these setbacks, Aberdeen's progress in

the league began where they had left off the previous season. They won seven of their opening fixtures and drew the other, before eventually losing at Celtic, when the hangover from the defeat in Berlin a few days earlier hit them straight between the eyes. The fixture computer had been unkind. But it hardly upset them. They brushed off that defeat and set off on another run that would take in eight successive victories and a draw to shoot them to the top of the table.

After a dubious start that had his critics crowing, Frank McDougall was now striking a rich vein of form. He seemed to have shrugged off his 'attitude', had lost weight and was actually enjoying himself. The coastal air was clearly driving energy into his lungs and forcing a smile across his face. Two goals against Hearts sparked off a flurry of goals as he scored in the next seven matches. Then Dundee United arrived at Pittodrie and made off with a 1–0 win. A fortnight later in the return United pipped it again, and suddenly the championship was wide open. Sandwiched in between had been a draw with St Mirren.

But if anyone thought Aberdeen were set to throw away the title they had landed so convincingly the previous season, they had to think again. They would lose only one more league match that season, away at Celtic. The goals came thick and fast: five against Morton, Rangers and Hibernian; four against Dundee, Dundee United and Dumbarton. McDougall was a man possessed. He struck a couple of hat tricks and rounded off the season with an impressive total of 22 league goals in 27 appearances. He also netted a couple more in the Scottish Cup. Aberdeen finally won the title at a canter, clocking up a record number of points for the Premier League and breaking the record they had set the previous season. They had lost just four games and had scored 89 goals, one short of the record.

Ferguson was ecstatic. So many changes had been forced on them by transfers and injuries that at the start of the campaign he had reckoned privately that they could not conceivably retain the championship. Yet here they were nine months on, notching up more points than the previous year's side. It said much for the spirit he had engendered at Pittodrie and for the young players he was steadily introducing into the first team.

But the one trophy Aberdeen could not retain was the Scottish Cup. Three successive triumphs was probably enough for any manager. It couldn't go on forever, though it very nearly did. The Dons marched to the semi-finals with wins over Alloa, Raith and Hearts before facing their old rivals Dundee United at Tynecastle. In truth Aberdeen should have wrapped up the game long before the final whistle as they missed glaring opportunities, but it ended goalless, and the two met again days later at the same venue. This time it was not so tidy. Tempers flashed, frustration began to show and Ferguson himself emerged with little credit. Neale Cooper was sent off, along with United's Davie Dodds, and a late goal settled the event in United's favour. A further source of controversy was a hotly disputed penalty when United's Malpas appeared to have blatantly handled the ball in the area. The crowd clamoured for a penalty but the referee had failed to spot it. 'The only man in the ground who didn't,' snarled Ferguson afterwards. The Aberdeen manager was seething; it was the familiar 'hot-headed' Fergie again. His rantings sounded like sour grapes, but there was no escaping the fact that after 23 cup ties Aberdeen had finally been beaten. However, it wouldn't be long before the Dons returned to Hampden and struck up winning ways again.

By the end of the season Ferguson could hardly complain. They had lifted the championship and were in with another shot at the European Cup. To strengthen the squad for the new 1985–86 season, Ferguson decided to bring in the former Rangers man Jim Bett, an exile abroad, playing

Belgian football with Lokeren. Scottish international Bett would prove to be an astute signing, bringing clarity and balance to the Dons' midfield. Yet there was also a significant loss, with Dougie Bell deciding to quit Pittodrie. To make matters worse, he joined rivals Rangers, the first major player Ferguson had sold to an Old Firm rival.

Aberdeen's season was off to a mixed start. After seven games they had only three victories to their credit, having lost one and drawn the other three. The pattern for the season had been set, although they would always be in contention. There were also injuries. Some of the youngsters who had emerged had possibly been pushed too quickly and too soon. Of the victorious 1983 Cup-winners side, Eric Black, Neil Simpson, Neale Cooper and John Hewitt would all be affected by burn-out to one degree or another.

Then, on 10 September, the cruel and dramatic death of Scotland manager Jock Stein at Cardiff also dealt a blow to Aberdeen. Ferguson had been acting as an assistant to Stein for some time and had been sitting with him on the bench that fateful night in Wales. With the World Cup finals looming and a crucial decider against Australia on the horizon, there was really only one candidate for the job of national team manager. Ferguson accepted – though only, he insisted, until the finals were over, and on a part-time basis. Aberdeen did not want to lose him – although chairman Dick Donald would not have stood in his way – and Ferguson himself had no desire to take the job on a full-time basis. A compromise was reached that seemed to satisfy everyone, but it was hardly ideal. For much of the season Ferguson would be absent from Pittodrie, watching players south of the border as well as taking in the occasional international on the continent. Pittodrie would miss his dominating presence and careful application to detail.

Nonetheless, within weeks of his appointment Ferguson was already claiming a trophy, the Skol Cup – the one competition he had never won at Aberdeen. They reached the final where they faced Hibernian without even conceding a goal and then wrapped the match up inside 12 minutes with two goals. It was to be known as the 12 minutes final. They added a third on the hour and picked up the Skol Cup without having conceded a single goal.

Back in the league complacency set in. Ferguson's divided loyalties didn't help, nor did winning a trophy so early in the season – it seemed to suggest that they could sit back on their laurels. In the run-in before Christmas they lost three games and drew two more. For five months they would not have an away win, while at home dry rot had set in. One win in ten games: it was their worst run since Ferguson had joined the club. And yet despite their dismal form and lack of consistency they were still clinging to the shirt-tails of the leaders. Even though they had slipped from top spot to fourth, nobody seemed to be able to take advantage of their slump. But with the first signs of spring Aberdeen's form began to re-emerge, partly initiated by a fine run in the Scottish Cup and the European Cup.

In Europe, Aberdeen had opened with another visit to their old friends Akranes of Iceland. The last time the two sides had met in the opening round of the Cup-Winners' Cup, Aberdeen had struggled to overcome their part-time opponents. But this time, there was no such embarrassment; Aberdeen notched up convincing wins home and away. Next in line were Servette, the Swiss champions, with the first leg in Switzerland. It turned out to be a dour game that did little to encourage anyone to watch football. Watching paint dry might have been more entertaining. However, in the return leg a Frank McDougall header was enough to edge the Dons into the quarter-finals – but it was a close thing. After that goal Servette brushed away the cobwebs and produced what Ferguson described as 'the finest football I have seen from a team visiting Pittodrie for a European tie'. It was some compliment.

If Ferguson could have had a choice of the quarter-finalists he would undoubtedly have plumped for Gothenburg. All the senior names had been avoided, the Swedes were just emerging from their winter hibernation and Aberdeen held fond memories of the Ullevi stadium. But all that was balanced by the fact that Gothenburg had recently won the UEFA Cup and in Glenn Hysen and Johnny Ekstrom had players who would soon shine on the world stage. The first leg was also scheduled for Pittodrie. It got worse. Goalkeeper Jim Leighton and striker Frank McDougall both cried off with injuries, leaving the Dons scratching around to find a team. Yet in the 16th minute Willie Miller swept them into the lead. Gothenburg came back to level the score shortly before the break. Then with 11 minutes remaining Hewitt struck to put Aberdeen 2–1 ahead. But there was to be a cruel finale as Johnny Ekstrom, in the final seconds amid a shrill of whistles, threaded his way through the Dons' defence to level the scores. Ferguson was furious that his defence had so complacently lost concentration. Gothenburg now had two away goals. It meant that Aberdeen simply had to win in Sweden. It was not beyond them, but they had left themselves with a mountain to climb.

This time the Ullevi was not so friendly. Aberdeen's attack force barely had a sight of the ball. Their defence held out admirably but just couldn't get the ball beyond their midfield to take any advantage, and so the game petered out into a goalless draw. Aberdeen were out, unbeaten, and cursing ever more their desperate luck at leaking that last-gasp goal at Pittodrie.

If Europe brought no prizes, there was at least to be some domestic consolation. In the league Aberdeen's encouraging spring form had dissipated when it was most needed, their European Cup defeat weighing heavily on their shoulders. In their final five games they could manage only one win to finish the season in fourth spot, six points adrift of champions Celtic. Yet the Dons' progress in the Scottish Cup continued unabated, with early round victories over Montrose and Arbroath before the quarter-finals produced a draw at Dundee. The Dons won the replay, albeit luckily, and then swept Hibs aside to face Hearts in the final at Hampden.

Shortly before the final came sensational news. Eric Black was set to sign for the French club Metz. He had conducted the deal privately and the first anyone heard of it was when it was announced publicly. Aberdeen was aghast, Ferguson speechless. Black was promptly dropped for the big game. Fortunately, in John McMaster there was a ready-made replacement. It took Aberdeen only five minutes to sort Hearts out. A breakaway by Hewitt and they were a goal up. Hearts never recovered. Shortly after the interval they added a killer second goal and then a third with 15 minutes remaining. It was the first time Aberdeen had won both domestic cups in the same season. They were to be the last trophies Aberdeen would win under Alex Ferguson.

CHAPTER NINE

Fergie's Tartan Army

Jock Stein seemed immortal. The burly, larger-than-life manager of Scotland was a legend. Stein had also been the manager of Celtic when they became the first British club to lift the European Cup in 1967. His club went on to become the first side to win nine successive Scottish league titles and to write themselves a chapter or two in the history books. Then in October 1978, after a brief residence south of the border with Leeds United that lasted just 44 days, Stein was appointed manager of the Scottish national squad. His task: to rebuild and prepare Scotland for the next World Cup finals in 1982. But Stein enjoyed only moderate success. Scotland qualified for Spain but, with Brazil and Russia in the same group, were always struggling to progress any further.

After that Stein's next task was qualification for the 1986 finals in Mexico. He had steered Scotland to the brink of a fourth consecutive appearance in the finals when on the evening of Tuesday 10 September 1985 they faced Wales at Ninian Park in Cardiff in a crucial decider. A win for either side would put them into the finals, but a draw for Wales would see them eliminated. A draw for Scotland, however, would put them into a play-off with Australia. In the event, a Davie Cooper penalty ten minutes from time gave

Scotland a 1–1 draw to keep their World Cup dreams alive. But on the bench, amid all the drama, manager Jock Stein was suddenly taken ill. Alex Ferguson, his assistant, was sitting by him. There were only minutes to the final whistle when Stein rose from the bench and then suddenly collapsed into the arms of trainer Hugh Allan. The Big Man was hurriedly carried down the tunnel to the treatment room, few of the players aware of what had happened. There is a photograph of Ferguson walking on to the pitch at the end of the game with laughing, smiling players surrounding him, but Ferguson's face is white and express-ionless, his eyes staring into space as he gently pushes someone aside. It hardly took a doctor to realise that Stein had suffered a major heart attack. It wasn't long before the news filtered through to the dressing room that Stein was dead.

The whole of Scotland felt his death, and Ferguson was devastated. Coming from a different generation, he may not have been the closest of friends with Stein, but there was the respect, the insight, the knowledge that Stein was a giant of a man who always believed his teams should produce attractive, exciting football. Much of Stein had rubbed off on his young assistant.

'He never spoke of his own success, and the ordinariness of his lifestyle made it a pleasure to work as his assistant,' said Ferguson. 'The last words he spoke to me were, "Whatever the result, let us not forget our dignity. Win or lose, we must keep our dignity."'

The World Cup finals were only nine months away. Scotland needed to find a new manager, and fast.

Ferguson's association with Scotland had begun when he took on the role of Stein's sidekick. As one of the most accomplished and experienced managers in Scottish foot-ball at that time, Ferguson had been a natural ally to Stein. He knew the current Scottish scene as well as anybody and could keep an eye on players north of the border while Stein could concentrate on the English players and the foreign travel. At 43 years of age Ferguson had already claimed more honours than Stein at the same age. They made a formidable duo. It was a tragedy that Stein's death robbed Scotland of such a resplendent partnership, one of so much potential and unfulfilled ambition.

Ferguson was always the obvious choice to succeed Stein. He might not have been capped at full international level, but then, neither had Stein, though unlike Stein he had at least represented his country at minor international level. He'd operated as his assistant, knew the Big Man's game plan and was himself highly respected within the Scottish game. Furthermore, the job needed someone with his authority, someone who could command the respect of experienced players like Dalglish and Souness, now turning their hands to managerial work themselves.

However, Ferguson's acceptance wasn't quite so straight-forward. Aberdeen were challenging for domestic honours again and now was hardly the time to desert them – yet the chance to take Scotland to the World Cup finals in Mexico was not one he could refuse. Ferguson was torn: it was the dream of every manager to be in a World Cup finals. The Scottish FA were accommodating, and a compromise was worked out. Ferguson agreed to do it on a part-time basis until the end of the World Cup finals – assuming that Scotland qualified. Walter Smith was appointed as his assistant to help relieve some of the pressures. Aberdeen had little option but to accept the situation. They were flattered and knew that, as the club's historian Clive Leatherdale succinctly put it, 'half a Fergie was better than none'. Nevertheless, his presence around Pittodrie was missed, the club losing 'much of its buzz without his day-to-day supervision'. It would show as well – the Dons finished the season with 44 points, their lowest tally for seven years. But there were compensations as they lifted both the Skol League Cup and the Scottish Cup.

Taking over from Stein meant stepping into the shoes of a legend. It was also equivalent to being handed the poisoned chalice. Ferguson's first task was to ensure Scotland's qualification, and that meant beating Australia. The entire nation seemed to regard this as a foregone conclusion, but Ferguson knew that when it came to Scotland nothing could be regarded as a simple formality. To lose would be a disaster, a humiliation the Scots would take years to recover from and would never forget. The Glasgow mafia would never forgive him. It was the kind of gamble you could do without at the start of a career as a national manager, even if it was only temporary and part-time. Remember Zaire, Iran and New Zealand, people warned.

Still, Ferguson was not one to shirk a challenge. And so on 20 November 1985 Scotland lined up against Australia at Hampden Park while Alex Ferguson sat nervously on the touchline. He'd had only one game to test his proficiency, a friendly against East Germany at Hampden, which had ended in a goalless draw with little wisdom gleaned.

Scotland's performance against Australia was hardly outstanding but it did produce a two-goal cushion – just about enough, Ferguson reckoned, to take them to the World Cup finals, although it took Scotland almost an hour before they produced their first goal. Ten days later they set off on an 11,000-mile round trip to Australia for the second leg. A two-goal margin might have looked comfortable enough, but with dramatic changes in temperature, jet lag and hard, bumpy pitches to take into account, almost anything could happen. Ferguson's biggest problem had been securing the release of the Anglos for the match. The long journey meant nine days away from home, but the English FA, not always the most accommodating, at least agreed to revoke the rule that obliged clubs to play full-strength teams. Four key Anglos travelled, although Dalglish, now player-manager at Liverpool, remained at base with his club. Souness arrived later to find illness and injury creating havoc, and after his exhausting journey, he wasn't in much condition to play himself.

Back home, almost one and a half million were said to be watching the match on television that morning. In the end they would not be disappointed but there were enough heart-stopping moments for them before lunch. Time and again Aberdeen's Jim Leighton was the saviour as Australia unexpectedly took up the challenge. Scotland would be grateful for a 0–0 draw. There was relief all round.

Ferguson was philosophical. 'I would have preferred to have gone to Mexico with a wee bit better performance,' he told the press, 'but the whole section for us, since the defeat by Wales in March, has been a hard struggle with a lot of tension and nerves.' Scotland's victory was dedicated to Stein.

For their efforts, the Scots were awarded a place in the toughest group of all in Mexico. Their opponents were none other than West Germany, Denmark and Uruguay. Groans could be heard all the way down Sauchiehall Street as the draw was made. The group was even christened the *Grupo del Muerte*, the group of death. And so it was. But at least there were no unrealistic expectations. There was no repetition of the silly cavorting around Hampden in an open-topped bus that Ally MacLeod and his team had indulged in as they departed high on adrenaline for the 1978 finals. Everyone recognised that they were up against it. It was a tricky situation for Ferguson. On the one hand he didn't want to demoralise his troops before they had even kicked a ball by suggesting that they were on mission impossible, while on the other he didn't want to go around boasting that Scotland were going to do this, that and the other to the opposition.

Ferguson had just four games to prepare. The first was against Israel at Hampden, a 1–0 win, which again proved little. The next was another emotional evening for Scottish football as Dalglish earned his 100th cap for his country. Ferguson generously invited him to captain the side that night as they took on Romania. It did the Liverpool man a power of good. He almost scored in the first minute and then helped provide two Scottish goals in an impressive 3–0 win.

Next came two savagely testing games, first against the Auld Enemy at Wembley and then six days later against Holland. For the England game Ferguson was without four of his key Anglos – Sharp, Strachan, McAvennie and Dalglish. They were also to miss the next game. Their presence at Wembley might just have turned events. As it was, Scotland lost 2–1, conceding their first goals since Ferguson had taken charge. The trip to Holland provided a further selection headache as three Celtic players were withdrawn from the squad. Ferguson was down to the bare bones but gave a first cap to both Ally McCoist and Robert Connor. In the event Scotland performed remarkably well, earning a goalless draw against the side that had surprised everyone by failing to qualify for the Mexico finals.

If Scotland already faced an uphill task in Mexico with the quality of opposition, Ferguson's problems were hardly helped by the last-minute news that his top man Kenny Dalglish was dropping out. Dalglish was injured and about to undergo surgery. Steve Archibald was drafted in to replace him.

Ferguson had already incurred the wrath of some with his squad selection. Fourteen of his 22 players came from the Scottish League, with only three of them from the two Glasgow giants. Most seemed to come from the provincial clubs of the north-east coast – Dundee United and, of course, Aberdeen. It was a genuine tartan army. Surprisingly left at home were David Speedie and Mo Johnston. Ferguson had also taken the brave (some call it reckless) decision not to take Dalglish's teammate Alan Hansen. His critics regarded the highly experienced Liverpool man as one of the few world-class players Scotland boasted.

Stein had already had reservations about Hansen, who always seemed to be injured. He was a liability, but under pressure they had chosen him for the game against England a few months previously. In training for the match Hansen had pulled up short after one lap of warming up and come limping off. 'What's the trouble?' asked Ferguson. 'It's my knee, it's gone,' replied Hansen, adding that he was off back to Liverpool. As far as Ferguson was concerned that was it when it came to Hansen. Whatever the views over Hansen, the absence of Dalglish was an unquestionable blow to Scotland.

Scotland had not only been the last country to qualify for the finals but were also the last to arrive, flying in just days before they kicked off.

Ferguson's 22-man squad for the finals was: Leighton (Aberdeen), Gough (Dundee United), Malpas (Dundee United), Souness (Rangers), McLeish (Aberdeen), Strachan (Manchester United), Aitken (Celtic), Bannon (Dundee United), Bett (Aberdeen), McStay (Celtic), Goram (Oldham), Nicol (Liverpool), Narey (Dundee United), Albiston (Manchester United), McAvennie (West Ham United), Archibald (Barcelona), Sharp (Everton), Nicholas (Arsenal), Sturrock (Dundee United), Cooper (Rangers), Rough (Hibernian).

They arrived, after a couple of weeks' acclimatisation in Santa Fe and Los Angeles, on the first day of June, and kicked off their challenge against Denmark three days later, sporting the worst-designed shorts ever seen on a World Cup stage. The Danes were considered one of the strongest members of the group, a glance at their line-up revealed a batch of players who in the years ahead would become familiar with football fans across Europe: Laudrup, Molby, Olsen and Nielsen, to name a few. Scotland, fielding nine Scottish League players in their line-up, lost 1–0, although the Scots created enough chances in the first half to have settled the game by half-time. Sadly they missed the goal-poaching of Dalglish. After that defeat it was a case of whether they could go home with any points.

Four days later they faced the ultimate test as they lined up against West Germany in Queretaro. It was made worse by the late withdrawal of Alex McLeish. Ferguson surprised the media pack with the inclusion up front of Steve Archibald, who had played only one game in the previous ten weeks and hadn't scored for Scotland in four years. Seventeen minutes into the match, McLeish's absence seemed almost irrelevant as Scotland shot into an audacious lead against the would-be finalists. Ferguson could barely believe it. He was off his bench punching the air and hugging anyone within a couple of yards of him. Five minutes later the Germans equalised and the sad truth began to dawn. The Scots held out until half-time, but five minutes after the interval Germany took charge, and without some fine goalkeeping from Jim Leighton they might well have trailed by three or four goals. Nonetheless, it had been a sterling performance from the Scots against one of the most adept sides in the world. Any criticism would have been churlish.

Two defeats, and Scotland should have been out of the finals and on their way back to Glasgow, but with Uruguay thrashed 6–1 by Denmark and managing only a draw with West Germany, Scotland still had slender hopes of qualifying in third place. To do so, they had to beat the Uruguayans. A draw would not be enough. McLeish was still out recovering from the dreaded Montezuma's Revenge, while Souness's ageing legs had turned to jelly after his display against the Germans; he wasn't even picked to sit on the bench. Ferguson would regret his error.

Scotland's record against Uruguay did little to boost their confidence. The South Americans had knocked them out of the 1954 World Cup finals, while the two other games against them in 1962 and 1983 had been tempestuous affairs, best forgotten for their brutality. History was about to repeat itself.

The game was scheduled for Friday the thirteenth. After just one minute it looked as if the omens were against the South Americans as Jose Batista was ordered off for a cruel tackle on Gordon Strachan. The Scots were delighted to see a referee imposing his authority on the game at such an early stage. With just ten men to beat and 89 minutes in which to do it, Scottish hopes suddenly soared. But if they thought the Uruguayans were about to go soft, they had another think coming. Being down to ten men, the South Americans might have been expected to show a bit more restraint, but they went into the tackle just as ferociously, pulling virtually an entire team back into defence. The tougher they tackled, the more Scotland's game fell apart. They were classic South American tactics: stifle the game, stop the opposition passing and hang on for a draw. Ferguson might have considered throwing on another attacker after the sending-off, or indeed, at any point in the first half hour, but it would have been a risky decision. Eventually Charlie Nicholas came on for Sturrock but he too came in for the same scabrous treatment and couldn't find the net any more than his colleagues.

The game ended goalless. Uruguay had bickered and battled their way into the next round but they had hardly won any admirers in the process. As for the Scots, they trooped off disconsolately, itching to go home. In the end they had failed to find the key to unlock their opponents' back line. They must have wondered how Denmark had ever managed to put six goals past them. Yet the Scots had always been the underdogs, their hopes raised by stirring performances against the Germans and the Danes.

As for Ferguson, he'd had enough. It had been a challenging experience but not the kind he'd want to go through too often. The responsibilities were frightening with so much focused on one competition. It was a long, painful slog, and if you didn't make it, you were out, considered a failure. 'I didn't enjoy it that much,' he admitted. 'There was a conflict of interest with six Aberdeen players in the squad. I chose the wrong side against Uruguay. I should have kept Souness in.'

'The World Cup finals are hard work,' he told the media. 'For the manager there is the thinking about the football and dealing with the press as well as keeping an eye on the players. For the players there is the need to cope with the boredom and length of time away. Players have to be prepared to make the sacrifice, and a manager too has to make sacrifices. Your family is going to suffer from the sacrifice. You need that support . . . at times you'll be bored, at times you'll miss the wife and kids . . . but the World Cup finals are worth the sacrifice.

'The problems of the national job are inherent,' he added. 'You don't have time to prepare. Players are a long way away, playing abroad, but for a small country like ours qualifying for the World Cup is a success.'

Ferguson recognised that while Scotland could produce the likes of Baxter, Law, Dalglish and Souness, players who all glittered on the home stage, that did not necessarily make them world-class stars.

And so he returned to his normal duties – back to the relative peace of Pittodrie, the friendly Aberdeen media, and the players he knew intimately. But the experience had whetted his appetite. He came home convinced that he wanted to move on. Little did he know that he was about to be offered one of the biggest prizes in English football.

CHAPTER TEN

A Taste of Bitterness

Back in the summer of 1984 Alex Ferguson took a phone call from Irving Scholar, chairman of Tottenham Hotspur Football Club. Tottenham were looking for a new manager. Was Ferguson interested in becoming the new boss of Spurs?

'Yes, I certainly am,' answered Ferguson

Over the next few weeks Alex Ferguson was to come within a whisker of moving to White Hart Lane.

It wasn't the first offer from England either. Three years earlier Wolverhampton Wanderers had tried to lure him away from Scotland. Ferguson had again been interested and had even gone down to Molineux to talk with the directors. After all, Wolves was one of the most romantic names in British football, although at the time they were struggling and looked to have lost their way. They needed someone to focus their direction and ambition. But what Ferguson saw at Molineux was enough to put him off. The stadium was deserted, in a state of disrepair, and nobody seemed to have any ambition. The directors also did not seem to know what they wanted. He wasn't even sure if they were really offering him the job or just interviewing him. In the end they did offer him the post, but after what he had seen, he had little trouble in turning it down and taking the next train back to Aberdeen.

Tottenham was a different matter. He liked the idea. They were a big club, well run, recognised for their style of football. Ferguson was keen. He talked with Scholar on a number of occasions and was suitably impressed by him. They even discussed wages, a club house, transfer fees and so forth. It looked to be all settled. But there was one stumbling block – the length of contract. Spurs would offer only a two-year deal; Ferguson wanted five years. Scholar later increased the offer to three years, but Ferguson was still not happy. It had to be five years or nothing. It was a measure of the importance he attached to thinking in the long term. So the deal fell through and Ferguson decided to remain at Pittodrie, but he had not abandoned the idea of moving on, merely decided to leave it dormant for the moment.

Scotland might have been eliminated at the first hurdle in Mexico, but the World Cup finals had proved an enormously enriching experience for their manager. Ferguson had been on a world stage and had clearly enjoyed it. Returning to Aberdeen was comfortable in many ways, but the adventure had left him hungry for greater challenges. Fortunately one was about to come his way.

Aberdeen could sense the uncertainty. Their man was now the focus of attention in Scotland. They knew about all the offers and equally knew that he had been sorely tempted by both the Tottenham and Rangers jobs. It seemed that almost every other week his name was being linked with some managerial post somewhere. It was only a matter of time before the right club put the right kind of deal in front of him.

There can be little doubt that Ferguson was now even more convinced about his next move. In truth he'd achieved as much as he could at Pittodrie. He as much as admitted it in his book *Six Years At United*. 'I felt I had not achieved enough, and once you start striving in football it's time to chuck it all in. So I was ready,' he confessed.

He'd won three Premiership titles, four Scottish Cups, one Scottish League Cup and the European Cup-Winners' Cup. It was a remarkable record. Yet Aberdeen were and always would be a provincial club with finite resources compared with Alex Ferguson's infinite ambitions. That wasn't their fault. It was simply a matter of geography. With a local population of just over 200,000, it would never be able to attract huge support. It had a neat all-seater stadium, but attendances rarely topped the 15,000 mark. Only Celtic and Rangers, with their vast army of travelling supporters, were able to swell Aberdeen's gate beyond 20,000. Aberdeen would always be short of supporters and consequently short of money. They could compete in Scotland, but as their European results illustrated, it was a different matter when it came to football on the continent. They had performed heroically the previous season to reach the last eight of the European Cup and had only been eliminated on the away-goal rule. Yet that result only put into perspective Aberdeen's hopeless cause. They were always going to be labelled 'giant-killers'.

There were other problems as well. Vice-chairman Chris Anderson had died, leaving the club with a huge hole to plug. Anderson had been a visionary and loyal supporter of Ferguson. Chairman Dick Donald, sensing Ferguson's restlessness, offered the manager a directorship which he was happy to accept. Then there were player problems – not disciplinary ones, but transfers. Eric Black had gone to the French club Metz and Neale Cooper to Aston Villa, while Frank McDougall had quit the game through injury. Black and McDougall between them had netted 79 goals in the previous two seasons. Replacing them was going to be a major headache for the manager-cum-managing director.

He went to see Dick Donald and told him that this would be his final year at Pittodrie. 'I want to quit at the end of the season, I need a new challenge,' he told him. The chairman, unsurprised, asked if he had somewhere else in mind, and on hearing that he hadn't, said, 'Well, I don't think it's a good idea to think of moving without another job. The only job you should leave us for is Manchester United. They're the only club who could satisfy the challenge you want.' Ferguson nodded. 'If Manchester United ever come in for you, then you have my word that you can go,' promised Donald. It was a speculative but astonishing suggestion.

The first month of the new season was encouraging enough. They were beaten by Dundee United on the opening day, but that was followed by a string of tolerable results. Then came September, and the gloom set in. First Celtic prised open their hold on the Skol Cup, and defeats by Hearts and Rangers in the Premiership seriously dented these ambitions.

To counter this, Ferguson made a rare foray into the transfer market, going to Switzerland to sign Davie Dodds from Neuchatel for £200,000. It seemed a good move at the time, even though it cost the club far more than they could really afford. Ferguson had always been a manager who bought at the cheaper end of the market and encouraged youngsters through his youth scheme. Dodds had not long left Dundee United to join the Swiss club, but the move had not worked out, for reasons that became apparent when he pulled on an Aberdeen shirt. The man who had once been such a thorn in the flesh of the Dons now looked only half the player. It had been a gamble, and in his early days Dodds did not look too impressive, scoring just four goals in 27 outings. Ferguson came in for some waspish criticism from fans, his signing being described as both 'stop-gap' and 'short-sighted'. The situation wasn't helped by the fact that Dundee United were their closest rivals. The fans simply weren't accustomed to it.

There was worse to come. Aberdeen had been drawn against the unpretentious Swiss club Sion in the European Cup. It looked a comparatively effortless tie, a sort of warm-up game that would whet the appetite for stiffer competition to come. A few seasons earlier they had put eleven goals past Sion on their way to picking up the Cup-Winners' Cup. But if Aberdeen thought this was going to be another walkover they were sadly mistaken. At Pittodrie Sion had the audacity to take a first-half lead. The Dons equalised through a penalty and Wright made it 2–1 with just ten minutes remaining – but the fact remained that the Swiss had scored a vital away goal. Two weeks later came the most humiliating moment in Ferguson's career as Sion slaughtered Aberdeen 3–0. After just four minutes the Swiss were a goal up, and ahead on the away-goal rule. They added two more goals and Aberdeen were out of Europe. Jim Bett had also been sent off in the process.

Ferguson was furious. But although he raged at his players, once he'd calmed down and begun to reflect more soberly on the evening's events he could come to only one conclusion. The team was disintegrating before his eyes.

Players were ageing, fresh blood was slow in coming through the youth ranks, and Scottish football was shifting into a new era as far as money was concerned. The old order was set to return. Rangers, under their charismatic new manager Graeme Souness, would be the force in Scottish football over the next decade, and nobody would be able to afford to live with them – certainly not Alex Ferguson's cash-conscious Aberdeen. With hindsight it's easy to see, but his remaining at Pittodrie would probably have made no difference. There was no competing with Rangers, who could sell out to crowds of 40,000 and more, and splash out huge sums on players. The signs were already there. Souness had spent a million pounds bringing in England internationals Chris Woods and Terry Butcher before the season had kicked off.

It was always going to happen. Sooner or later Ferguson would be tempted by a big-money offer from south of the border. He might have gone to Ibrox a couple of years earlier had the political conditions been more acceptable, but there was little indication then that the bigotry and prejudice were ever going to end. It would take an outsider, a lad from Edinburgh who had never played any of his football in Scotland, to change that. But now, out of the blue, came an offer from Manchester United – perhaps not the most successful club in England, but certainly the richest, the best supported and the club with the greatest potential.

Whether or not Ferguson was 'tapped' before Ron Atkinson had been fired is a matter of conjecture. The speed of his appointment suggests that there was some contact. The official United line has always been that there was none, and Ferguson has always claimed that the call came out of the blue. However, the Aberdeen chairman Dick Donald remained convinced that 'feelers' had been out before Martin Edwards phoned to request official permission to talk to their manager. Crick and Smith, in their book *Manchester United, The Betrayal of a Legend*, claim that Martin Edwards and director Maurice Watkins had a secret arrangement to meet Ferguson in a Glasgow hotel on the evening before Atkinson was dismissed. Whatever the truth, it is of little significance now.

The fact is that United asked Ferguson to be their new manager and he had little hesitation in accepting. Money was no problem. Ferguson was hardly earning a fortune at Pittodrie, and United could almost match the figure with their receipts from programme sales alone. In time Ferguson would learn to be a little more canny when it came to his salary.

Informing the club that he was leaving was the most difficult task, and he was happy to let the back pages speculate that United were after him. It was obviously a tempting prospect, and nobody could blame him for accepting it. Nonetheless, it was still a wrench for Ferguson. He'd made his home on the windy north-east coast and been made welcome. Aberdonians may have a reputation for dourness but they had all been friendly. Aberdeen was a small city, yet Ferguson had achieved so much while he was there. He'd smashed the Old Firm monopoly, brought domestic and European glory to the city, and given the fans football with flair. One simply had to look at the Aberdeen players who would go on to manage – Miller, McLeish, McGhee, Strachan, Rougvie. Perhaps only Don Revie had produced so many potential managers with his famed Leeds side of the sixties. It spoke volumes for Ferguson's style, for his ability to pass on ideas and generate enthusiasm.

The only sour note was to come when Ferguson appointed Archie Knox, his number two at Aberdeen, as his assistant at Old Trafford. Knox had returned to Pittodrie during the close season, a move that many reckoned would eventually see him installed as manager. It seemed the chairman was almost resigned to losing Ferguson and that Knox's return affirmed the succession. But it was not to be. Knox did not want the job: he was going to Old Trafford as the gaffer's lieutenant, turning down the chance to be general at Pittodrie. The planned succession had fallen apart.

Aberdeen were left high and dry. Knox agreed to hang on until a new manager had been appointed, but given the time that this took it is clear that nobody on the board had thought beyond Knox. It was two weeks before Aberdeen finally appointed Ian Porterfield to the job. As Knox took his seat on the bench at Pittodrie for his first game 'in charge' against St Mirren, the stands stood and roundly booed him. The biggest cheer of the afternoon came at half-time when the tannoy announced that Oxford United were beating Manchester United. It was a sad end to what had been such a productive and happy relationship.

CHAPTER ELEVEN

In the Shadow

On a chilly November morning Alex Ferguson, contract in his pocket and as keenly dressed as ever, strolled out through the tunnel at Old Trafford and stood thoughtfully at the edge of the dugout. In front of him stretched the luscious green turf of the pitch while above him the sun was slicing through grey Manchester skies. Dark clouds moved relentlessly overhead, passing over the Manchester Ship Canal to make their way steadily east towards the Pennines, just about visible in the grey distance. A seasoned Lancashire cricket follower at the other Old Trafford would have diagnosed rain in the air. The silence of the occasion was broken only by the drone of a petrol-driven lawnmower imperiously making its way up and down the pitch, occasionally halting before spinning and beginning another length. A touch of early morning frost glistened on the grass. The groundsman over the far side looked up and stared at the small band of people gathering by the touchline, ready to pounce at anyone trespassing on his sacred territory.

Ferguson hesitated by the touchline, not wanting to incur the wrath of his groundsman at this early stage. Behind him a small band of photographers and journalists kept a respectful distance, while ahead of him in the old north stand the executive boxes reflected the autumn sunshine.

To his left the vast terracing of the majestic Stretford End, home of the most fanatical and vocal United supporters, disturbed the symmetry of this graceful stadium. To his right was the opposition terrace with its threatening ironwork, a stark reminder that not everything about this game was quite as beautiful as you might like. Behind the journalists and photographers towered the south stand, a sign of the future with its executive boxes and dining facilities. It was a neat contrast with the past. And then just above his eyeline was the directors' box, Sir Matt's seat and the press box. Ferguson glanced up at the giant roof, its muscular shell almost encircling the ground. All in all, it was an impressive sight. Here was a stadium capable of holding almost 55,000 fans, as swanky an arena as any in Britain. It might not hold as many as Hampden or Ibrox, but its facilities were second to none. It could take your breath away, even scare you.

The sight of this empty mausoleum was liable to send a shiver of nerves down the back of the staunchest viewer. Like anyone, Ferguson could be intimidated. He surveyed the prospect with mixed feelings. This was the moment he had been waiting for. Yet as he glanced up, soaking in its history and its pedigree, he must have wondered if he was up to the job.

Plenty of others before him had failed: Wilf McGuinness, Frank O'Farrell, Tommy Docherty, Dave Sexton, Ron Atkinson. The latter had only recently arrived in a blaze of publicity, ushering in a golden era, but it had soon lost its shine; while Docherty, full of Scottish exuberance and mischief, had succumbed to the temptations of the flesh and paid for it with humiliating exposure in the tabloids, upsetting United's Catholic dignity. All had lived and suffered in the shadow of one man: Matt Busby. You could almost sense that shadow falling across the pitch. Resplendent on his own special throne up in the directors' box, Busby could sit in judgement on his successors. He

A smart young boy – Alex aged seven (*Mirror Syndication International*).

An early Fergie hotshot, Dunfermline v Partick Thistle (*Mirror Syndication International*).

was a king judging his princes, and not just on their results – the style was crucial too. Busby unconsciously breathed life and death into this club. Ferguson was dazzled by it all. There was fear in his heart but he deliberately covered it up.

For now at least he had friends, and the press seemed to include themselves in that category. They slapped his back, congratulated him on his appointment, introduced themselves, offered home phone numbers and, above all, a fair hearing. In time he would reflect on that and wonder whatever had happened to that old English promise of reason and decency.

BBC radio commentator Alan Green remembered the occasion well. He'd known Ferguson up at Aberdeen and had arranged to witness his arrival at United and grill him about what was generally considered the most tortuous job in British football. As the other journalists moved away, Green, like a slippery inside forward, seized his opportunity. Ferguson was standing motionless, his eyes fixed on the floodlights. 'Do you realise what you're taking on here?' asked the BBC man. Ferguson seemed barely to hear him. If he did the words certainly never sank in. 'Isn't this fantastic?' was all he could offer. He was bemused by it all, a child in a room full of toys. It was all he had ever wanted.

Green nodded in agreement, but with his knowledge of Old Trafford sensed then that all might not be quite so straightforward. Ferguson had taken on a task that was certainly more challenging than any he had ever undertaken. The manager might have been warned about the Busby shadow, his influence and paternalism – indeed he had already met the man, now a legend – but he could still never have guessed at how influential he was and just how destructive his presence could be.

There was moreover another warning that had not been passed on, another challenge that would soon come to weigh heavily on him. It came from 30 miles away, from the same direction as those leaden skies, from Merseyside. He'd experienced it once at Aberdeen, and that had been bad enough. Over the next few years it would haunt him far more than Busby ever would. Already it had cost Ron Atkinson his job and would come within a whisker of costing Ferguson himself the most daunting position in soccer.

If Matt Busby had been a thorn in the flesh of many an Old Trafford manager, then surely Liverpool Football Club had been like a hot blade in a festering wound. Manchester United Football Club might have had some special claim to being the nation's favourite club since Munich, but when it came to winning trophies there was no contest. Liverpool were simply supreme. By 1986 they had already won four European Cups, two UEFA Cups, and sixteen league championships. They were far and away the most successful club in British football, and one of the finest on the European stage. United might have won the FA Cup a few times since the mid-sixties, but when it came to polishing the championship trophy they trailed miserably behind Liverpool and their almost equally impressive neighbours, Everton.

Try as they might United had made little impression since the glory days of Best, Law and Charlton. They'd spent millions of pounds in a desperate bid to build a championship-challenging side, signing huge cheques each season to bring in the likes of Gordon Strachan, Bryan Robson, Frank Stapleton, Ray Wilkins, Gordon McQueen and Joe Jordan, almost every one of them a British record buy, and yet success had still eluded them. They had packed their massive stadium to the rafters most weeks with the most loyal of followers, yet had been unable to repay their loyalty to the extent that was demanded.

Manchester United was a big club in every sense of the word. It always had been, though it had not always been as

The first cup is the sweetest – Alex Ferguson v
(*Mirror Syndication International*).

Fergie gunning for goal, Rangers v Dundee 1968 (*Mirror Syndication International*).

Ferguson of the Rangers; when he signed in 1967 he was Scotland's most expensive player (*Daily Record*).

Outpacing Celtic's Billy McNeill in the Scottish Cup final 1969 (*Colorsport*).

Fergie, the bad boy, being escorted off the field by Falkirk trainer Ronnie McKenzie after being sent off once again (*Aberdeen Evening Express*).

Manager of Saint Mirren, with Tony Fitzpatrick and Derek Hislop (*Mirror Syndication International*).

Ferguson's move to the manager's job at Aberdeen in summer 1978 brought him to the big time (*Mirror Syndication International*).

Pittodrie can be cold (*Colorsport*).

Pure joy. Ferguson and Archie Knox after winning the European Cup-Winners' Cup in 1983 (*Aberdeen Evening Express*).

As promised. Ferguson and Mark McGhee welcome back fans from the *St Clair* after the triumph in Gothenburg (*Aberdeen Evening Express*).

Gordon Strachan is doused in champagne after another Aberdeen triumph (*Mirror Syndication International*).

An open-top parade through Aberdeen, after beating Hearts 3-0 in the Scottish Cup Final 1986 – Ferguson's last trophy at the club (*Mirror Syndication International*).

popular as it is today. The club had been playing league
football since 1892, the year Gladstone led his Liberal Party
to a fourth general election victory. The Labour Party had
not even been formed and would be a further eight years in
the waiting, while Queen Victoria was in the 55th year of
her reign. But the roots of United went back even further,
to the year 1878, when a group of railway workers,
employed at the Lancashire and Yorkshire Railway
Company's carriage and wagon works at Newton Heath,
clubbed together and formed a football team. They named
it Newton Heath. United's roots were firmly set among the
industrial workers of the north, a far cry from its later
direction. Football was the emerging popular culture of the
working classes, particularly in the north and the Midlands.
Here was a simple game – healthy, comradely and exciting
– encouraged by Methodism, teetotalism and the social
organisations of Victorian England.

Newton Heath were an immediate success, shooting up
rapidly from their railway roots, turning professional and
joining the Football Alliance in 1889. Now the opposition
was tougher – Nottingham Forest, Grimsby Town, Sheffield
Wednesday and the famous Brutal Bootle, as they were so
fondly known. It was a tough division, but within a few
years Newton Heath had outgrown their weekly opponents
and were clamouring at the door of the newly established
Football League. However, it would take three more years
before the lords of the league agreed that Newton Heath
were worthy of admission. Finally in 1892, as they enlarged
the First Division and added a Second Division, the former
railway workers' club was given the nod, even admitted to
the top Division.

They kicked off their league history with a classic tie
against the mighty Blackburn Rovers, the most famous club
in the land at that time and five times winners of the FA
Cup. Within a minute Newton Heath were a goal down but
they battled back, eventually losing 4–3 as a torrential

rainstorm struck Lancashire. There would be little else to cheer that season as Newton Heath wound up in 16th place and were lucky to escape relegation. They were not so lucky the following season.

There followed ten years of misery, as if a wandering gypsy had placed a curse on the club. Not only were they transfixed in the Second Division but they almost went out of business as their crippling debts mounted. The story has it that it was a dog that saved the club, a shaggy lumbering St Bernard who belonged to the Newton Heath captain, Harry Stafford. The dog had been loaned out for a bazaar the club was holding to raise essential funds. One evening it went walkabout and was later found roaming the streets by the licensee of a nearby pub who just happened to be a friend of local brewer John Davies. When Davies saw his friend's find, he took a fancy to it, and bought the dog. Legend has it that the dog pined for its true owner and Davies, feeling pangs of guilt, set about discovering who that might be. It didn't take him long. Stafford told him of the club's plight and Davies promised to help. Thanks to his generosity, within a year he had rescued the club from the bankruptcy court just as it was set to go out of business. Suddenly Davies was president of the club and with typical northern entrepreneurial gusto set about resurrecting its fortunes. A year later the club had even changed its name to Manchester United and appointed a secretary-cum-manager, Ernest Magnall, who would have a profound effect on its future development. He was the Busby of the Edwardian era. United were on their way.

By 1905 they had escaped the Second Division and three years later Manchester had its first ever glimpse of the league championship trophy. The following year the FA Cup was added to their burgeoning sideboard of honours as they overpowered Bristol City at the Crystal Palace. In 1911 they were champions again, inspired throughout the period by the enigmatic Welsh wizard Billy Meredith and the resolute

Charlie Roberts. However, the sensational, almost treacherous departure of Magnall to Manchester City in 1912 was sweet revenge for City, who years earlier had seen half their famed Cup-winning side walk out and join United.

By now United, showing flashes of the ambition and vision that would become their hallmark, had moved into a swanky new stadium, the pride of the Football League. It had originally been designed to hold 100,000 spectators but had to be scaled down as the costs of development mounted. Designed by that noted football architect Archibald Leitch, the new stadium at Old Trafford boasted the plushest facilities of any club in the land, with even a billiard room for the players. But United had been built on Magnall's managerial acumen, and his sudden departure was to wreak havoc on the side. Charlie Roberts, football's first ever *catenaccio*, was the next to go, and with the coming of war and a betting scandal involving the players, United's fortunes disappeared over the Balkans. By the time the war was over Magnall's fine team had all but disappeared, and their star striker Sandy Turnbull had been killed on the Somme. They were about to tumble into decline. During the inter-war years they were the butt of the music hall comedians who joked about the yo-yo side as United slipped into the Second Division and then rose again, only to crash once more into the lower division. There followed a supporters' boycott, new managers, record defeats and the narrowest of escapes from the ignominy of the Third Division North. Gates plummeted to little over 20,000 to match the side's miserable fortunes until the Second World War rescued them from any further embarrassment.

By the time football resumed, United had a new man in charge, a buoyant, bonny-faced Scot who had played all his football with rivals Manchester City and Liverpool. He was a respected wing half, the kind who stood his ground, a motivator, whose influence on United would be more far-reaching than any man before or since. At first the signs were dismal. Old Trafford was an eyesore, wrecked by German bombs, neglected by the absent ground staff. Six years of war had taken their toll. The weeds sprouted healthily on the terraces; a small tree had taken root on the pitch. It was not fit for playing on. So, Busby and United abandoned their famous ground and went off to play at neighbouring Maine Road while the directors prepared Old Trafford for a brighter, more distinguished future. It didn't take long in arriving. Busby had soon moulded a useful team together, focused around his quietly spoken but inspirational captain, Irishman Johnny Carey. In his first season in charge they narrowly lost out on the title, finishing as runners-up, just a single point behind champions Liverpool. It was much the same story the following two seasons as United again ended in the runners-up spot. If nothing else, Busby had at least created a consistent side. In 1948 they picked up the FA Cup, beating Blackpool, Matthews and all, 4–2, in a glorious, unforgettable display of sweeping football. It was what the game was all about. But still the title eluded Busby. It didn't arrive until 1951, by which time they had been runners-up yet again. They also narrowly missed out on another Cup final, eventually losing a bravely contested semi-final replay. One title, four runners-up spots, one FA Cup. It wasn't bad for a manager still a novice in his trade. By the time he had learnt the business, there would be no holding United.

By the late forties the team of Crompton, Carey, Chilton, Cockburn, Rowley and company had grown weary. Some had been recruited in the pre-war years. After the 1951 title it was time for fresh blood, but Busby had to look no further than to his reserves and his youth sides. In came a young defender, Roger Byrne, and a tireless Belfast boy, Jackie Blanchflower.

Busby had instituted a revolutionary youth scheme at Old Trafford, aimed at recruiting the finest young players in the land. It was to prove rich territory as the youth side

picked up five successive FA Youth Cups. Here was a vein
to be tapped. Busby had little hesitation in giving his
youngsters their opportunity and they were to reward him
with two consecutive league titles and an FA Cup appearance before tragedy struck at Munich. They had also just
reached their second successive European Cup semi-final.
Busby's Babes were all but wiped out in the terrible plane
crash. Busby himself defied death, though only just, but
skipper Roger Byrne, the lion-hearted Duncan Edwards and
the wispish goalscorer Tommy Taylor all died at Munich.
And there were others: Geoff Bent, Eddie Colman, Mark
Jones, David Pegg and Bill Whelan also died, while Jackie
Blanchflower and Johnny Berry would never play again.

England, having qualified for the World Cup finals in
Sweden, were also robbed of the backbone of their side.
But with the disaster, a legend was born that was to turn
United into a national institution. The club would be
admired for its spirit and determination; Busby would be
venerated for his courage. Throughout the world they
attracted a new following.

'United Will Go On' rang the message, and so they did,
but it would be another seven seasons before they rose to
their former glory and it would be a very different United.
Only Bobby Charlton and Billy Foulkes survived from the
Busby Babes era, but another youngster, George Best, had
arrived to carry on Busby's tradition of exciting young
players. Often loquacious, Best, like Cantona, was a law
unto himself. His individualism, not always professional,
caused endless headaches, but equally his boundless talent
outmatched that of any other post-war British footballer.
Alongside Best was the redoubtable and almost equally fun-
loving Aberdonian Denis Law, another man of shocking
talent. United's attack was completed by Charlton, always
the professional, always the steadfast one whose energetic
contributions brought a consistency that was at times
lacking from his colleagues. It was this trio with their

romantic, unpredictable ways who, perhaps even more than the Busby Babes or the disaster at Munich, helped usher in a new generation of support: Law, Best and Charlton. The names would trip off the tongue, always to be associated with the United side of the sixties. They would lift the FA Cup, the league title and then, in 1968, on a memorable night at Wembley stadium, the European Cup as they sank the Portuguese champions Benfica. Busby's dream had been fulfilled. Follow that, as they say. Sadly United couldn't.

Busby, growing old and weary, decided to call it a day and bowed out, handing over the reins to his young assistant and former captain Wilf McGuinness. But it never worked; McGuinness could not make the long leap from dressing room to manager's office. He had too many friends, too many stars. They gave him grief, and in the end the board brought an unhappy period to a swift conclusion. Above all, George Best had become ever more wayward in his later years, expending his abundant talents on wine, women and song. It was sad but that was the way of Best, always a law unto himself.

After the youthful inexperience of McGuinness the board, now wilting under player and fan pressure, persuaded Busby out of retirement to help stem the slide towards self-destruction, but it was always a stop-gap arrangement until a suitable replacement could be found. Months later, in June 1971, they found their man, opting for the very opposite of McGuinness, appointing a manager of maturity and experience. The man was Frank O'Farrell, the respected boss of Leicester City, one of the country's most attractive sides. He was almost a younger version of Busby with his soft smile and quiet, courteous ways. Busby himself stepped aside and upwards, appointed to the board. But still it didn't work. O'Farrell was a stranger in the camp. The players found him remote, rarely seeing him, unable to form a rapport or much respect for him. Best continued with his shenanigans, infuriating his own team-mates, often absenting himself from training and even matches. O'Farrell tried to face up to the problem, dropping the wayward genius and then transfer-listing him, but Busby demanded conciliation. Best was always worth another try, he argued, and he himself volunteered to heal the wounds. It worked briefly but the damage had been done in his undermining of O'Farrell.

After that it was never the same. The rift between player and manager was greater than ever. And in the end, just eighteen months after appointing O'Farrell, United ditched the pair of them, as the club yet again slid ominously towards the relegation zone. The board had already set their sights on a young Scot, Tommy Docherty; flamboyant, motivated, with a love of the unpredictable. In many ways United and Docherty were suitably matched. The team, suddenly acquiring a Scottish dimension, opted for a brave approach. They might have been heading for the Second Division but they did it in style, never showing a hint of inhibition or fear. There was no 'play it safe' with Docherty. It was not his style. Sadly this very recklessness was to be his undoing. After guiding them back into the First Division and a famous FA Cup final victory over Liverpool, Docherty's love-life hit the front pages. He had been having an affair with the wife of the club's physiotherapist. For what was predominantly a Catholic club, Busby himself being a fervent Catholic, it was all too scandalous, and Docherty was duly sacked. It might have been the beginning of one love affair but it was the end of another. His affair with United was over.

It was time for yet another reappraisal and yet another Busby figure. Into the breach stepped the phlegmatic, craggy-featured Dave Sexton, late of Queens Park Rangers. Schoolmasterly, conservative, thoughtful, Sexton was a stark contrast to Docherty. You would never have caught Sexton whooping it up with his players or dancing a jig around Wembley. There was something of Ferguson in

Sexton, a man who believed in fair discipline, hard work and commitment, with little time for outlandish excesses. But Sexton was never given the time to make his mark. There was always somebody to remind him of the heady days of Docherty, especially the fans, with whom he never really established any kind of rapport. He snapped up some exciting young players, gambled expensively in the market and reached an FA Cup final, but he could not make much progress where it counted.

United had not picked up a league title since 1967 and with the passing of each year, another seemed even further away. Old Trafford had become obsessed with the championship. Their failure to win it was not made any easier by a Liverpool side that was winning everything in sight, including more European Cups than United. United had been eclipsed by their Lancashire neighbours and it hurt. Liverpool were now one of Europe's top clubs; United had been forgotten. Sexton paid the price, sacked as the 1980–81 season drew pitifully to a close.

With Docherty's memory still swirling around the Stretford End, the board did yet another U-turn, this time hiring an equally extravagant figure in West Brom's Ron Atkinson, though not before they had tested out Lawrie McMenemy at Southampton. McMenemy wisely turned United's challenge down, but not so the flamboyant Atkinson. The Liverpudlian might have had a champagne image yet with limited resources had groomed a coterie of youngsters at West Brom, already catching the eye of the England selectors. Atkinson was duly appointed and swiftly recruited Hawthorns youngsters Bryan Robson and Remi Moses to the United cause. At least there was more excitement under Atkinson as he motivated players and fans alike. You felt you were getting your money's worth. There were even steps towards rekindling the famed Old Trafford youth system, which seemed to have died as expensive recruits were enlisted. Sixteen-year-old Norman

Whiteside was given his chance but other youngsters were
not, notably Peter Beardsley and Frank Stapleton, the latter
discarded as a teenager only to be re-signed for a £1 million
fee years later. The former would harry United for the next
ten years, winning championship honours with Liverpool
and then proving just as stinging with Newcastle.

There were successes under Atkinson: he lifted the FA
Cup twice, reached a European semi-final and a League
Cup final, and in the league was never out of the top four.
But it still wasn't good enough. Liverpool continued to run
away with everything and Everton were also notching up
more domestic honours than United. Atkinson was never
given enough credit, and in November 1986 he made way
for the man now draped in a United scarf and shivering in
the centre circle at Old Trafford.

If Ferguson was nervous about the task facing him he
did not show it that morning. He was as confident as ever,
smiling for the cameras, slapping shoulders with old
acquaintances. If you can't be confident on your first day,
when can you be? He smiled again as the press photographers gathered around, clutching their long lenses, ready
for another pose. Alan Green was not the only one to
wonder just how long the honeymoon would last, how long
it would be before Ferguson was under fire, like all his
predecessors, from fans, the board and of course the back
pages. Green thought he looked a good choice, but there
were nagging worries about his lack of knowledge about
the Football League. He'd never worked in England, so
wouldn't really know the clubs, the players, the tactics.
Privately Ferguson shared that concern. Coming to English
football was like stepping into another world. Martin
Edwards had taken something of a gamble in appointing
the Scot, and his reputation was as much on the line as
Ferguson's. The question was whether he would hold his
nerve when the going got tough.

The long shadow of the main stand now stretched across

the pitch as the sun edged its way bravely from behind granite clouds. The coterie of photographers and journalists in the centre circle was breaking up. They thanked him for his patience and began to make their way back towards the players' tunnel, deep in conversation. Ferguson followed, chatting to one or two of them as they strolled across the pitch, suddenly becoming obscured in the midday shadows. Busby's shadow was everywhere, its imperious presence always a threat.

CHAPTER TWELVE

Tough at the Top

It wasn't the best of starts. And if Ferguson had had any premonition of the enormity of the job he had undertaken it would soon be amply confirmed. United were languishing second from bottom of the old First Division when he moved in. It was only November but already they were out of contention as far as league honours were concerned. They were also out of the League Cup, beaten 4–1 by Southampton in Ron Atkinson's final game in charge. There was not a lot to play for; just the FA Cup. But at least everyone knew that, and it gave him a season's grace to begin rebuilding.

Just how big that job would be was emphasised in his first game as he took his new charges to Oxford United and lost 2–0. In Aberdeen they cheered. The following week they drew at Norwich but then came home to Old Trafford to notch up their first victory under Ferguson, 1–0 against Queens Park Rangers. Even for the usually optimistic Ferguson it came as something of a relief. From then on there was a gradual improvement, including a pre-Christmas 1–0 win over Liverpool at Anfield, which generated some back-slapping around Old Trafford. Yet the following day they lost 1–0 at home to Norwich. United were capable of beating the best but equally capable of losing to the worst. Later in the season they repeated the Liverpool scoreline at Old Trafford, though it was a rare win in an end-of-the-season slump. The bizarre contrast of results only underlined the problem. Against the most difficult sides they could show spirit and determination coupled with a sense of adventure, but they could only do it now and again. They were incapable of repeating it week after week. When the league points were finally totted up United were in 11th spot, 30 points behind champions Everton. They also took an early exit in the FA Cup, beaten at home by Coventry City.

That first season Ferguson was in awe of Old Trafford. Norman Whiteside remembers how he used to come up to him and Bryan Robson when they were training and just say, 'Big place this, big place.' Peter Davenport also recalls how nervous Ferguson was. 'He was like a kitten. I remember the first time he announced a team. He went through it and he said, "Right, we'll have Clayton, Remi and Kevin in midfield and up front we've got Frank, Peter and Nigel. Okay lads?" And there was a moment's pause, then Robbo said, "Nigel? Who's Nigel?" and Fergie points at me and goes: "Him, Nigel Davenport."'

A few months after his arrival, having had a little time to size up the problem, Ferguson sat down with the board to discuss developments. He had assessed the side and now knew what he wanted. He told them straight: 'I need nine new players if we are to win the championship.' It came as something of a shock to the directors, who had expected to be told they would only need a player or two in order to put up a realistic challenge. There was a look of disbelief on their faces as Ferguson explained. At least one board member wondered if they had employed the right man for the job; they had never anticipated anything like this. After all, Ron Atkinson had been given the go-ahead to spend in the transfer market and had signed quality players at a high price. Big Ron had cost them a staggering £4.7 million in his five years; now a new manager was asking for more money. Somehow they had imagined that Ferguson would create a team out of nothing – another heavy spending spree had never come into their calculations. One director asked him to explain.

'There are too many older players,' explained Ferguson, 'too many the wrong side of 28. Of course many of them are experienced internationals and still have much to offer, but collectively they have lost their magic.' He listed them one by one: Remi Moses, Mark Higgins, Gary Bailey, Kevin Moran and Arthur Albiston.

'There's nothing wrong in having a few older experienced professionals,' Ferguson told them, 'but we've got far too many. We need more youngsters coming into the side and at the moment there are too few. You've just got to look at the injuries the older players are picking up to know that you cannot rely on them. It's bound to lead to inconsistency.'

There was a moment's silence as the board digested this unwelcome news. Martin Edwards was supportive, but he more than anyone knew that United could not really afford a massive outlay of cash. Ron Atkinson had been given a free hand to sign whoever he wanted and had splashed out heavily on players such as Bryan Robson, Remi Moses, Peter Davenport, Colin Gibson, Terry Gibson and John Sivebaek, and it had all been to no avail.

However, Ferguson was ready to compromise. 'More players can go,' he told them. The manager had already started a clear-out. One of the first to leave had been Peter Barnes. 'Not my kind of player . . . not a good team player,' Ferguson stated. Now he added a few more names to his provisional list of departees. There was Jesper Olsen, a fine individualist but also careless and lightweight, and not one to rely on when the going got tough. But the top name on the list came as something of a surprise to the board. Frank Stapleton, said Ferguson, had proved to be a disappointment. His pace had all but disappeared; he seemed morose, rarely contributing to the laughter of the dressing room. Ferguson could never figure out why he seemed so downhearted. Moreover, he had not signed a new contract, so Ferguson was all for letting him go. In the end Stapleton reached an accommodation with the club and stayed, although it was against Ferguson's better judgement. But it would not be for long; in the close season he was sold to the Dutch club Ajax.

The fitness of Remi Moses was already cause for concern. The former West Brom player had serious injury problems, enough to make him miss half the side's outings that season. He would survive just one more season when again he would miss half the campaign. Eventually he retired in June 1988. Arthur Albiston would survive another year but would only make half a dozen appearances. Terry Gibson also moved on during the summer of 1987, joining Wimbledon for £200,000.

Ferguson was in the market for quality players, but it was to be a season of lost opportunities. Almost the first man he set his sights on was John Barnes of Watford. Surprisingly Ferguson had never seen Barnes play, but when the then Watford manager Graham Taylor rang United to inform him that Barnes would probably soon be available, he jumped at the opportunity. Taylor told him that there was continental interest, and if Barnes was to stay in England someone would have to move fast. Taylor also told him that he had informed a few other top clubs of Barnes's availability. Ferguson consulted with his chief scout, Tony Collins, but they could only uncover a couple of reports on him, both of which marked Barnes down as inconsistent. The scouting staff were cautious, not prepared to commit themselves, leaving Ferguson in a quandary. Lacking the backing of his scouting staff, he decided to let the chance slide. He would regret it for the next five years. But if there was a lesson to be learned from the experience it was that the scouting staff needed to be improved. It would not be long before Tony Collins left to be replaced by Les Kershaw.

A similar conundrum occurred with Gary Pallister. The Middlesbrough central defender had come to the attention of a number of top clubs. Liverpool had been interested in him for years, but when Bob Paisley had been quoted a fee of £1 million the Merseyside club had backtracked and Pallister had remained at Ayresome Park. He had continued to give impressive performances and Ferguson decided to put in a bid. He phoned the Middlesbrough manager Bruce Rioch and was told the price would be far below his previous valuation, probably around half a million pounds. On the one hand that was good news but it also posed an intriguing question. Why was Pallister suddenly worth half of what they had been quoting a year or so ago? The truth was that Middlesbrough were simply being more realistic, regretting perhaps that they had not come to a compromise with Liverpool.

Ferguson decided to test the waters and offered £400,000. Middlesbrough said no, but United were given an indication that if they went a little over £500,000 they might get their man. Again Ferguson consulted with his scouting staff, and again they proved hesitant. It was impossible for Ferguson, like any manager, to spend too much time watching any single player. No manager has enough time. They have to rely on others to act as their eyes and to form an opinion. After all, that is what scouts are paid for. Given everyone's hesitation, Ferguson decided to give Pallister a miss. When he did finally sign him Pallister's valuation had gone up again, with United forced to pay a British record fee of £2.4 million.

Peter Beardsley was also on Ferguson's shopping list that summer. The bubbling Newcastle man had once been on United's books, an early Atkinson signing for £250,000. But Beardsley had failed to live up to his promise, and in the end Atkinson had offloaded him to Vancouver Whitecaps without his having played a league game. Eventually Beardsley returned to England, joining his home club Newcastle United, where he enjoyed a prolific goal-scoring partnership with Kevin Keegan. This brought Beardsley to most people's attention, including that of Alex Ferguson. The United manager called his opposite at St James's Park and was quoted an astronomical fee of £3 million. It was more than United could afford. Three weeks later Beardsley joined Liverpool for a little under £2 million with Ferguson never even invited to put in a counter offer. The fact was that the Beardsley deal had been struck with Liverpool months earlier.

Although Ferguson drew a blank in England he was more successful when he returned to his homeland. At least with Scottish players he could trust his own instincts. He had seen most of them regularly over the years and had watched them develop or fall by the wayside. Top of his Scottish hit-list was Brian McClair, the Celtic striker whose contract was up for renewal. United desperately needed someone capable of netting 20 goals a season. Peter Davenport, signed by Ron Atkinson for a fee of just over £500,000, had failed to produce the goals that his high fee had suggested. Ferguson had watched McClair from close quarters in Celtic/Aberdeen clashes, and although he had not initially been impressed by the striker he had seen him develop over the years into an effective marksman. McClair was keen to move, to follow in the tradition of top Celtic players moving south. The only snag was that his club were looking for a £2 million fee, while Ferguson was reluctant to pay an inflated price. In the end United signed McClair but opted for a tribunal to settle the amount. They got their man in July 1987 for £850,000. Ferguson was well pleased to have put another one over on his old Glasgow rivals. Ten years later he would look back on that deal with much satisfaction; McClair was still making the odd appearance. It was one of the best pieces of business he ever concluded at Old Trafford.

Ferguson's other signing that summer of 1987 came as a surprise to many. This was Viv Anderson, the Arsenal and England full back. Ferguson was looking for experience and they did not come much more experienced than the former Forest man. At £250,000 he was a snip, but Anderson was never in the same league as McClair. His best footballing days were already behind him and although he would give adequate service, he would make only 63 appearances for the club before moving on.

There was also one other player Ferguson fancied at around that time but who never made it to Old Trafford – Marco Van Basten. Ferguson was a great admirer of his. So Jesper Olsen, who was a close friend of Van Basten's from his days at Ajax, was politely asked to make a phone call and sound him out. Unfortunately Van Basten had just signed a new contract. It was a non-starter but it had been a nice thought. On grey days Ferguson would muse at what might have been if Van Basten had come to Old Trafford.

Apart from the signing of McClair and Anderson it had been a lean summer for Ferguson, and at times this would show in team performances. He had earmarked certain players for possible signing but had failed, for one reason or another, to lure them to Old Trafford. Instead, his top targets Barnes and Beardsley ended up at Anfield, as would the league title.

However, Ferguson had learned an important lesson: United's scouting system needed to be overhauled. He had to be sure that he was being given quality advice, advice that he could depend on. During the close season his scouting staff had sat on the fence once too often and consequently the club had missed out on key players. Ferguson felt unable to trust them. They were reluctant, possibly because he was a new man at Old Trafford, to commit themselves. Even the most expensive, high-profile signings can end in disappointment, and nobody was willing to be associated with a signing that did not succeed. Perhaps in the past United had signed too many expensive players who had not made the grade: Garry Birtles, Peter Davenport, Ted McDougall and Jesper Olsen had never lived up to their back-page big-cheque reputations, and they had cost the club millions. Among the scouting staff there was now a fear of recommending yet another failure. And yet the scouting system was crucial to any club – especially one like United, which buys and sells in the transfer market as much as any club in the country. Ferguson decided a clean sweep was necessary. In the old days, United knew they could rely on Billy Behan's recommendations as he sent a stream of players like Johnny Carey, Johnny Giles and Billy Whelan across from Ireland without anyone else from the club having seen them. That was the kind of trust Ferguson longed for at Old Trafford. It would take time, but eventually he installed Les Kershaw as chief scout, describing him as a man who was 'prepared to throw his hat into the ring and make a judgement'.

Ferguson's first full season in charge at Old Trafford, 1987–88, was to be full of ambition but short on pedigree. United performed well enough, showing plenty of early promise, but could never quite match a rampant Liverpool inspired by their summer signings. United would eventually settle for second spot, nine points behind the champions and eight points ahead of third-placed Nottingham Forest. But they had never really been in contention and had not managed top spot all season. At any other club, barring Liverpool, it would have been called an impressive performance but it was not good enough either for the fans of United or for Alex Ferguson. To make matters worse the cup competitions brought little joy, with United knocked out of the FA Cup in the fifth round at Arsenal, and out of the quarter-finals of the League Cup by Oxford United.

Ferguson kept his counsel for the first few weeks, saying little, criticising nobody. Then they played Wimbledon away and lost. It proved to be a turning point in Ferguson's approach. In the dressing room after the game he let fly, his legendary temper ringing off the walls like scatter bullets. It was just as Gordon Strachan had warned them. But the main culprit for the afternoon's events could not be found. Peter Barnes had been substituted with half an hour to go after an abysmal display that rated high on the all-time list of poor performances. After laying into everyone he could find, Ferguson went in search of the principal culprit to give him a one-to-one rollicking. But Barnes could not be found. Ferguson looked everywhere – in the showers, the toilet, the bar – but no Barnes. Eventually Ferguson cooled, and went off upstairs to perform other duties. As the dressing room door closed, the door to the showers quietly opened and there was Barnes. He'd been hiding in the bath for more than 30 minutes, ducking under the freezing water every time Ferguson came in looking for him. 'He was blue with cold,' remembered Strachan.

In the dressing room the players christened Ferguson the 'hairdryer' because you were always likely to get a blow dry from the torrent of hot air that came in your direction as you got your rollicking. 'He'd stand so close to you as he let fly,' remembers one player. 'It was nose-to-nose stuff.'

In the early days the Ferguson hairdryer was in constant use. 'You used to try and make sure you weren't the man with the ball as half-time approached,' Mark Hughes once recalled. 'He seemed always to pick on the last mistake before the whistle and explode at that person. It used to scare the living daylights out of us but it was only because of the tremendous will to win that he had.'

On the credit side, close-season signings Brian McClair and Viv Anderson had settled well, making a visible difference. McClair was top scorer with 24 goals and had been ever-present throughout the season, bringing a fresh sense of urgency to the attack with his unbounded strength.

United might have done better but for an injury to Paul McGrath in mid-autumn. Ferguson could already see the need for a long-term replacement and had earmarked Terry Butcher for the task. He had all but agreed a deal with Ipswich and the player himself when the England defender broke a leg. Ferguson was back to square one – such is the life of a football manager.

He set his sights on Steve Bruce of Norwich instead, finally securing his man for £800,000, though not without a considerable amount of wrangling with Bruce's club. Bruce immediately slotted in the central defence, even breaking his nose on his debut, and was to remain there for the next nine years, although his early performances did not always suggest such promise. There were moments when Ferguson and United must have wondered if Bruce was really the man for the job, but as he grew more experienced, so he became more authoritative.

Ferguson's dilemma now focused on how to make that final leap from second spot to top, made all the harder by a Liverpool side looking invincible under Dalglish. More would clearly be expected of Ferguson in the coming season. His first full season had promised much and although it had failed to deliver, there was enough potential to suggest that United could finally clamber over that last hurdle. But in order to do that it was evident that new blood was needed. As usual the summer was spent wheeling and dealing in the transfer market.

Ferguson's chief concern was his defence, and in particular his goalkeeper. The United defence had conceded 38 goals in the previous season, not all due to poor goal-keeping, but certainly not helped by a switch in keepers midway through the campaign: Gary Walsh had suffered a couple of serious head injuries and had been replaced by Chris Turner. For all his experience, Turner was suspect when it came to crosses, unsettling defenders with his hesitation. With Walsh still injured, Ferguson desperately needed cover. Rather than buy a second-string keeper, he decided to opt for a goalkeeper he could trust, someone dependable and with experience. Walsh was still young enough to bide his time in the reserves. Ferguson decided to return north, to his old club Aberdeen, and for a British record fee for a goalkeeper of £450,000, lured Scottish international Jim Leighton south of the border for another stint with his former manager. Leighton would generate confidence and management to the back four, although, as it turned out, his stay would be short-lived.

The biggest headline-grabbing signature that close season was Mark Hughes, the United favourite whose £2.5 million transfer in August 1986 to Barcelona had left United fans shell-shocked. His Spanish sojourn had proved disappointing and 18 months later he had been loaned out to the German club Bayern Munich, where his self-esteem and confidence had been briefly restored. A move back to Old Trafford was always on the cards. Hughes wanted it, and so did the fans. Although Bayern were keen to turn his loan into something more permanent, it was a battle United were always going to win. Ferguson had made a bid for Hughes at the end of the previous season but had been turned down by Barcelona manager Terry Venables. This time it was different. Hughes was clearly surplus to the Spanish club's requirements and at little over £1.5 million was a bargain. It was good business, especially as Ferguson also decided to unload a few players not now needed by United. Out went Chris Turner, Arthur Albiston and Graeme Hogg. He also decided to offload Kevin Moran to Sporting Gijon on a free transfer.

Despite the clearout, Ferguson was still largely dependent on the squad brought together by his predecessor. As the new season wore on it would become increasingly clear to him that tinkering with the squad – introducing new players here and selling a few players there – was not going to resolve United's underlying problem. He needed almost to start with a clean sheet, to begin all over again. But first he had to resolve a more serious problem that was repeatedly raising its ugly head.

CHAPTER THIRTEEN

The Drinking Club

When Alex Ferguson marched into Old Trafford, Tommy Docherty had warned him to relax his disciplinary approach if he was to keep his job. 'It's no good being a hard man who scares players stiff if they are going to play covered in goose pimples from the manager's last ear-bashing,' advised the former United and Scotland manager. Ferguson may have read his advice; he may even have heeded it for a time in the intimidating atmosphere of Old Trafford, but after a while he knew it was time to bang a few heads together.

Gordon Strachan warned everyone as well. The first thing the former Aberdeen midfielder did on hearing of Ferguson's appointment was to go around the dressing room shaking everyone's hand. 'Bye, bye, that's me on my way,' he said, 'I'm out of here.' Strachan knew Ferguson well. 'I told them all what he was like,' he later confessed to journalist Jim White. 'But he was like a pussycat for the first few weeks, three months even. They were all looking at me 'cos I'd made him out to be Hannibal Lecter or something. Then we played Wimbledon away, and that afternoon they all looked at me again and you could see them thinking, "Yup, Gordon, I take your point."'

Drink is an unseemly part of the culture of football.

157

Amateurs, semi-professionals and professionals alike all enjoy a pint after the game. Even Friday night five-a-side 40-year-olds like to adjourn to the pub for a few jars after running up a sweat. It's part of the camaraderie, the socialising, lads together; there's nothing wrong with that. After a heavy workout a drink is vital, although it doesn't have to be alcoholic. Managers recognise, more than anyone, that it can be good for morale, building team spirit. It can also help players to put a bad game behind them, as well as being a suitable way to celebrate. But there are limits. And at Old Trafford one or two of Alex Ferguson's charges were beginning to exceed those limits.

Ferguson had inherited a demoralised and ill-disciplined squad when he took over from Ron Atkinson in November 1986. Atkinson himself had had troubles with the team, although his own champagne lifestyle hardly set a glowing example. In his final season he had fined seven players for an after-hours drinking session on a pre-season trip to Holland. That had been followed by a punch-up between Jesper Olsen and Remi Moses that ended up with the Dane needing hospital treatment and eleven stitches. The club described it as 'a clash of heads'. Indeed it was, but nobody wanted to talk about just how the heads had managed to clash. And so it went on.

Every journalist in Manchester had heard the stories; fortunately, not too many others knew. There was a bond of silence. The local newspapers said little and the worst tales rarely leaked out much beyond the reception desk at the *Manchester Evening News* or Granada Television. The trouble was that many of the yarns were true.

The players seemed to imagine that drinking in a wine bar in an exclusive area of south Manchester would somehow make them anonymous, that nobody would notice them or be the slightest bit concerned about their behaviour. Unfortunately the same wine bar was frequented by more than one local journalist with an in at Old Trafford.

The tales were horrific. Even *Red Issue*, the United fanzine, joked openly about Paul McGrath's drinking habits. Bottles of champagne were reported to be stacked high on tables, star players were seen carried out legless, there was after-hours drinking. It did the club's reputation little good, although few stories ever reached the headlines. They might have got away with it under Ron Atkinson, but it was dangerously foolish to imagine that new manager Alex Ferguson would not get to hear of it. Other managers, fond of the champagne, might have tolerated it, even initially encouraged their behaviour. But not Ferguson.

In his first week in charge at Old Trafford he had called all the players together for a meeting one morning at United's training ground The Cliff to lay down some basic rules. He had heard the rumours and just wanted to let them know that he was not going to tolerate excessive drinking and clubbing. 'Tell them from the start,' he thought, 'then there will be no excuses. Everyone will know the boundaries.'

McGrath noticed the difference from his predecessor almost immediately and at the time made a simple but astute comparison. 'Under Ron Atkinson life was demanding but more relaxed. Where he would yell at you for stepping out of line and give you another final warning, the new boss will steam in first time and hit you with everything he's got.' But still the drinking went on – just in a more surreptitious way.

Ferguson was plugged into the Manchester gossip and the drinking stories from the start. Gordon Strachan had warned him early on. Strachan, on his own admission, had never been able to drink more than a pint or two, but when he joined United was persuaded to go out with the drinking set. He was in for a shock; it took him almost a week to recover. He never went again and was always amazed at how some players could manage to kick a ball on a Saturday after such heavy drinking during the week. Arnold Muhren, the former United Dutch international, had also written about it after leaving United, horrified by the contemptuous attitude of his fellow professionals. Ferguson had been a manager long enough to know that drinking went on in every club but what he heard about United set alarm bells ringing. It seemed worse than anything he had so far encountered.

When supporters heard the whispers they were equally stunned. The drinking may have largely been confined to mid-week sessions but it was hardly the kind of example to set within the club, especially where there were young players. It only added to their frustrations. What was more, it involved some of United's top players, household names, internationals who should have known better. It was restricted to a clique of players, but efforts were always being made to drag others into their group. By the summer of 1988 Ferguson decided that things had to change. He was not against the players going out for a drink after an exhausting match, or enjoying themselves, but he was not going to tolerate them abusing his generosity or the club's public image.

Ferguson knew their names and approached each one separately. He told them in no uncertain terms that while he was no puritan and was perfectly happy for them to enjoy a drink, he was not going to allow the kind of bingeing that had been reported to him. It had to stop, he told them bluntly. Manchester United was not going to be known as a drinking club, rather than a football club. Standards had to change.

But change would not be quite so easy. One of the drinking gang, Paul McGrath, had already travelled too far down the road for a simple U-turn. In 1989 McGrath was part-way through a two-year driving ban following a positive breath test after a crash. He had been well over the limit. It was not a good time for the Irish defender. Ferguson hauled him in and tried desperately to resolve the problem, suggesting treatment, pastoral care, and any kind of medical help the club could give. Martin Edwards spoke with him. Matt Busby was also asked to talk to him and even the long-suffering Mrs McGrath spoke with the manager. But McGrath seemed hellbent on destroying himself.

McGrath, however, denies that Busby ever spoke to him. And nor, he claims, did the club doctor or the supposed parish priest. But in his book *Ooh Aah Paul McGrath* he does admit openly to the drinking sessions. 'He's [Ferguson] right about the drinking binges myself and Norman [Whiteside] would go on,' he writes. 'We'd be in this pub or that pub and all the time somebody would ring Fergie at the club and give him a progress report. Usually by the end of the night we wouldn't have a clue if we were in Hale or Altrincham – and we'd care even less.'

On the tour of Malta in May 1987 McGrath and Whiteside were reported to have spent the night drinking and arrived late at the airport the next day. They were each docked a week's wage. Earlier that year on another trip, this time to Dublin, Gordon Strachan, Billy Garton, Paul McGrath and Kevin Moran were all fined for arriving late for the team bus. Like most football clubs, their trips abroad to play friendlies always seemed to end in trouble. At one point McGrath and Whiteside were hauled into Martin Edwards's office. Both players had already received two written warnings and a verbal warning after being spotted out drinking mid-week. Ferguson was also convinced that McGrath had appeared on a local television show while drunk. By all accounts it was not the friendliest of meetings afterwards as McGrath and manager traded words.

However, it wasn't just McGrath's drinking that troubled Ferguson. The player had undergone eight knee operations, missing numerous games in the process. Ferguson decided the club would be better off without him. He was offered a five-figure settlement to wind up his contract, and with it, effectively, his career. The deal was said to be worth

£100,000 with the additional promise of a testimonial in Ireland. It was tempting and McGrath came within a whisker of accepting it. After talking it over with some of the other players, however, he promptly told Ferguson and Edwards where to stick their offer.

The problem would continue for a couple more years. There would be appalling moments, such as the week-long pub crawl McGrath went on with his drinking pal Norman Whiteside. As the week progressed United supporters were ringing in to tell the manager where the two had been spotted as they visited one pub or club after another. Ferguson was almost to put a map of Manchester on the wall of his office and stick pins in the various places they had been seen. Although it had its funny side, come the end of the week there was a more serious problem. Whiteside was injured and therefore excluded from playing on the Saturday but McGrath was pencilled in to play. On the Friday before the game McGrath was unable to train and the following day reported ill, claiming he was unfit to play. After the week's bingeing it was little wonder, but it left Ferguson with no choice but to name Deiniol Graham as his 13th man, after the lad had played in the A team that Saturday morning. It was the final straw for Ferguson. After that he was no longer prepared to tolerate McGrath's excesses and it would only be a matter of time before he went.

The local papers had been restrained but the national tabloids eventually caught up with him. After a testimonial for his pal Kevin Moran, the *Sunday Mirror* told its readers in August 1988 that McGrath had ended up 'wide-eyed and legless, sitting alone at a table in a bar of a Cheshire hotel'. It may or may not have been true but it was certainly not the kind of image Alex Ferguson wished United to be associated with.

Finally, in July 1989, McGrath left Old Trafford and signed for Aston Villa for £400,000. United had gained a healthy surplus and rid themselves of a problem, though not everyone saw it that way. McGrath was recognised as a battler whose commitment, when he was fully fit, was a mighty bonus to the side. Ferguson would have his critics as McGrath left but he knew the genuine reasons and was prepared to stand by his decision.

McGrath, of course, saw it differently. Years later, he explained: 'I was playing at the back when Ferguson came in. In his first game he moved me into midfield, then he dragged me off at half-time. The writing was on the wall and we never really saw eye to eye. It just went from bad to worse.

'I didn't really think there was much point battling against the man,' he went on. 'It just seemed I wasn't in his plans, at least that's what I think he was trying to tell me.' Yet for all his hell-raising McGrath went on to give sterling service to Villa before joining Derby County at the beginning of the 1996–97 season. He had also played in two World Cups since being sold by United. At the age of 37, with dodgy knees and what must have been an even dodgier liver, Paul McGrath was still playing Premiership football. It's a funny old game, as someone once said.

Norman Whiteside, however, was a different proposition. An outstanding young player, he had been dogged by injury. His long lay-offs and subsequent depressions had led him down the late-night road into clubland. Ferguson was always more tolerant of Whiteside, partly because of his age but also because the manager understood the frustrations of injury. But at times even Ferguson was more tolerant than perhaps he should have been. He rated Whiteside highly and has gone on record as saying that with 'one more yard of pace he would have been one of the greatest players ever produced in British football'. But Whiteside's continuing knee problem and his off-the-field behaviour would finally be the undoing of his Old Trafford career.

Ferguson's decision eventually to allow both McGrath and Whiteside to leave was crucial to the fortunes of the club. The two players needed to be separated for their own good as well as United's. Ferguson was laying down the law, letting everyone know the standards that were expected of them. From that moment on a new atmosphere began to evolve at Old Trafford. Players knew where they stood on the drink question and just how far they could go.

Yet Whiteside and McGrath weren't the only culprits. Bryan Robson had also been banned from driving and was known to be one of the regulars at the now infamous Hale Wine Bar. However, Robson was a true professional – and his transfer would have caused a minor earthquake around Manchester. He also seemed to have the ability to shrug off a few drinks and play with as much zest and ability as anyone in the country, but it did leave you wondering just how good he might have been without them. Yet it seemed that even Robson might be jettisoned in the hope of ridding the club of its drinking image. When Martin Edwards and Alex Ferguson spoke to Newcastle United in 1988 about the transfer of Paul Gascoigne, Newcastle were left in no doubt that they could consider any United player in part exchange, including captain Bryan Robson. Quite what the Manchester public would have made of losing Robson is an interesting question to ponder. It would certainly have put added pressure on Ferguson to succeed – and had success not been instant, the loss of Robson would have been quickly used as a whipping stick.

Ferguson would wrestle with these problems for much of the 1988–89 season as United failed to make an impact on the league. They began badly enough, drawing their first game and then losing at Anfield. They put that right by winning their next three only to come a cropper in an appalling autumn as they failed to win another league game until mid-December. All they seemed capable of was drawing, with a sequence of eight draws in nine games.

They plunged down the league towards the relegation zone. There was little for Ferguson to be pleased about, although at least Mark Hughes was hitting the net regularly. Brian McClair, on the other hand, would not begin to score consistently until after the New Year, managing only three goals before January. By then United's fate had been sealed. Six victories in seven games lifted them up the table and into third place, but they were always well adrift of the pacemakers. Eventually they ended the season in eleventh spot, 25 points adrift of champions Arsenal. They had lost 13 games. The cups brought little satisfaction either. In the League Cup they were dismissed at the early stages, going out to Wimbledon, while in the FA Cup they reached the quarter-finals, thanks mainly to an easy passage. The sixth-round draw seemed to have brought them a golden opportunity with a home tie against Nottingham Forest, but United lost 1–0 and their season was all but over.

The fans were scathing. In its May 1989 edition the United fanzine *Red Issue* asked angrily, 'When is Mr Ferguson going to realise that he doesn't know what he is doing and return to that quiet backwater, Aberdeen?' It went on to demand entertainment and claimed that Ferguson had transformed United into a 'very mediocre team playing lacklustre football, obsessed with negative defensive play and totally lacking in flair'.

The 1988–89 season had been a bitter disappointment for Ferguson, who after the previous season had hoped his side might again challenge the leaders. Instead they struggled, uninspired and lacking in ambition, despite multi-millions spent in the transfer market.

Ferguson was now having to be more careful in the transfer market. 'If we buy now it will mean going into the red,' he was told at one board meeting. 'We're not saying we can't buy but we have got to be prudent. We cannot afford to get it wrong . . . we still have a big squad on high wages, so there are limits beyond which we shouldn't go.'

When he had arrived at Old Trafford he had been promised the earth, but the resources available did not match his expectations. 'I came here thinking I would have the luxury of buying players,' he said. 'I have done a lot of hard work at youth levels, but to win the league we need to buy players. I'm disappointed we haven't had that kind of money.' It clearly annoyed him, especially since he'd been outsmarted by his Merseyside rivals. 'Liverpool have bought the best and what sticks in my gullet is the difference between them and us. I respect them but I don't like being second.'

The growing financial tensions between Martin Edwards and Alex Ferguson would come to a climax over the possible signing of Paul Gascoigne. Ferguson was desperately keen to sign the young midfielder, whom he saw as a focus for his new side. Newcastle had also indicated that they would be prepared to sell. But when Edwards and Ferguson met Gascoigne's advisers they were somewhat shaken by the young man's demands. Not only did he want a £100,000 signing fee but he was expecting a salary of £125,000 a year, plus £5,000 for every England cap he won. On top of that there was to be a club car, a house and a huge slice of any ongoing transfer fee. They were rumoured to be the highest demands ever made in the history of English football. It would have raised the United overdraft to around £4 million at a time of record high interest rates. Quite what happened next remains shrouded in mystery. It seems clear however that Edwards was not as enthusiastic about the signing of Gascoigne as Ferguson. The manager went on holiday to Malta, hopeful that the deal would be completed. Edwards also went off for a week's holiday, and in the meantime Gascoigne signed for Tottenham. Edwards claimed that he did not understand what had happened and that they had tabled a bid that matched Tottenham's.

In his meticulously researched book on United's finances, Michael Crick claims that Gascoigne's adviser refutes

Edwards's claim. 'It was in their power to match Tottenham's offer and the fact is they didn't,' he insists. And so Gascoigne was lost. In the murky world of football you can never be certain. Perhaps Edwards was prepared to back Ferguson's enthusiasm for the Newcastle man, but it was not a moment for any hesitation.

Above all Ferguson felt sorry for the fans. Gates had tumbled, with only a couple of league games all season over the 40,000 mark, although 55,000 had turned up to see United in the quarter-finals of the FA Cup. Somewhere there were 15,000 or more fans missing for most league matches. But before it was to get any better it would get worse.

CHAPTER FOURTEEN

Silverware

Ferguson's problems lasted deep into the 1989–90 season. There seemed no respite. United suffered three successive defeats in August and September and then more before the autumn was out. A 5–1 humiliation by Manchester City sent Ferguson into hibernation. In early December they faced Crystal Palace and lost their seventh match. A week later against Tottenham they lost again, two successive league defeats at Old Trafford. Any hopes of the league had fast disappeared over the horizon. The knives were out for Ferguson. To add to their troubles, they were drawn away to Nottingham Forest in the third round of the FA Cup. It looked a hopeless task but United, mustering up enough energy and commitment, and with their own Red Army of fans playing their part, surprised everyone with a 1–0 win. Ferguson was delighted. United's season, and his United career, had finally been kick-started.

But, after the glamour and the excitement of the Cup, it was back to the daily grind of the league programme. Two more defeats followed and then came the fourth-round tie at Hereford. It might not have been quite as daunting as their trip to Nottingham but Hereford had scalped more than one big name in their history. It was by no means an easy tie, with a major Cup upset always on the cards. When

United arrived they discovered the car park was flooded, and the pitch was little better with pools of water in the goal areas and out on the flanks, not the kind of surface that helped a ball-playing side like United. Instead it favoured the long ball, running at defences and simply hoping that the bounce of the pitch would fall in your favour. It was gambling rather than science. In the end United won, but they left it late and for much of the game looked edgy and ready to settle for a replay at Old Trafford. Still, at the final whistle they could heave a sigh of relief: at least they were through to the next round.

By the time United came to take on Newcastle in the fifth round they were on the back of a run of eleven league games without a win. They were now serious relegation candidates. Earlier in the season it had seemed probable that results would pick up and they would steadily climb out of danger, but it was now March and they boasted just 28 points from 27 games. It was hardly the kind of inspirational form they needed for a visit to St James's Park, even though Newcastle were then a Second Division side. They still had fanatical support and a rich tradition in the FA Cup. What they didn't have was luck, although for more than a moment or two Ferguson must have wondered if United were running out of their own quota of good fortune. United took the lead through Mark Robins and led until half-time, but just as they were beginning to dominate, Newcastle equalised from a penalty. United then made it 2–1 through Danny Wallace but Newcastle fought back to equalise for a second time. It was end-to-end excitement, but eventually it was substitute Paul Ince who, with his first touch, set up the goal for Brian McClair. United had squeezed through into the quarter-finals. More importantly, you could see the confidence beginning to ooze back and the smiles returning to the dressing room. They were even about to break their duck in the league.

The quarter-finals brought United yet another away tie,

though this time it involved only a short hop across the Pennines to Sheffield United. Four away ties: United were certainly having to do it the hard way, even if the opposition was again from a lower division. But in fact their trip to Bramall Lane turned out to be considerably easier than they had feared, or than the 1–0 score line suggested. Thanks to Brian McClair, United were into the last four; Old Trafford was beginning to buzz again.

There were further signs that United's luck was genuinely turning when the draw for the semi-finals kept them apart from the First Division challengers, including the favourites for the Cup, Liverpool. The Merseysiders were drawn to play Crystal Palace while United faced Oldham at Maine Road in an all-Lancashire derby. It turned out to be a day of breathtaking excitement. First Crystal Palace surprised everyone by beating Liverpool 4–3, then later that afternoon United and Oldham fought out a televised semi-final that had the nation's football fans sitting on the edge of their seats for another two hours. It was a game that could have gone either way as the balance swayed one way and then the other. Finally, it ended 3–3 and the two sides had to face each other again.

In the replay, Oldham again pursued United relentlessly but there never seemed much doubt that United would eventually win through. Even when Oldham forced them into extra time, United's name seemed already to be written on the trophy. In extra time Mark Robins popped up to knock in United's winner after Mike Phelan had squared the ball to him. Robins had saved them yet again. He was the toast of Old Trafford – but not for long.

Unfortunately, the youngster did not get the reward he might have expected as Ferguson decided to leave him on the bench for the Wembley final. Robins's Old Trafford career would never be quite the same again. His six goals in the final run of the season had saved United, but it was clearly not enough to guarantee him a first-team place. He would linger around Old Trafford for a few more years, but the urge for first-team football eventually took him to Norwich. As if the decision to leave Robins out of the starting line-up had not been difficult enough, Ferguson was to face an even greater dilemma a few days later.

United's opponents at Wembley, Crystal Palace, had already had the better of United at Old Trafford. Managed by old-boy Steve Coppell, they had enjoyed a mixed season, eventually finishing in 15th spot, on the same number of points as United. It was not going to be an easy final, Palace having already shown their worth by beating Liverpool in the semi-final. They would not disappoint at Wembley either.

By the time Ferguson and Coppell led their sides out at Wembley, United had edged their way out of the relegation zone. Their Cup exploits had helped boost confidence and four successive wins in the spring had lifted them up the table, although at the final count they were still only five points from the drop into the Second Division. It had been a close shave. And at the top Liverpool were champions.

United kicked off as Wembley favourites, but an early goal by Palace rocked United back on their heels and it took a thundering header from Bryan Robson to level the scores. By the interval there was little to choose between the two sides but then after the break a kindly deflection in the penalty area left Mark Hughes with an easy opportunity to put United back in the lead. That was the signal for Palace to introduce substitute Ian Wright. With almost his first touch the man who would later lead the Arsenal attack hit a memorable individual goal to force extra time. Then in extra time Wright again tipped the balance in favour of the London club. Suddenly it began to look as if Ferguson's luck was running out. Perhaps United's name was not written on the trophy after all. Apart from the semi-final against Liverpool, Palace had enjoyed an easy run in the Cup, and even against Liverpool they could count themselves fortunate. But then, just as the final whistle loomed and fingernails were being bitten down to the quick, up popped Mark Hughes to save United's embarrassment. Palace were devastated. United had escaped from jail yet again but the fingers were pointing at goalkeeper Jim Leighton.

After the game Jim Leighton sat in the dressing room with his head between his hands. 'I knew he was a beaten man,' says Ferguson. Leighton had been a worry all season. Archie Knox and Ferguson had had countless discussions about the keeper. Time and again they had toyed with the idea of dropping him but each time had stuck with their man. After the semi-final they had faced the same dilemma but had decided to leave him in for the replay. Yet Leighton had never looked comfortable. He was his own worst judge. He knew when he had played badly but lacked the ability to put it behind him for the next game. Instead, he would lose confidence, worry all the more, and inevitably it would show. Confidence is a goalkeeper's keenest asset; the lack of it his greatest enemy. On a couple of occasions Ferguson had rested Leighton in order to give Les Sealey an opportunity but he had always restored the Scottish keeper. He had even considered playing Sealey in the final game of the season at home to Charlton, but at the last minute had opted for his Cup final line-up with Leighton hanging on to his place.

Ferguson knew Leighton well and also recognised that at Aberdeen he had been protected by an outstanding defence and a highly successful team. At United the defence was vulnerable and he was exposed. As the last man in the line of defence, the goalkeeper is always liable to take some blame. United had struggled all season, and as the goals slipped past Leighton there was a tendency by some to make him the scapegoat. It did nothing for his confidence.

After the final, Ferguson once again reviewed the situation. His instincts told him what had to be done. They had stuck with Leighton for the first game, despite their initial doubts, but now it was time for a change. It was obvious that it would not be popular, either with Leighton or indeed with the fans. It might even unsettle the defence – there is nothing more likely to unnerve the back four than chopping and changing the last man. Defenders have to develop an understanding with goalkeepers, to be aware of their positioning, their calls, their temperament and to be able to guess accurately how far they will venture from the goal-line to collect crosses. Suddenly to throw an on-loan goalkeeper into the pressure-cooker atmosphere of a Wembley Cup final was hardly ideal. It was a huge gamble. But often that kind of gamble has paid off in a Cup final. It was a risk worth taking.

The night before the replay Ferguson took Leighton on one side and told him that he would not be playing the next day. It was to mark the end of Leighton's love affair with Manchester United and, inevitably, with Alex Ferguson. The two men went back a long time, to the heady days at Pittodrie. Leighton would never play for Ferguson again and in February 1992 was transferred to Dundee United for £200,000. Ferguson admits, in hindsight, that if he had known the way it would affect Leighton he would not have made the same decision. It almost wrecked Leighton's career and cost him two years of his footballing life. The easy decision was to play Leighton, the hard decision was to drop him. Ferguson could understand his disappointment. After all, he too had been left out of a Cup final lineup.

Ferguson was to be vindicated. In the replay Sealey acquitted himself well, saving superbly in the first half and commanding the United defence like an old trouper as United came under intense second-half pressure. Sealey looked as if he'd been there all season; the United defence reacted accordingly. United were always the better side. Palace had let their chance slip and the game was settled by a single goal coming from Lee Martin on the hour as he burst diagonally into the area. United had won the Cup for a record seventh time.

It was the beginning of the beginning. Ferguson had picked up his first trophy with United. He had ended a season that for the most part had been a nightmare with some silverware in the boardroom. It gave rise to a wave of optimism for the forthcoming season, especially as their Cup win offered him the chance of trying his hand in Europe again. But it had been a narrow squeak, with luck playing more than a small part. Ferguson still had to look enviously up at the top of the league table. Liverpool were champions yet again, for the 18th time. Fortunately it was to be the last time he would see his Merseyside rivals heading the table at the end of a season. The Cup win had bought him time, but just how much was anyone's guess.

On a warm Saturday afternoon, early in the next season, United lined up against Nottingham Forest at Old Trafford. It was to be the day Alex Ferguson peered yet again down the barrel of a gun. United had kicked off the season in dismal form: two defeats and a draw in their first seven games, including a grating 4–0 thrashing by the champions at Anfield. Ferguson might have picked up the FA Cup a few months earlier but it counted for little in the high-pressure world of Old Trafford. What mattered more than anything was the need to go one better than Liverpool and win the league title – and already Liverpool had shown United that they were not even contenders when it came to dreaming of such honours. Liverpool still reigned supreme. By 5 o'clock Forest had hammered home the message as United crashed to their third defeat of the season. Any hope of the league title was fast disappearing down a long black hole.

Of equal concern was the reaction of the crowd. With ten minutes remaining and a clueless United clearly heading for defeat, all that you could hear around Old Trafford was the sound of seats being upturned as the fans streamed out of the ground. It was not the kind of noise to engender much faith in the future. In the boardroom after the game, there were disgruntled looks. Any side managed by Brian Clough was a difficult proposition, but this was no exceptional Forest side. United should be doing better.

Although Martin Edwards would deny it, there is little doubt that the thought must have crossed his mind: should United get rid of Ferguson? At the beginning of the year he had given Ferguson a guarantee that his future was safe. Ironically, that reference had come just hours before United faced Forest in a crucial third-round FA Cup tie. United had won that day and gone on to lift the Cup. But now, after a season that had kicked off with such high hopes, the nightmares were reappearing. The fans had demonstrated their feelings in no uncertain way. Ferguson knew that they might not always be as loyal as they had been in the past. Next week there might be more empty seats. That would mean a drop in revenue, and United was a business as much as a football club. They could ill afford to lose their support.

Ferguson might have picked up his first trophy with United but he still faced overwhelming problems. The Cup win only disguised the truth. The fact was that you only had to win half a dozen matches to lift the FA Cup. An appalling season in the league was testament to the fact that all was not well, and only a bright end-of-season run had saved United from the unthinkable – relegation. Admittedly, long-term injuries to key midfielders Bryan Robson and Neil Webb had not helped, and their return to the side had brought about a marked upturn in fortunes. But there were still problems at the back. To help put that right Ferguson had recruited Irish full back Denis Irwin from Oldham Athletic for £625,000 during the summer. After his sterling efforts in the Cup final, Ferguson had also offered Les Sealey a new one-year contract. But it was obvious to Ferguson, and just about everyone else, that

Sealey was not the long-term solution to United's goal-keeping problems. And after being dropped for the Cup final, Jim Leighton was certainly not in the mood to guard United's creaky defence. On the bright side, however, one or two youngsters were coming through. Lee Martin, for one, looked promising. A YTS trainee from the age of 17, Martin had already picked up England Under-21 honours and was being hailed as a future full international with a glittering career ahead of him at Old Trafford. Sadly, it was not to turn out like that.

That Saturday, as Ferguson made ready to go home following the defeat by Nottingham Forest, he must have felt more than ever that he was fumbling in the dark shadow of Busby. Never short of confidence, he could still do with a little inspiration from somewhere. Neither Neil Webb nor Paul Ince had, as yet, shown their true capabilities. Webb, bought for £1.5 million, had been sidelined for much of the previous season with a serious Achilles tendon injury, picked up while he was on duty with England, and although he had returned to the fray, Ferguson had to admit that in all honesty he looked only half the player he had with Forest. Paul Ince was equally disappointing, yet to settle and assert himself, as was Gary Pallister. In time they would prove to be inspired signings, which was more than could be said for Danny Wallace, who was eventually eclipsed by the emergence of Ryan Giggs.

Over the next few weeks it would get no easier. In their next league fixture United entertained high-flying Arsenal at Old Trafford. They lost 1–0 again. As if that was not humiliating enough, a mass brawl of United and Arsenal players not only brought condemnation from the media but also led to a hefty fine from the Football Association and the loss of one more point. Ferguson could almost feel the nails being hammered into his coffin. The fracas summed up, far more than words could, the frustration that had crept into Old Trafford. Luckily the public missed the most disgraceful scenes which took place in the tunnel. Ferguson himself had not been far away from the action. Not only were the players at each other's throats, but Ferguson was squaring up to the Arsenal manager George Graham, while Arsenal's number two Theo Foley was appropriately eyeing United's number two Archie Knox. The players meanwhile were involved in a mass brawl, with Norman Whiteside defending the United flag.

Although Ferguson was to describe the incident as 'more handbags at dawn than a brawl' it nevertheless brought the club into disrepute and provoked a few back-page headlines they could have done without. United were lucky that most of the action had taken place away from the public gaze and after the final whistle. It might have been 'handbags' on the pitch, but if the cameras had caught the action in the tunnel, the punishment might have been even more severe, with some of the staff reprimanded as well.

Even so, Ferguson complained bitterly about the treatment being meted out to both clubs. He reckoned they were being made scapegoats and that other punch-ups went both unreported and unpunished. He believed it was because United and Arsenal were high-profile clubs that the FA felt obliged to dish out the severest punishments. Perhaps of more concern to Ferguson was that he was put in the position of doling out punishment to his own players when he really believed that the incident should have been forgotten. McClair, Ince and Irwin were all fined in what was tantamount to a public-relations exercise designed to satisfy the back-page clamour for action.

A week after the Arsenal fracas United drew 3–3 at Manchester City to keep the debate about Ferguson's future well and truly alight. United had dropped to sixth in the table and were already a massive 14 points behind leaders Liverpool.

United and Ferguson were in serious trouble. They had progressed into the third round of the League Cup after a comfortable win over Halifax Town, but then on the last day of October found themselves drawn against Liverpool at Old Trafford. It was to be a defining moment in Alex Ferguson's Old Trafford career. If United lost, then the demands for his head would be heard all the way down the M62. Ironically, it was to be his opposite number, Kenny Dalglish, who would suffer the most as United gallantly upset the form book by beating Liverpool 3–1. One incident stood out above all others. As a ball was skied towards the touchline, Dalglish came out of the dugout to volley it back. He missed. The Stretford End roared with laughter. Within five months Dalglish had quit Anfield. Liverpool's defeat that evening had played its part in his departure, adding to the burden of pressures he faced. But for Ferguson it meant a stay of execution.

In Europe too United were making steady progress. In the opening round of the Cup-Winners' Cup the Hungarians Pecsi Munkas were brushed aside to give them another comparatively easy tie, this time against the Welsh Cup-winners Wrexham. Again United had no trouble and were into the quarter-finals having barely broken into a sweat. If they'd had a tougher draw against more formidable European opposition Ferguson could well have been facing an even more troublesome autumn. By the time the quarter-finals came around his problems had eased considerably, thanks to a good run in the League Cup and an improvement in their league position. After losing to Chelsea in late November they would not lose another league fixture until late February, when they undermined all their good work by losing three successive games in a sequence of seven matches without a win. Any hopes of catching the league leaders quickly disappeared and at the end of the season United had to be content with sixth place, 24 points behind champions Arsenal.

A little more consistency had crept into their game but they had still lost ten league fixtures and drawn 12. Their minds had been elsewhere by the New Year. By then they were through to the quarter-finals of the League Cup after a stirring 6–2 win at Highbury against League leaders Arsenal, thanks to a devastating hat trick from Lee Sharpe that signalled his arrival on the football scene. They were also into the last eight of the European Cup-Winners' Cup and were about to embark on a useful run in the FA Cup as they reached the fifth round before losing away to Norwich.

United's League Cup run took them to Southampton for the quarter-finals, and after a 1–1 draw United finished off the south-coast side 3–2 at Old Trafford, with Mark Hughes hitting a hat trick to take them into the last four. In the two-legged semi-final they faced Leeds United, winning both games to earn Alex Ferguson a second Wembley final.

Meanwhile in Europe, United entertained the French side Montpellier, and although they only managed a draw at Old Trafford, they snatched a 2–0 win in the south of France and were into the last four. Ferguson's experience in the competition with Aberdeen was telling. Clubs were watched, dossiers drawn up, hotels tested and plans made. Nothing was left to chance. It had paid off against Montpellier when the press had predicted an exit for United after their Old Trafford draw: in France, with a full-strength team once more plus a little luck, United had battled defiantly and proved everyone wrong. As if Ferguson was not enough of a talisman, United then got the luck of the draw, avoiding both Barcelona and Juventus. Instead they faced Legia Warsaw, with the first leg away from home. When Legia shot into an early lead there was a brief moment of anxiety for United, but an instant equaliser from Brian McClair plus a couple more goals in the second half virtually ensured a place in the final. It was hardly surprising that at Old Trafford United could barely raise their game. It ended in a 1–1 draw – but what did that matter? United were set to face Barcelona in the final in Rotterdam.

By then United had also faced Sheffield Wednesday in

the League Cup final. United were odds-on favourites but that was to discount the fact that Wednesday were managed by Ferguson's predecessor, Ron Atkinson. If anyone could tactically outwit United, Atkinson could. And that was precisely what he did. United might have dominated the match but it was Wednesday who scored the crucial goal. Ferguson was hardly generous in defeat. 'They [Wednesday] were never in the game,' he wrote some years later as he blamed the press for over-enthusing about Wednesday's victory. But the fact was that United had probably underestimated their opponents, assuming that they could brush them aside as they had Legia a few days earlier. There was a vital lesson for them here: to stop believing their own publicity.

In the event, Ferguson was not able to brood for long over their defeat by Sheffield Wednesday. Now his task was to focus on the European campaign – yet the following day, even that was to be pushed from the forefront of his mind. A bombshell was heading his way, coming from an entirely unexpected direction.

CHAPTER FIFTEEN

An Old Married Couple

It was a miserable trip back from Wembley. The rain spluttered down, adding to everyone's misery as the team coach slipped on to the North Circular and began to head towards the motorway. Ferguson sat alone, chewing over his disappointment, and making plans for United's forthcoming European encounter. The occasional car packed with United supporters sped past with the fans waving enthusiastically at them, but inside the coach there was an air of gloom. The television had been switched off. A few card games were going on towards the rear but generally there was an overwhelming silence. Some players slept, others read. Ferguson tried to grab a little sleep himself, still wondering where they had gone wrong. Perhaps they had simply taken Second Division Sheffield Wednesday too much for granted. Archie Knox was unusually quiet. Defeat in the League Cup final had taken it out of them.

As they pulled off the M6 and neared the Cheshire homes of most of the players, Ferguson could never have guessed that the next day would bring another blow, almost as bad as their Wembley defeat.

'Walter Smith's on the phone,' shouted his secretary the following morning as he bounced into the office following a light training session. Ferguson had kept a couple of tickets for the final aside for the Rangers manager but at the last moment had received a fax to tell him that Smith would not be coming. He assumed that the phone call was an apology or explanation. He was right, but it was not quite the explanation he had anticipated.

'There's no way I can tell you this easily,' began Smith. Ferguson wondered what was coming. 'I've offered Archie Knox the job as my assistant here at Ibrox.'

'And what's he said?' asked Ferguson.

'He's interested,' replied Smith. 'And we'd like to know if he can be relieved of his contract.'

Ferguson was stunned. He had known Knox for years. Why would he want to leave United? 'Well, officially the answer has to be no,' he snapped. 'He's under contract here.' But even as he was speaking, the United manager knew that contracts meant little and that if someone wanted to leave, whether they were players or staff, there was not much point in holding them against their will. Everyone had to be pulling together.

He came off the phone disappointed that his number two and friend wanted to leave, angry that Rangers had made what was tantamount to an unofficial approach and annoyed that after their defeat the previous day and with a European semi-final just days ahead of them, he was having to waste time sorting out another crisis. It was clear enough why Rangers were after Knox. Following the appointment of Graeme Souness as manager of Liverpool, Rangers had promoted his assistant, Walter Smith, to be their new manager. That promotion left a gap on the Rangers coaching staff. Ferguson had simply never imagined that Archie Knox was in the frame.

He immediately dragged Knox in. 'What's going on?' he asked.

His coach was apologetic. 'I'm sorry, but I couldn't really say anything before the Wembley game.'

'But are you really interested?' asked Ferguson incredulously.

'Yes,' replied Knox simply.

'But why?' Ferguson was astonished.

'I guess it's the money,' Knox answered. He was already one of the highest paid assistants in the game.

Ferguson looked at him. 'If that's all it is, I'm sure I can sort something out. I'll talk to Edwards, see what I can do. It can't be the football. You know as well as I do that the football up there is crap. It's a lot worse now than it was when we were at Aberdeen.'

Knox seemed to agree. Within hours Ferguson had fixed up to see Martin Edwards. As he had suspected, there was no problem about improving Knox's contract.

'If that's what you want,' said Edwards, 'then fine. We'll up his salary.'

But it was still not enough. Rangers were dangling a huge carrot in front of Knox. They wanted him, and if necessary they would go into an auction for his services. Ferguson talked to him again. He could barely believe that Knox was really interested in going to Ibrox. Surely Manchester United was a bigger club than Rangers, and with just as much ambition.

'They don't come any bigger than United,' he told Knox. 'This club has a great future. Things are really going to start happening here. Why go to Ibrox? You know as well as I do that there are only two teams in Scotland, and at the moment there's really only one. Okay, so you'll win the league with them, and probably the Cup as well. So what? Where's the challenge in that? You'll soon see the short-comings when it comes to Europe.'

Knox was wavering and they agreed to talk again later that week. Ferguson was surprised that the money seemed to be such a factor, surprised also that Knox didn't seem to share his belief in United. If that was the case, maybe it would be better if they parted company. What was even more bizarre was that Knox and Rangers wanted the deal settled immediately, when United stood on the brink of European success.

'Can't you even wait until the end of the season?' Ferguson asked when they had their talk later that week. The answer was no – Rangers wanted him immediately. A decision had to be made; there was no point in arguing any more. Ferguson and the club had done all they could. They had offered him a substantial improvement in salary and it was still not enough. When word leaked out, everyone was just as puzzled as Ferguson. Knox was well liked and nobody could understand why he should want to desert them when they were on the brink of another success.

Perhaps Ferguson should not have been so surprised. It was the second time his assistant had left him. At Aberdeen Knox had quit Pittodrie shortly after they had won the Cup-Winners' Cup, to become the new manager of Dundee. At the time Ferguson had encouraged him to make the move. After all, he was taking a step up from a number two job to become a fully fledged manager. They'd talked about it in the past and Ferguson always knew that if a good offer came his way, he would leave. There was no harm in that. People have ambitions and you cannot stand in their way. But this was different. Knox was not taking a step upwards – if anything, Ferguson reckoned, it was a step down.

In the end Ferguson and United had no alternative but to let Knox go. All that had to be done now was for Rangers and United to settle compensation, but it left a nasty taste in the mouth. Ferguson had lost a trusted friend, someone he had worked with for a long time and who knew his ways. It would be difficult to replace him. When the manager had come to Old Trafford, one of his first requests had been to appoint Knox. The board had agreed and Knox was Ferguson's first signing. 'One of my best,' he said at the time. The two men had worked together for a couple of years at Aberdeen and had known each other even longer.

Aberdeen's triumphs owed almost as much to Knox as they did to Ferguson. And Ferguson would be the first person to acknowledge that.

When they arrived at Old Trafford the pair of them had been visibly shocked by the training set-up. 'It was simply not good enough,' said Ferguson. The standard of fitness was not what it should be for players playing 60 games a season. Knox was told to sort it out. He took charge of fitness and soon put in place a new regime aimed at sharpening up the United squad to make them the fittest in the league. It didn't win him too many friends, especially first thing in the morning.

Knox was a typical dour Scottish Calvinist, unremitting and hard-working. He formed a strong link with Ferguson. They had an understanding; men with similar values. It had been a remarkably successful partnership as they picked up trophies galore north of the border. Yet despite the closeness it was to come as a shock when Archie Knox walked out on Manchester United. Ferguson and Knox have rarely spoken to each other since their parting. It all happened so suddenly.

Ferguson now had to begin the task of finding a replacement assistant just as United's season moved to a climax.

Brian Kidd had been a shrewd member of Manchester United's European Cup-winning side in 1968. Playing alongside Law, Best and Charlton, in one of British football's most exhilarating attack forces, he had picked up a league championship, as well as a couple of England caps. On the surface Kidd was a star. He had the medals to prove it, and when he left United it was for a massive six-figure fee, although he had never wanted to leave Old Trafford. He just didn't feature in new manager Tommy Docherty's plans. Kidd was also to figure in three more £100,000 transfer deals that took him to Manchester City, Everton and Bolton Wanderers. After that it was downhill most of the way as he opted to briefly blaze the footballing trail across America. Then it was back home to become assistant manager with Preston North End. But United, his first club, always remained his first love.

Despite his glamorous career there was always something refreshingly unpretentious about Kidd. He was never a star-struck, star-studded player. He never hit goals at the kind of rate you expect from out-and-out demon strikers – only 70 in a total of just over 250 games for United – and even in the heady days of Best, there was no talk of Kidd frequenting night clubs, modelling clothes or getting into trouble. He had his feet firmly on the ground, his mind focused on the game. In many ways he was the forgotten man of United's outstanding side.

When he did return to Old Trafford it was to help the Professional Footballers' Association run the Football Community project, rather than for some high-profile job with the first team. Not that this was an unimportant job. It was simply the kind of quiet, unassuming role that suited Kidd down to the ground. He could merge into the background and unobtrusively get on with the job to the best of his ability. Professional was the word to describe Kidd, always willing, rarely complaining, glad to be of help wherever he could. Occasionally Ferguson would ask him to represent the club by visiting junior clubs and local schools, and later he also asked him to help out with the B team on a part-time basis and to assist at the club's School of Excellence.

Kidd helped train the schoolboys and would be sent to talk to parents of potential signings. It always went down well with the parents to have a member of the famed '68 side taking an interest. Kidd was an intelligent man, the kind of person the parents felt they could trust. They could natter about the old days, swap a few stories about Best, Law and Charlton, and of course Busby. And usually Kidd would return to Old Trafford with a signature in his pocket, representing a promise from the parents. In more recent years Ferguson has unashamedly used Brian McClair to fulfil that role, a player whom today's generation of fathers are more likely to relate to.

In October 1990, when the club's youth development officer Joe Brown retired, Kidd was appointed in his place and made director of the School of Excellence. At that stage both Manchester City and Oldham Athletic were arguably a shade ahead of United with their youth development schemes. Ferguson wanted United, with the help of Kidd, to reassert itself and become the top choice of youngsters in the region. Other centres of excellence were set up around the country, and Kidd was told to go and spend two or three days a month in Ireland – a traditional source for United, which seemed to have dried up – to unearth the best Irish lads.

By Christmas 1990 the club was beginning to reap the dividends. 'Next season we have the best group of school-boy players coming to Old Trafford we have ever seen. I am particularly thrilled by the quality of the boys who will soon be here, and I see it as a result of our reorganisation,' Ferguson told the *United Review*. At the end of the previous season he had released most of the youngsters on their books and urged his scouting staff not to bring him the best in their streets but the best in their towns. Nobby Stiles had also been drafted in to help.

Ferguson did not have to look far for his new number two. With hindsight Kidd was always the obvious choice although at first it did not seem quite so obvious. Ferguson had mulled over a number of other possibilities before he finally decided on Kidd. The role of assistant was crucial. Although Ferguson was a hands-on manager who liked to devote his time to his players, it was not always possible. Other managers – Dave Sexton was one – would rarely be spotted on the training field, preferring instead to leave the training and day-to-day work with the players to their coaching staff, but that was not Ferguson's style. He enjoyed the dressing-room rapport, the jokes, the mickey-taking. He'd sit and watch, grinning to himself. Yet there would still be days when he would not be available to take training, when he would be away from Old Trafford on business – looking at other players or teams, attending FA hearings, and so forth.

The job of any manager, especially at a big club, is varied and time-consuming, and often the bulk of work with the first team can fall to the assistant. For this reason it is essential for the manager to have a coach he can trust, a man who can carry on the work without anyone spotting that the manager is not around. Ferguson had always been able to trust Knox; it was a special relationship. He wasn't going to rush into appointing someone else, and it would be a few months before he finally decided on Kidd.

Kidd was blissfully unaware of Ferguson's interest in him. The idea of becoming his number two had never even occurred to him. Surprising though it may seem, there isn't always a great deal of gossip and speculation at football clubs. It's not like the political world, or even some parts of the business world, where every move, every promotion, is analysed and debated. In any other business the departure of Archie Knox would have had the staff huddled in corners laying odds on the successor. But not in football. What's more, once he'd finally been approached by Ferguson, Brian Kidd didn't even want the job. 'I was so content with what I had,' he claimed, 'getting a great apprenticeship alongside Eric Harrison, working with the kids and getting a good quality of young player coming through, that I didn't want to change.'

Taking on the role of number two was not only a super-human challenge but an appalling risk. Ferguson still hadn't won the title and his job remained on the line. Kidd could sense that Ferguson was moving in the right direction, building the club up from the bottom, but the fans didn't always appreciate that, and unless trophies were won, nobody would be interested. It was all about putting silverware in the cabinet. If Ferguson was sacked, and at Old Trafford that was always a possibility, his number two would probably find himself on the scrap-heap as well. The job would also mean more work, more travelling, more pressure. What was the point? He didn't need all the hassle.

Kidd was hesitant. But Ferguson was not going to let him slip away that easily. Debating the issue was pointless, so Ferguson just told him: 'You're my new number two whether you like it or not. I need you to help me.' Of course he always knew that Kidd, a good pro, would accept it and delight in the challenge. There was never any question of his refusing. And so a partnership was born that in time would rival the famed partnership of Busby and Jimmy Murphy.

Kidd's role was to prove crucial, especially as so many of the youngsters he had helped bring to the club in the first place and developed on the training ground progressed through the ranks to challenge for first-team places. It was an astute move by Ferguson, although at the time he could never have fully realised the implications. Kidd knew the youngsters well, better than Ferguson ever could, as he'd worked with them so closely for so long. And when the time came to blood them in Premiership football, Kidd could confidently recommend them and tell Ferguson that they could be trusted.

Kidd's great strength is his unique relationship with the players and his knowledge of the youngsters. Having been a professional himself, he understands the issues that worry them, and sympathises. 'Brian commands total respect from the players because he is not only a great trainer and motivator, but he knows what it's like to be out there,' says Ryan Giggs. 'Everyone at the club feels the same way about him.'

Ferguson and Kidd have struck up a rapport. Both are

intelligent men; professional, hard-working, responsible and committed. It's not a unique relationship – plenty of football clubs have two men at the helm who work closely and well together – but you would have to go a long way to find a team that work better than Ferguson and Kidd. They complement each other: Ferguson the occasional hothead – although he's mellowed over the years – and the more placid Kidd. In some ways it bears a resemblance to the Shankly/Paisley relationship, rooted in honesty, trust and balance.

There's an element of democracy running through Ferguson's managerial style, although the ultimate responsibility for decision-taking always rests with him. He sits at the top of the managerial pyramid, and beneath him at the various levels are separate teams, each with a certain amount of autonomy, but each answerable to him or the next line of management. Ferguson is a born decision-maker. He doesn't shirk responsibility but, like all good decision-makers, he consults carefully before deciding.

The democratic approach is also applied to United's scouting system. If chief scout Les Kershaw strongly recommends a player, then Ferguson insists on taking his opinion into account. You pay someone for their opinions, because they have a supposed expertise. If you won't take their advice, then it hardly seems worth paying out for it. It's the same with Jim Ryan, who has travelled from one side of Europe to the other sizing up hundreds of possible recruits. It was Ryan who recommended Solskjaer; Les Kershaw had seen him as well. So Ferguson took their advice.

'I think most managers, a lot of the time, have to live on their own,' Ferguson recently told *Four Four Two* magazine, 'but I confide in Brian because he's my assistant and we have a healthy relationship in the sense that while I'm not for people to agree with me, I'm for opinion, for another angle, and Brian's very good for that. He's honest and we try and operate our side of the club, run our side of the club between us, without having to depend on anyone else.'

It is this relationship which, at the end of the day, has been as quietly crucial to United's success as any other development. And there is little doubt in the corridors of Old Trafford that Ferguson's eventual successor will be his current number two, though how long before that happens is anyone's guess. Back in the mid-nineties Manchester City tried to lure Kidd away to Maine Road, but Kidd was not interested. It's difficult to imagine him leaving the club where his heart lies. 'We argue like cat and dog,' says Kidd. 'But I think it's healthy to have different views and opinions. We're like an old married couple.'

In the last days of the previous relationship, when Walter Smith made his fateful phone call signalling the end for Ferguson and Archie Knox, United had been on the point of taking off for Rotterdam, for the European Cup-Winners' Cup final. They had not played in a European final since 1968, when they had become the first English side to lift the European Cup. Now they had the opportunity to add some more European silverware to their cabinet. It would also be more than welcome after the five-year ban that had kept English clubs out of European competition following the Heysel disaster.

Ferguson's biggest problem was with his goalkeeper. Sealey had been injured and temporarily replaced by young Gary Walsh, but there were doubts about Walsh's ability. He had not always looked confident when he had been given his opportunity between the posts, and although he had been at Old Trafford for a few years he had never managed to secure the goalkeeper's shirt for himself. Injuries and inconsistency had meant infrequent appearances. Ferguson opted to give Sealey a late fitness test, which Sealey duly passed.

Ferguson's other problem was whether to play Neil Webb

or Mike Phelan in the midfield. For most of the season the midfield had been a question of which three to draw out of Phelan, Webb, Ince and Robson. On this occasion Ferguson opted to leave Webb out of his starting line-up. Since his horrific Achilles injury, Webb had never looked the same player. At times he lacked that extra yard of pace, and he never seemed quite as confident as he had before. The decision to drop Webb was to spell the beginning of the player's disillusionment with Ferguson and Old Trafford. It would not be long before the pair had a public split, and in November 1992 Webb returned to Nottingham Forest.

The final itself turned out to be a night of triumph for United. Barcelona, one of the most respected and popular club sides in Europe, boasted players such as Dutch international Ronald Koeman, Michael Laudrup and the Spanish star Goicoechea in their line-up. It was a sizeable task for United, but on a night full of adventure and spirit they proved that they were up to the job. One man in particular had something to prove. His time at Barcelona had ended in disappointment and a loan spell to Bayern Munich, but in Rotterdam's Feyenoord stadium, Mark Hughes set out to show Barcelona just how wrong they had been in offloading him so nonchalantly.

It was the Welshman who conjured up both goals. From a Bryan Robson free kick in the second half, Steve Bruce headed the ball goalwards with Hughes edging it into the net. Seven minutes later he struck again, this time latching on to a delicate through ball from Robson before finally rounding the goalkeeper and drilling it into the back of the net. Koeman pulled one back for Barcelona, yet although there was general panic in the final ten minutes as the Spanish side suddenly leapt to life, United were able to hang on to win their second European trophy.

Perhaps more importantly, Alex Ferguson had won the European Cup-Winners' Cup for a second time. It was a remarkable achievement, but it was just the beginning.

Manchester was ecstatic. A vast army of Red supporters, the likes of which Ferguson had never seen before, turned out to greet their returning heroes. For miles the streets were lined as the convoy edged its way from Manchester's International Airport towards Old Trafford. The *Manchester Evening News* estimated the total crowd at something like half a million. Whatever the figure, it was a vast crowd, bigger than anything seen in the city since the days of Best, Law and Charlton. As Ferguson soaked in the breathtaking atmosphere he could hardly help but feel that here was a vast army of support for United that was still untapped. United were indeed the best supported club in the land. It begged the question as to how many would line the streets if they ever won the title. It would not be long before he discovered the answer to that question.

There was one other development that season that few recognised at the time as a pointer to United's future. All season Ferguson had been quietly crowing about a youngster in their reserves. The 17-year-old, a former England Schoolboys captain, was one of a number of promising lads emerging through the school of excellence. Another was Ferguson's own son Darren. Both lads had been playing in the reserve side which topped the Pontins League. Against Sheffield United in late February, Darren had been given his chance in the first team, coming on as a substitute. Then in the following game, at home to Everton, he was given a full debut. Also blooded that day as a substitute was the 17-year-old who was about to light up the skies around Old Trafford. His name: Ryan Giggs.

CHAPTER SIXTEEN

Fergie's Fledglings

In his biography of Matt Busby, Eamon Dunphy argues that the ultimate test in football is to measure achievement against resources. Matt Busby unquestionably passes that test. But perhaps Alex Ferguson passes it with even higher marks. Ferguson has almost unlimited resources at hand, yet has chosen the path that Matt Busby pioneered, by developing his own players rather than simply buying in talent.

In the 1950s money was just as scarce at Old Trafford as it was anywhere. In post-war Britain there were few televisions, even fewer car owners, almost no foreign holidays, and not much else in the way of household goods, other than the essentials. Wages were low; rationing had only just come to an end. It didn't cost much more than a couple of shillings (10p) to have a top seat at Old Trafford. United would make the occasional foray into the top end of the market but they were never among the so-called 'millionaire' clubs like Sunderland, Arsenal and Everton. Like many other managers, Busby had to concentrate on producing his own talent – but he did it with more endeavour, cunning and flair than anyone else. He wasn't going to do what other clubs did by concentrating on their own patch. Instead, he set up a comprehensive scouting system to tag players throughout the land, as well as in the Greater Manchester area. Young players were tracked, vetted and encouraged to come along for trials. They came in their hundreds, with scores of them joining. Not all made the grade but there were enough at first to encourage Busby to develop the system even further.

By 1953 it was clear that something extraordinary was fermenting at Old Trafford when the youth team gave a devastating performance in thrashing Wolves 7–1. Everyone was agog; even Busby was impressed. They looked so mature, so confident, so full of themselves. He decided to throw some of them a first-team shirt. There was nothing to lose and everything to gain. The expectations would soon trickle through to the rest of the juniors.

It turned out to be an astonishing assembly line of talent. One by one they emerged. Duncan Edwards, perhaps the finest of all United's youngsters, was one of the first to appear in that initial batch, along with Eddie Colman, David Pegg, Liam Whelan and Albert Scanlon. Others quickly followed – Bobby Charlton, Bill Foulkes, Dennis Viollet, John Doherty, Kenny Morgans, Ian Greaves and so forth. The list of those progressing through the youth ranks and into first-team football was breathtaking. They joined the likes of Roger Byrne, who had signed as a youth player in 1949 and had become skipper and an England international, and Jackie Blanchflower, brother of Tottenham star Danny.

Busby seemed to have no hesitation in giving them their chance. Nor did they let him down, winning the championship in 1956 and 1957. He looked to the long term, perhaps helped by an era that allowed managers the luxury of more time and space to experiment. Busby had been there since 1945 and was as safe as houses. It was to contrast with his successors, who were later forced to think in the short term as they crashed headlong into the transfer market seeking instant success instead of developing their own talent.

The Munich disaster destroyed not just United's
blossoming youth but the whole ideology that lay behind
the plan. United had to get back on their feet quickly; it was
a question of survival. Immediately after the disaster they
had to spend heavily just to field a team. The conveyor belt
had been ripped in two. In came Stan Crowther, Ernie
Taylor and, some months later, the golden boy Albert
Quixall, a record buy for £45,000. Perhaps Busby felt guilt
after seeing so many of his young players killed, but the
emphasis on developing his own youngsters was never the
same. There would be others emerging but never in similar
numbers. Instead he looked to buy in quality, signing Law,
Stepney, Herd, Setters, Crerand and others for huge fees.
The United youngsters had won five FA Youth Cups during
the 1950s but would not win another until 1964. The ten
years after Munich saw the emergence of George Best,
Jimmy Rimmer, John Aston, John Fitzpatrick and others,
but the constant flow was never the same.

After Busby it grew visibly slower. New managers had
to prove themselves quickly. Expectations were high. They
couldn't hang around waiting for young players to mature,
couldn't throw them into the first team with the same
confidence. McGuinness came and went, so too did
O'Farrell, Sexton, Docherty and Atkinson; five new faces at
the top in eleven years. None of them had time to wait;
everything became short term. It was impossible to develop
long-term plans: none of them felt secure enough. The
solution was buy, buy, buy. O'Farrell spent £500,000,
Docherty forked out £1.5 million, Sexton £3.6 million and
Atkinson £4.7 million. It doesn't sound much by today's
prices but at the time it was a king's ransom. When
Docherty arrived he found the youth system in disarray. 'It
was a disaster,' he claims, 'and there was no official chief
scout – they'd let things go.'

Docherty did try to introduce youth into the side,
blooding 17 youngsters, but only three of them established

themselves. The quality was no longer there; other clubs were competing better in the youth market. By 1978 the entire youth scheme was under threat. Sexton had introduced just a handful of youngsters to the first team, and in 1978–79, for the first time since the war, not one home-grown player made a debut. According to Harry Gregg, coach at the time, 'United had become a different club altogether.' There were more imports than home-grown players. The spirit and the bonding that the youngsters gave to a club as they grew up and developed together had been shattered.

Ferguson changed all that. He insisted on laying down a long-term plan that would benefit United in the future. Of course, he would still have to go out and buy players, but as time went on a youth system would begin to supply the players. He was confident that he could do it. After all, he'd done the same at St Mirren and, with even more national and international success, at Aberdeen. Of his European Cup-Winners' Cup-winning side, only three players had been bought in. The others had either been there when he arrived or had come through the youth and reserve ranks. He had turned Aberdeen into the envy of Scottish football and was capable of plucking the best Glasgow-born youngsters from under the noses of Celtic and Rangers. To achieve the same success at United required a pact with those upstairs: they had to believe in his philosophy. It was pointless putting so much energy and resources into building up a youth system if in two or three years he was to be castigated for failing to produce instant success. It was a long-term plan that needed a five-year commitment. Fortunately he was given such a commitment, although in December 1989 it was almost curtailed as anger on the terraces and carping criticism in the papers put his job on the line.

Ferguson turned the youth policy upside down as he discovered that United had more scouts in Scotland than in

200

Manchester. The scouting system was overhauled, as even rivals Manchester City had stolen a length on them. The anomaly had to be reversed: Brian Kidd, Nobby Stiles, Eric Harrison and Jimmy Curran were given the task of laying the foundations for United's future.

It has been said that Bobby Charlton used to take time off work just to stand on some windy touchline watching an unknown 14-year-old lad playing in a United juniors match. Charlton would return to Old Trafford drooling about the precocious skills he'd just witnessed. The young lad he'd seen could grab the ball and begin to run with it, slithering one way, spiralling another. He could take a defender on the outside or cut inside with equal proficiency and had the maturity of a 20-year-old. Charlton hadn't seen the like since George Best. He could scarcely comprehend what he was seeing in one so young. It wasn't long before the name of Ryan Giggs was brought to Alex Ferguson's attention.

Old Trafford has always gloated over its stars. The Busby Babes boasted Byrne, Taylor and Edwards; then in the sixties it was Best, Law and Charlton. Even Tommy Docherty's side boasted the exhilarating skills of Coppell, Pearson and Macari, while in more recent years it had been Hughes, Robson and Whiteside. Old Trafford has always thrived on thrilling young players, the kind of men capable of turning a game single-handed, of displaying a flash of genius to leave you with a warm memory on a wintry afternoon.

Ferguson first saw Giggs play just a month or so after he had joined the club. It was Christmas 1986 and Giggs, by then on the United books, was playing in a training match. Ferguson remembers it well. 'It was like watching one of those little cocker spaniels chasing a piece of floating, wind-blown waste paper around the park.'

From the moment he first saw Giggs play, Ferguson knew that they had a potential gem. Of course it doesn't always work out. Young players can sometimes be sidetracked, or maybe don't develop physically as they should, or even lack that edge of determination or rudimentary spirit needed to carry a player to the highest level. You only have to look at the line-ups for United's own FA Youth Cup-winning sides to see how many of them fail to make the grade into the professional game. History is littered with players described as 'the next George Best'. But it was soon apparent that Giggs was not going to fall by the wayside.

It was Viv Anderson who was to highlight that Giggs really had what it takes. Giggs was a mere 15-year-old, yet playing against Viv Anderson at The Cliff in a training game, the youngster gave the England international an afternoon he would not forget in a long time. For an hour or more Anderson was chasing and puffing as Giggs twisted and turned. Anderson became angrier every minute at the cheek and energy of the teenager, then finally lost his cool and began to go in harder than he should have. But was Giggs troubled or deterred? No. His concentration never wavered one inch. It left everyone watching in no doubt whatsoever that Giggs would make the grade. He was brave, spirited and crafty.

Giggs was the son of Danny Wilson, a rugby fly-half of some distinction with Cardiff and Swinton, but when his parents separated, young Ryan assumed the name of his mother. He was born in Wales; hence his decision to opt for Wales rather than England, even though he had already played for England Schoolboys. Giggs was gifted from the start, walking at seven months, running at one. By the age of 14 he was captaining England Schoolboys and was virtually a full-time sportsman. Fortunately, his school recognised his extraordinary abilities and allowed him to pursue them, without putting too much pressure on him about his school work. It was obvious to everyone that young Ryan Giggs was going to make it big, though at one stage the question was who with. It was Manchester City who initially latched on to him, inviting him to their school of excellence, but his heart was always with United. Eventually Ferguson's new youth initiative spotted the youngster and signed him up. He was only 13 at the time.

Giggs was groomed for the top. He soon became a member of the United Youth team and made his first appearance in the United programme in October 1989. The United youngsters had just returned from Italy after winning the prestigious Grossi Morera trophy. They were dubbed 'Harrison's heroes' and Giggs was referred to as 'associate schoolboy Ryan Wilson'. He was not in the team photo since he was back at his school desk when the team picture was taken, but was shown instead in a separate shot, the first of many that would appear in the *United Review*. Interestingly the only other youngster in the team photo who would make it to become anything like a regular United first teamer would be Darren Ferguson. Ian Wilkinson also had one game for the first team, in the League Cup, but that would be it. Nobody else made it.

A year later the press latched on to the young lad, even though he had yet to play in the first team. One Sunday newspaper predictably labelled him the 'new George Best'. Ferguson was seething. 'I was appalled,' he wrote in the *United Review*. 'Ryan will be his own man and doesn't need saddling with this kind of expectation. He also has to be given time. I won't be rushing him either . . . patience is the word.'

Ferguson was insistent that young players had to be protected. It was something he had learned the hard way at Aberdeen. The team that won the European Cup-Winners' Cup had boasted five youngsters between the ages of 17 and 18, and by 1990, when they should have been in their prime as players, not one of them was playing regular first-team football. One had been forced to quit the game through injury while the others had all suffered continuous injury problems which had robbed them of their best years in the game. The lesson was not lost on Ferguson. 'No one thought any harm was being done at the time,' he claimed, years later. 'But it's easy to see otherwise with the benefit of hindsight.' Now he was ever mindful of the burn-out factor.

He had been criticised at one point in the 1990–91 season for leaving Lee Sharpe out of the side. The 19-year-old had been particularly effective and at least one newspaper had questioned his omission. 'I don't want him burned out through over-playing as a teenager,' was Ferguson's swift response to that criticism. 'I want him still playing for me when he's 26 or 27.'

Twelve months on and young Ryan Wilson, or Ryan Giggs as he had by then become known, was tossed into the first team in March 1991, and named as a substitute against Everton at Old Trafford at the age of 17. Ferguson took the view that if he was good enough, he was old enough. The time was also right, since there was little at stake by that stage and the pressure would not be on him. Darren Ferguson also made his full debut in that game. It was time to give the youngsters an airing. The manager told Giggs to just go out and enjoy himself, play his normal game, and not to do anything foolish.

Coming on in place of Denis Irwin, Giggs did not let his manager down. Even though United lost, he played with style. And in his full debut against Manchester City two months later he rewarded his manager with the only goal of the game, scored in front of 45,000 at Old Trafford. The lad seemed to relish the big occasion. Of course the press had a field day. As far as they were concerned he was the new George Best. But rather than let everyone get carried away, Ferguson wrapped his gem safely up in cotton wool and stored it away. The following week Giggs was back with the reserves playing in front of a couple of thousand.

At Pittodrie the shortage of quality players had forced Ferguson, on more than one occasion, to play a youngster when a day off might have been a wiser prescription. But at

Old Trafford he did not have to resort to such measures. He could afford to play someone like Giggs for one match and then leave him out the following week. It would be the same later with players such as David Beckham, Nicky Butt, the Nevilles and Paul Scholes. None of them would be played week in week out until they were old enough and strong enough – physically and mentally – to withstand the rigours of the game.

It wasn't until the following season, 1991–92, that Giggs was to emerge as a player of undeniable quality. He was in from the start of the season, named as substitute, and after a couple of games was pulling on the number eleven shirt to take his place in the opening line-up. It didn't take him long to show that his starring role against City the previous season had been no fluke. Giggs had arrived. What's more, he had all the qualities the media love – enigmatic good looks, daring skills, even a smattering of charm – he was the perfect role model. Schoolgirls adored him, schoolboys looked up in envy and parents were admiring. Before the season was out the commercial boys at Old Trafford had realised that Giggs was a gift from heaven. It wasn't long before they were selling Giggsie towels, Giggsie duvet covers, Giggsie this and Giggsie that. Anything with Giggs on it was a sure seller. Overnight his precocious talents had turned United into a star attraction. The boy would soon be worth a fortune.

Not surprisingly, United were instantly besieged by the press with requests for interviews. Could he appear on television, was there any chance of a photo-call, could they have an interview . . . ? Ferguson however had different ideas. He was not going to allow his gem to be passed from hand to hand. A blanket ban was put on Giggs talking to the press.

'I needed to protect him,' insisted Ferguson. 'My prime concern was the clear risk of a repetition of the George Best scenario or a Gazza syndrome. So I bolted the Old Trafford door and made sure Ryan was safe inside.'

It didn't go down well with the press. Some of the tabloids and various television companies continued to harass him and the club for interviews, but Ferguson stuck by his decree. There would be no interviews until he said so. And as other youngsters such as Lee Sharpe, David Beckham and the Neville brothers emerged, Ferguson continued to adopt the same strategy. Fortunately, Giggs has always been in a very different situation from Best. Best was vulnerable from the start, having left his Belfast home to come to live in Manchester at an early age. He had money, looks, fame and the run of Manchester. Giggs has been far more tightly controlled. Fortunately he has lived much of his life in Manchester. It's his home town and he still lives close to his mother and relies on her a great deal. He's a sensible lad who could do without all the publicity. The ban saved him hassle and kept him focused on football.

With all the publicity Ferguson needed to keep Giggs's feet firmly on the ground. Having had three teenage sons himself, Ferguson was well aware of the pressures and difficulties such kids face. He could appreciate the temptations, especially in a big city, but had enough experience of his own to know how to deal with the situation. Just because Giggs was in the first team did not entitle him to avoid the menial tasks that others of his age at the club were having to suffer. Like them, he was put to doing enough of the regulatory sweeping and cleaning to make him realise that he wasn't such a superstar when it came to Old Trafford.

Yet there was little doubting that Giggs was a superstar. 'He is the most precious, skill-blessed player I have ever had in almost twenty years in management,' wrote Ferguson in his book *Just Champion*, 'the greatest talent I have ever been asked to manage.' Today Ferguson might want to take stock of that statement in view of the impact that Eric Cantona has made at the club. But it is doubtful that he would want to change it that much.

As Giggs flitted one way and then another, squirming past confused defenders in television slow-mos every week, so the word spread to the footballing capitals of Europe. AC Milan were quick on the scene, making a £10 million bid. At the time it would have been a world record fee for a player, but Ferguson was having none of it. 'Forget it,' he told them politely, perhaps too politely. Weeks later they were back again with their middle man repeating the offer, but Ferguson would not even contemplate it. Giggs was not for sale, full stop. He was already playing for Europe's top club, what could he possibly gain by going abroad? Other calls of interest would filter through over the years but the answer was always the same: 'Thank you but no thanks.' Eventually Italy and Spain's top bosses got the message. Ferguson had other plans for the youngster. His devilish cunning was going to be a major factor in United's bid for the championship. Without him United would be tossing away any hope of the title.

Giggs was the first in an assembly line of young talent that would pour out of Old Trafford, justifying Ferguson's policy. In 1992 they won the FA Youth Cup for the first time since 1964. Then a year later they were losing finalists, before winning it again in 1995. By then success was permeating through the club, from the first team to the reserves, and to the A and B sides as well as the youth team.

The youngsters brought a sense of spirit and continuity to the club as they steadily progressed from one team to another. They knew no fear, because Old Trafford had always been their home. For new players it could be overwhelming, as indeed it had been for Ferguson when he arrived, but the youngsters never seemed to suffer or feel it in the same way. 'When Andy Cole first came here, he was totally overawed,' says Wilf McGuinness. 'The kids knew no different and that's why they progressed better at the time than Cole.'

However, winning the Youth Cup didn't guarantee first-team chances or recognition. Many failed to make the grade; others enjoyed just a handful of first-team appearances. Some, like Lee Sharpe, moved on, bringing in a handsome profit.

Ferguson himself likes nothing better than working with the kids. Even at Aberdeen he would be putting in the time with them. 'He was fantastic with the lads,' remembers one of his Aberdeen scouts. 'There is nobody better than him at working with young boys. He's like a magnet – he attracts them towards him. They all want to do something for him.' It was to be much the same at Old Trafford.

By 1997 the list of successes was growing by the day. Giggs was by then a seasoned Welsh international while the Neville brothers, Philip and Gary, had picked up England honours; so too had Nicky Butt and Paul Scholes, while David Beckham was looking every bit another Bobby Charlton as he too won an England call-up. Added to that were others such as Simon Davies, John O'Kane, Chris Casper and Ben Thornley who had played in the first eleven and looked certain to become fixtures in the side in the years ahead. The assembly line seemed set to run and run.

CHAPTER SEVENTEEN

Almost There

With the FA Cup and the European Cup-Winners' Cup firmly under his belt, Ferguson was now convinced that his team were ready to seize English football's mightiest prize. But as he spent the summer basking in the glory of his side's victory in Rotterdam, the manager still had some nagging worries.

United had never resolved their goalkeeping problem. Leighton, Sealey and Walsh had given accomplished service but none could be described as outstanding. Ferguson had only to glance down the road to Anfield to see what a difference a consistent goalkeeper could make. At Liverpool, Ray Clemence and Bruce Grobbelaar had kept goal over a period of 20 years, and their consistency and continuity had reaped rich dividends for the Anfield club. In that time United had fielded half a dozen keepers with only Alex Stepney worthy of comparison with the Liverpool duo. A safe pair of hands in goal had to be the starting point for any aspiring manager.

Ferguson's hand was now being forced. Leighton was still bitter after being dropped for the Cup final, his Old Trafford career in tatters. Added to that, Sealey was demanding a two-year contract while Ferguson was only prepared to offer him one year. The manager's attentions turned to the transfer market and in particular to Denmark. He had tried in the past to sign the Brondby and Danish international goalkeeper Peter Schmeichel, but with the Dane under contract and a prohibitive fee being demanded, United's interest had waned though it had never been forgotten. However, in the summer of 1991 the rumour coming out of Denmark was that Schmeichel was out of contract and keen to join United. Ferguson was alerted and promptly sent goalkeeping coach Alan Hodgkinson off on a spying mission. 'Make sure you see him in at least half a dozen games,' Ferguson told him. Hodgkinson was soon back. 'So what do you think?' asked Ferguson. 'Is he really as good as we originally thought?'

'He's the best keeper in Europe,' replied the former England man confidently. 'He's got everything – size, agility, intelligence, and is a brilliant organiser of a defence.' Ferguson did not need to hear any more. Within a couple of weeks the Great Dane was on his way to Old Trafford, signed for £500,000. It was a snip. Schmeichel was about to become one of the most influential players at Old Trafford. His arrival in the United defence brought not only dependability and confidence but organisation as well. At times he could be as much a pain for his own defenders as he was for attackers. His yelling and berating of his defence might have brought smiles to the terraces and scowls to his colleagues' faces, but it was effective. Defenders soon recognised that they could trust him.

Schmeichel was not the only important purchase that summer. Although Giggs provided plenty of pace on the left, Ferguson felt that some width on the other side could be the key to United's title chances. With Giggs on one wing and someone else operating on the right flank, defences would be torn apart. But who could fit the bill? Ferguson and Kidd mulled over the possibilities. None of the potential candidates was up for sale. Ferguson was about to give up but then remembered a video of a Ukrainian sent to him by a Norwegian journalist. They looked at it and were astonished by what they saw. The youngster was called Andrei Kanchelskis and was still only 21. With the break-up of the old Soviet Union he had become available for transfer. He was already an international and looked the part – on the video at least. Ferguson decided to investigate further. All the reports that came back were encouraging. Ferguson decided to have a look himself and went to watch him play against Germany. He was impressed. Kanchelskis was quicksilver fast, tricky and strong despite his lightweight appearance. At £650,000 he was cheap and worth a try. Ferguson invited him over for a week's trial towards the end of the 1990–91 season. Kanchelskis played one game that season, but a delay in his work permit meant that he didn't really put his roots down at Old Trafford until after the summer of 1991.

Sitting in his office one morning, Ferguson jotted the names of his principal players on a piece of paper and then scribbled their nationalities alongside them. There were two Irishmen, three Welshmen and a Scot, plus Schmeichel and Kanchelskis. The signing of the Ukrainian and the Dane had exacerbated a problem that was of growing concern to the United manager – the lack of English-born players in his squad. A new UEFA ruling allowed for only three foreign players, plus two 'naturalised' players (i.e. those whose careers had taken place in England even if they were qualified for other countries, such as Giggs and Irwin), to be played in any European competition. Furthermore, the ruling stipulated that Welsh, Scottish and Irish players would be considered foreign. Ferguson was clearly going to struggle to find a reasonable side to play in European competition.

A possible answer came while the club was on a pre-season tour of Norway, with the news that the England and QPR defender Paul Parker might be up for sale. Everton had been talking to him but although they had reached agreement with the club, they had apparently failed to reach any agreement on personal terms. Arsenal and Tottenham had now been alerted and were also rumoured to be preparing bids. Ferguson decided to move quickly. Within the hour he was on the phone to QPR and had been given permission to talk to Parker. Unfortunately, both Arsenal and Tottenham had also been given permission, and United were at the back of the queue, but Parker promised Ferguson that he would visit all three clubs and listen to their offers before making a final decision. It was as much as Ferguson could hope for. Parker duly arrived and was staggered to see more than 300 fans sitting in the stands. It was enough to convince him that United had ambitions. He duly signed for £1.7 million. Ferguson had added three established internationals to his squad for a combined sum of just under £3 million. It wasn't bad business, even though only one of them was English. There was nothing that delighted Ferguson more than wheeling and dealing in the market. He wasn't like Ron Atkinson, always gambling at the top end of the market, but preferred to swoop at the lower to middle end, picking up quality players cheaply and then turning them into multi-million-pound stars.

The manager had now grown so confident that his side could clinch top honours that he even went on to predict that United were ready to bring the title back to Old Trafford. 'I am confident about our chances and that we have laid the right foundations,' he told everyone on the first day of the new season. Later he would confess that 'I honestly thought we were ripe for a serious assault on the league championship. It was not a matter of getting carried away but simply a declaration of intent for the supporters.'

With hindsight it was a rash promise. He would not be able to deliver for another year, but at least the essentials were in place. It simply needed time. Thankfully he would not be reminded of his predictions too much, and the challenge that United were to make for the title ensured that his position at Old Trafford would remain safe.

United began the new season, 1991–92, in devastating form. Eight out of their first ten matches ended in victory with United soaring blissfully to the top of the table. Then came a couple of draws before their first defeat, away at Sheffield Wednesday. However, United soon picked up again, winning six of their next seven matches and sharing the points in the other. That run had ended with an impressive 6–3 defeat of Oldham Athletic at Boundary Park. By the end of the year United had dropped a mere 15 points, having been beaten just once and having drawn six. They had won their other 14 games. They topped the table, though only just, with Leeds United hanging on in second place. It was championship form. Sadly, the second half of the season was to prove disastrous by comparison.

The new year began appallingly as United crashed to a 4–1 defeat at home by Queens Park Rangers. It was a taste of things to come in the second part of their season. Following the game there were suggestions that the United players had been on a binge, and some claimed that Ferguson had still not fully resolved the drinking problem at Old Trafford. In fact there were still some players at the club who enjoyed more than was good for them, but on the whole the days when Old Trafford resembled a beer parlour were long gone. The result had come as such a shock 'that people just had to find a reason for it', insisted Ferguson, 'and some invented their own'. The truth was less interesting. Two goals within ten minutes had United facing an uphill struggle from the start. Ferguson also claimed that at least four of his side were suffering the early effects of flu and were well below par. Whatever the reason, the result gave a boost to United's chief rivals, Leeds United.

Over the next nine games Manchester United spluttered along, barely able to get themselves out of second gear. They didn't lose, but far too many points were casually tossed away. Yet they still led the chasing pack until a disastrous run-in saw the championship stolen from under their very noses. In their final eleven fixtures United could muster only three wins and four draws. The title slipped away from them as they lost three consecutive matches in late April, including a crucial 2–0 defeat at Anfield. It was the final blow; Leeds were champions by four points.

It was a humiliation for United fans. To lose the title anywhere was bad enough but to lose it at Anfield made it even worse. 'It was probably the worst moment I can remember as a United fan,' recalls lifelong United supporter Tim Bamford. 'It was the worst of all scenarios – the combination of Anfield and being pipped to the title. It took us months to recover from that.'

The critics sniped and in his book, *Six Years at United*, Ferguson was equally vitriolic, launching a stinging attack on one of them, the former United manager Tommy Docherty. 'He is what he is, a bitter old man,' wrote Ferguson, forgetting that to many Stretford Enders he remained a hero, still fondly remembered for his exciting blend of Scottish talents.

Ferguson was devastated to have come so close again. It seemed he might never be able to vault that final hurdle. Yet there was much for him to take satisfaction from. Kanchelskis had proved a stimulating addition. Even if he was not always able to reproduce the same level of commitment each game, his exhilarating chases up and down the right flank always had the Old Trafford fans out of their seats in anticipation and always posed a danger to defences. Giggs also was continuing to mature with each game, while Schmeichel had settled well and was already screaming at his own defenders. The problem lay with goals. United might have the best defence in the league, but when it came to putting the ball in the back of the net there was something lacking. Only 63 goals had been scored. Even Oldham, fifth from bottom, had managed that number. Brian McClair was top marksman with 18 league goals, but other contributions were limited. Mark Hughes netted a helpful 11 but nobody else came near double figures. It was the same old story. Since the days of Dennis Viollet, United had lacked a striker who could regularly fire 20 goals and more a season. Other clubs seemed to unearth outstanding strikers with uncanny regularity, but not United. In the past, United managers had tried to buy in top strikers, but they always seemed to arrive minus their shooting boots. Ted McDougall, Garry Birtles and Peter Davenport had all been expensive proven goal scorers, yet none had contributed much more than a handful of goals to the United cause. Ferguson worried about his side's goal-scoring ability. They needed to find someone who could hit the net regularly. As they drew up a list of possible solutions it was obvious that there was a general shortage of outstanding strikers, but it had been marked in their minds as a top priority.

If in the end luck had deserted United in the league, there was enough success elsewhere to suggest that Ferguson was constructing a side of considerable quality. Maybe they hadn't won the league trophy, but the season ended with two other trophies proudly on display in the Old Trafford boardroom.

Earlier in the season United picked up the European Super Cup. As a trophy it might not hold too much prestige, but to beat the European champions Red Star was enough to delight the Old Trafford faithful. It proved that United were well capable of living with the best, even if Red Star had outplayed them in the first half. Sadly, United disappointed when it came to the European Cup-Winners' Cup, going out in the second round to Atletico Madrid, thanks largely to a 3–0 defeat in Spain.

United's chief success was in the League Cup, the one domestic trophy they had never won. They began their campaign with a comparatively gentle tie against Cambridge United. After a 3–0 home win, United's progression into the next round was a foregone conclusion, and a 1–1 draw at Cambridge was more than enough to settle the contest. The next round brought slightly stiffer opposition in Portsmouth, who later that season would come within a whisker of reaching the FA Cup final, but at Old Trafford against United they went down 3–1. Neighbours Oldham were the next visitors but again presented few worries, with Andrei Kanchelskis hitting United's second in a 2–0 win. United were into the last eight, but Ferguson must have grimaced when he heard the draw. It couldn't have been tougher: an away tie with Leeds United.

By coincidence United were facing Leeds three times in the space of a fortnight with League Cup, FA Cup and league encounters, and all at Elland Road. The results turned out to be something of a mixed bag. United won the two cup encounters and drew the league game, but their success only added to a fixture pile-up that would be their undoing as the season gathered pace. Leeds, out of the two cup competitions, were left with just the league to concentrate on. After the victory over Leeds, Ferguson had the feeling that at last United would lift the League Cup, but privately he worried about the fixture congestion and the draining effect it might have on his players. He was to be right on both counts. In the two-legged semi-final they faced Second Division Middlesbrough and after a goalless draw beat the north-east side 2–1 in extra time at Old Trafford.

United's opponents at Wembley were Brian Clough's Nottingham Forest, four times winners of the trophy, six times finalists. What's more, they had already beaten United in the league. But at Wembley there was really only one team in it. United dominated for much of the game and although the match was settled by just one goal, United could, and should, have had more. In a way it only underlined United's failing: an inability to score goals. When the goal did come, again it was from McClair, who latched on to the flawless pass from Giggs. It was yet another piece of silverware for Ferguson.

United might not have won the league but they had given Leeds a run for their money, finishing just four points behind the new champions. Ferguson may have been disappointed but he could look back on his brief Old Trafford career with some gratification. He had picked up the FA Cup, the League Cup, the European Cup-Winners' Cup and the European Super Cup during his time, while the youngsters had just won the FA Youth Cup, which augured well for the future. Only one trophy now remained to be won.

CHAPTER EIGHTEEN

The Burden of History

The last time United won the league title, Harold Wilson was just into his second spell at Number Ten and a pint of beer would have cost you less than two old shillings. In those days the London underground was still a delight and Manchester was still a busy port. *Sergeant Pepper* was in the making and the Six-Day War was yet to break out. Since then, a whole generation had come and gone without ever knowing what it was to call their team champions. Wherever Ferguson turned he was reminded that twenty-odd years was a long time to be waiting to see the league championship trophy again. Winning the title had now become as much an obsession with him as it had with most United fans. 'There can be no lasting satisfaction until I have brought the championship back to this club,' he told United supporters. The burden of history needed to be lifted.

Ferguson knew that the lack of fire power which had knocked United off track the previous season had to be resolved. More than once after training, he and Brian Kidd pondered the problem, puzzling over just who might fit the bill. Others on the training staff offered their suggestions as well. Top of their list, they decided, was David Hirst, the big, bustling Sheffield Wednesday striker. Ferguson fancied Hirst and reckoned his explosive power in the box and his

lightning pace were just the qualities United lacked.
Ferguson put in a call to Hirst's manager at Wednesday,
Trevor Francis, but received no encouragement. Hirst was
not for sale. However, it would not be the last time Ferguson
phoned Francis. Also on the list was a young striker with
Southampton, Alan Shearer. He was only 21 but already
looked to be a blazing prospect. Ferguson called the
Southampton manager Ian Branfoot and was told that
Shearer was not for sale and anyhow looked set to sign a
new contract with the Saints. Branfoot promised to keep
Ferguson informed if the situation changed. As the summer
drew on and the nation gawped in admiration at the
Barcelona Olympics, Ferguson's search for a striker was to
become even more urgent.

With little on offer in the top flight, Ferguson began to
look around elsewhere. Eventually he hit upon Dion Dublin
at Cambridge United. A tall, gangly, awkward player,
Dublin had scored more than 50 goals in 150 appearances
at Cambridge. It wasn't an outstanding strike rate but it
was improving all the time. Ferguson viewed a series of
Cambridge videos and admitted that he was particularly
impressed by the range of goals struck by Dublin. He could
hit them first time, head them, volley them or poke them in
from a distance. What's more, Dublin was up for sale at £1
million. It seemed a snip and United duly paid up.

If the 1992–93 season was to be United's championship
year, as Alex Ferguson firmly predicted, then it hardly
kicked off with much belief among his players. In their first
fixture, across the Pennines at Bramall Lane, they lost 2–1.
Then in their second match, at home to Everton, their
championship hopes were put into perspective as they lost
3–0. In the dressing room before kick-off Ferguson had
ranted at them that they must win this game. They'd
already got their season off to a bad start, he told them.
This was crucial; a good win today would get the fans
behind them, and get them all in good spirits for the

forthcoming season. They couldn't afford to lose another match. But United had gone and lost. It was a disaster. The fans wanted to blame it on the lack of atmosphere, with the Stretford End pulled down and a building site behind their famous goal. Ferguson knew better. He bit his lip and put on a brave face in front of the press. They hadn't played all that badly, he told journalists, knowing that it would make little difference. They were sure to go to town with their headlines. He wasn't wrong either. The next day they slaughtered him on the back pages.

Ferguson had to admit privately that they weren't far wrong. Next in line was another home match, this time against newly promoted Ipswich. It was a chance for United to try to retrieve the situation, but hearts soon sank when United went a goal behind. Fortunately Irwin saved the day as the Reds salvaged a point, yet the situation was still desperate. United had dropped two home points and had only one point to show out of nine. It might have been early days, but instead of challenging at the top of the table, they were propping up the entire division.

For their fourth match United were away at Southampton. It was an awkward game, and with further disasters looming Ferguson decided to give new signing Dion Dublin a debut. It proved to be an inspired judgement as Dublin hit a late winner. With his aggression and pace, Dublin looked the part, providing that extra edge in the penalty area, but it was not to last. Following a 2–0 win over Nottingham Forest, United then beat Crystal Palace, but any pleasure from that result was tempered by a grave injury to Dublin, who was stretchered off with a seriously broken leg. It was effectively to mark the end of Dublin's Old Trafford career. Although there were initial worries that he might never play again, Dublin did eventually return to fitness but by then others had taken his place and he was to play only a handful more games for United before Ferguson sold him to Coventry City for a neat profit. Although

Dublin's injury was an appalling blow to the club, it turned out to be a blessing in disguise as it focused Ferguson's mind on finding a replacement. And the man who was eventually to step into his boots would have an influence beyond all others at Old Trafford.

United had soon knitted five successive league wins together, including a revenge 2–0 win at Goodison Park over Everton. But that run was to be followed by five successive draws, then a couple of defeats. Anyone who had been carried away thinking United might after all be potential champions was now brought back to earth with a bump. United slipped down the table yet again. International duty was taking its toll on the squad, while early-season injuries to Bryan Robson, Dion Dublin and Lee Sharpe had added to the despair.

It was time for action, time for Ferguson to make a move into the market. There was no alternative; something had to be done to stem the slide. Ask any manager whether they like being forced into the market and they'll tell you 'no', as it's much better to deal in your own time. Buy in haste, repent at leisure. Players have to be watched and carefully scrutinised, over more than a handful of games. But just occasionally an opportunity arises that demands a snap decision, and that's when you have to trust your instincts. Such an occasion was about to arise for Alex Ferguson. With Dion Dublin injured and a run of poor results, Ferguson needed to do something to get United's season back on course. And that meant signing a top striker. David Hirst still remained top of his hit list, but after the earlier approach, he now decided on a more formal bid. After a quick chat with the chairman, United decided to up their offer for the Sheffield Wednesday player and faxed a bid of £3.5 million to Hillsborough. Manager Trevor Francis reacted angrily: Wednesday were not interested in selling Hirst; end of story.

Then, out of the blue, came a phone call from Leeds

United, an inquiry about the availability of Denis Irwin. It was to lead to one of the most dramatic signings in the club's history. Irwin was not for sale, but as Martin Edwards chatted with his opposite number at Leeds, the deal that would bring Eric Cantona to Old Trafford was put into motion.

Cantona did not make his debut immediately since there were still formalities to be sorted out, but his presence was felt almost straight away. As United took on Arsenal at Highbury he watched from the stands and was, believes Ferguson, an uncanny influence. 'You got the sense that more than one player on the park was playing for his place, acutely aware that the Frenchman was a threat to their selection.' United won 1–0 and were on their way, their championship credentials restored. Cantona was named as substitute for United's next game, a 2–1 win over Manchester City. A week later he made his full debut at Old Trafford as United took on top-of-the-table Norwich. With Norwich nine points clear of United it was just as well they won 1–0 to stem any East Anglian ambitions. In their next match, at Stamford Bridge, Cantona hit his first goal for United as they drew with Chelsea. It wasn't long before the Frenchman was a fixture in the side, working his magic. United would lose only two more games that season.

Cantona's impact was splendidly demonstrated in their next game as they travelled across the Pennines to Hillsborough to face Sheffield Wednesday. In a game that even today is rated as one of the most crucial that season, United battled back from a three-goal deficit to salvage a 3–3 draw. And, fittingly, it was Cantona who hit the equaliser in a memorable encounter. United had now added a new grit to their performances, a determination not to lose. With Paul Ince leading by example, United shoulders no longer dropped when they went a goal behind. They were becoming more confident, more patient, more certain that they could recover from any deficit. In the past they would have lost spirit, become frustrated and given up. Like Ince, Cantona was another battler; a man not accustomed to being on the losing side too often.

United's 3–3 draw with Wednesday was to inject them with a crucial belief in their own strength. If they could fight back from three goals, they could do anything, Ferguson told them. It worked. In their next game they hammered five goals past Coventry and then four past Spurs to go to the top of the table. Everything was going according to plan until they travelled to Ipswich. Ferguson had a feeling it wasn't going to be United's day. The pitch was bone hard and an appalling error by Peter Schmeichel let Ipswich in for the opening goal. They even added a second before McClair hit a late consolation goal for United. A few more minutes and United might have grabbed an equaliser. It was an annoying defeat but it was a timely reminder that there was still plenty more work to be done before they could claim the title. United had to remain focused, determined and resilient. There could be no easing up.

Over the next few weeks United's form dipped and bobbed, with four wins, four draws and a solitary defeat at Oldham. It was a worrying period for Ferguson, who more than once wondered if the title would slip from their grasp yet again. However, there was still plenty of time to rectify things, and what pleased him more than anything was that the side were continuing to play adventurous football and create chances. Cantona had undoubtedly added a new dimension and in doing so had helped lift the burden off young Giggs. With Kanchelskis and Giggs providing the width and Cantona the invention, United were maturing into a side of exciting enterprise.

Aston Villa had now emerged as United's closest rivals, but a 1–1 draw with Ron Atkinson's side at Old Trafford temporarily put a halt to their gaining any ground in the championship race. Defeat for United could have been catastrophic, but whereas in previous seasons their final run-in had been full of nerves, self-doubt and over-the-shoulder glances, this time their concentration was focused and more self-assured. The final seven games were all won with only four goals conceded.

United had won the title long before the final game of the season. The telling moment came against Sheffield Wednesday. A goal down at Old Trafford with time running out fast, United looked to be about to relinquish their grip at the top of the table. The thousands who had already poured out of Old Trafford were about to miss one of the most sensational finishes of the season. The man who inflicted the damage was the inspirational Steve Bruce. With just four minutes remaining, he struck an equaliser and triggered an all-out United deluge for a winner. The minutes ticked by – 90 minutes, 92 minutes, 95 minutes, 97 minutes – and then with the whistle almost at the referee's lips, Bruce struck again. United had won 2–1. If ever Ferguson should complain about a referee adding on too much injury time, he would do well to remember that April afternoon and just how crucial it was to United's fortunes.

That result was another genuine turning point for Ferguson, pumping confidence into everyone at Old Trafford. There was suddenly a new conviction about United, a feeling that this time they could really do it. The determination that they had shown, plus the luck which had come their way, seemed to point towards an eventual title success. Everyone was pulling together.

What had also helped United's cause had been early dismissals from the two domestic cups and the UEFA Cup. In the League Cup they had gone out to Aston Villa in the third round, while in the FA Cup they had lost away to Sheffield United in the fifth. In the UEFA Cup they went out in the first round, losing on penalties to Torpedo Moscow. At the time those defeats had seemed harsh but in retrospect they were a blessing, allowing United to focus on the one trophy, and not to get sidelined or bogged down in fixture pile-ups.

Yet as the season drew to its conclusion Villa looked far from finished, even beating Arsenal at Highbury. United however kept their concentration and nerve, beating Coventry, Chelsea and then Crystal Palace. They were four points clear with only two games remaining. Ferguson was now learning about another kind of pressure: the sort brought by success. He'd experienced the lows at Old Trafford, but now the title was almost in the bag and the strain of cocking an ear elsewhere for other results was beginning to tell. He was just like any other supporter, unable to resist tuning in to find out how the opposition was doing. It was no good for the nerves. He decided to take a leaf out of Bill Shankly's book: don't worry about the opposition, just worry about your own side.

On Sunday 2 May, Villa took on Oldham in a game they simply had to win. Defeat or a draw would hand the title to United. The game was televised live but Ferguson decided not to watch, opting instead for a game of golf with his son Mark. The odds were on a Villa victory but then on the 17th tee a stranger wandered over towards them. 'Mr Ferguson?' he asked. Ferguson nodded politely, expecting to be asked for an autograph. 'Oldham have won,' the stranger said. 'United are champions.' They were the sweetest words Alex Ferguson had ever heard. A 26-year wait was over. Ferguson was the first United manager to pick up the trophy since Matt Busby. 'It was the day I truly became manager of Manchester United,' he said later, 'the moment when I could finally realise, even inwardly accept that I was the man in charge.'

That night the city of Manchester partied as it had rarely partied before. Crowds poured into the pubs, the noise of car horns drowned everything, flags waved. Ferguson rushed home only to find that a party had already begun at his house. The players were on the phone adding their congratulations and wanting to know if they could have a drink. Normally they were not allowed any on the night before a match but Ferguson relented. 'What the eye doesn't see,' he thought, reminding them that they did have a game the following evening and they shouldn't go too wild. It showed how much he could trust them.

The following night the championship came home to Old Trafford. Anyone who was there has described it as the greatest night in Old Trafford's long history. How they danced and sang! It was a mass party, with the fans determined to make the best of it, bent on letting Merseyside know that United were back and wouldn't be giving up the trophy for some time. Their opponents that night were Blackburn Rovers, managed by the former Liverpool player and manager Kenny Dalglish, a man who knew a thing or two about winning trophies. Dalglish was left in no doubt about what the fans reckoned to his former club.

Up in the stands in the directors' box one man watched in awe, as proud a fan as any, a broad grin stretching from one corner of his face to the other. It was Matt Busby. But now, at last, Ferguson could say that he had emerged from Busby's shadow. He was his own man.

CHAPTER NINETEEN

L'Enfant Terrible

Eric Cantona had rebel stamped all over him: a tortured look and temper to match; a thrusting chin, straight back and devilish eyes. And with his short-cropped hair, he resembled some nineteenth-century convict, pulled straight out of the pages of Balzac or Dickens. Cantona was no footballing saint. He was simply a man, often misunderstood, but equally the victim of his own wayward behaviour.

In an ebullient career that had swept him across France like the Mistral wind, he had left destruction wherever he played. At his first club Auxerre he thumped international goalkeeper Bruno Martini, then at his next club, Montpellier, he assaulted team-mate Jean-Claude Lemoult with a pair of his own over-sized boots. At champions Marseille he also had his moments, storming off in a huff during one match and ripping his shirt off in the process. At Bordeaux he skipped training, explaining pathetically that his dog had died. Here indeed was a sensitive man, though not sensitive enough of others' feelings, calling the national coach Henri Michel a 'shitbag'. He was fined by his club and then fined again as he hurled a football at a referee's head.

By now Cantona, not surprisingly, had acquired a reputation as a bad boy that far outstripped his reputation as a footballer. The French were growing weary of his antics, his monopoly of the headlines and his surly attitude. They even dubbed him *Le Brat*. At the disciplinary hearing after he had thrown the ball at the referee, Cantona lost patience and turned on his accusers, branding each of them 'idiots' to their face. At least it showed some bravery; you could hardly accuse him of hypocrisy. But it wasn't winning him friends, either in official circles or on the field. In France Cantona was just another footballer; a fine player but hardly unique, just one of many good players. Perhaps another manager might have tamed him but half a dozen had already tried and given up in the process. Maybe they had failed in refusing to listen to his own forthright but legitimate views about the game. Or maybe it was simply a lack of mutual respect.

There have been enough English and Scottish players in the same mould. One only has to think of Len Shackleton, once dubbed the clown prince of English football. In his autobiography, a chapter on football administrators was left blank. Shackleton and Cantona would have understood each other. They came from the same batch. They almost looked alike: tall, upright, handsome, full of swagger, always doing their own thing.

French football finally tired of Cantona's flippancy, and when Trevor Francis, manager of Sheffield Wednesday, hinted at some interest, Cantona was immediately despatched to the chilly Pennines of Yorkshire. It was French national manager Michel Platini who pointed out that English football might be worth a try, while it was his former Marseille partner Chris Waddle who recommended him to Trevor Francis. For Cantona it was a chance to begin afresh, in another culture where his reputation did not precede him. He arrived in Sheffield and enjoyed a week's trial but Francis was still undecided. Typically, when Francis suggested a second week Cantona told him where to put it. He was an established international and a week's trial ought

Ferguson after being appointed Manchester United manager from Aberdeen in November 1986 (*Mirror Syndication International*).

Ferguson lines up at Old Trafford with former Aberdeen stars Gordon Strachan and new signing Jim Leighton (*Mirror Syndication International*).

Running Scotland with Jock Stein in the run-up to the 1986 World Cup (*Mirror Syndication International*).

Caught you! Bob Paisley caught in the act of tapping Bryan Robson (*Mirror Syndication International*).

Ferguson with chairman Martin Edwards, whose loyal support helped him through the tough early years at Old Trafford (*Mirror Syndication International*).

The spirit of United past and present: Ferguson with Sir Matt Busby and the European Cup-Winners' Cup, May 1991 (*Mirror Syndication International*).

ABOVE: Ferguson with bargain-buy Cantona and record-breaking signing Roy Keane, two of his best moves into the transfer market (*Empics*); while Andy Cole, BELOW, another record signing, has not yet fulfilled the hopes put on him (*Mirror Syndication International*).

Ferguson and a worried-looking Brian Kidd, whose support and input have been vital factors in the management team at United (*Mirror Syndication International*).

He really can smile! United's 5-0 victory over Nottingham Forest on 28 April 1996 meant the title was almost won (*Mirror Syndication International*).

The Scottish connection. ABOVE: Ferguson collects his OBE with his family from Holyrood Palace (*Mirror Syndication International*). BELOW: He still goes back to Govan on a regular basis – here he tries out the Fergie's Fledglings of the future (*Mirror Syndication International*).

Ferguson hails the hero of the hour Eric Cantona after the FA Cup final victory over Liverpool on 11 May 1996 that secured a unique second Double (*Colorsport*).

From l-r: Philip Neville, Gary Neville, artist Michael Browne, Ferguson and David Beckham, in front of Browne's painting, *The Art of the Game*, which was bought by Eric Cantona in spring 1997. A fourth member of Fergie's Fledglings, Nicky Butt, is also depicted on the painting (*Mirror Syndication International*).

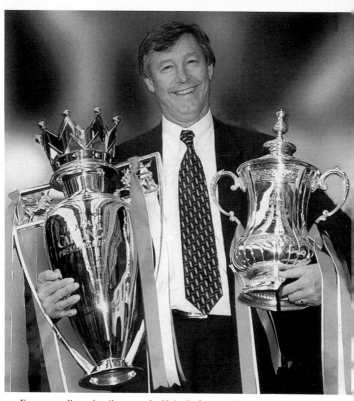

Ferguson collects the silverware for United's first ever Double in 1994 (*Mirror Syndication International*).

to be enough. He, the great Eric Cantona, was not going to hang around Yorkshire waiting for Trevor Francis and Sheffield Wednesday to make up their minds. Coming for a week's trial was humiliating enough without having to put up with an extension. It was insulting, the equivalent of Bordeaux inviting Gary Lineker for a trial and then doubting his qualities. It was beneath Cantona's dignity and he was, above all else, a proud man. Francis remained unconvinced and chose to let the chance slip.

Howard Wilkinson, on the other hand, a few miles up the road at Leeds, could recognise quality when he saw it and was prepared to take the risk. He'd heard the Cantona stories but was ready to give him the benefit of the doubt. Cantona was promptly signed for a million pounds while Francis ummed and ahhed in the background. Francis would soon regret his indecision – a bit like the man who failed to sign the Beatles.

Somebody once wisely suggested that it was better to be a lucky footballer than a good footballer. Cantona was fortunate; he was both. In his first season at Elland Road he was a championship winner as Howard Wilkinson's unfancied side stole the title from under Manchester United's noses. Cantona played his part – perhaps not as significant a part as he might have liked to suggest, but certainly without him, Leeds might have ended up in second spot behind United and the Eric Cantona story could have had a very different ending. To the Elland Road faithful Cantona soon became a folk hero. It was they who adopted the ooh-aah-Cantona chant.

But even with a championship medal pinned to his chest, it wasn't always a comfortable or easy relationship between player and team. His captain and team-mate at Leeds, Gary McAllister, has talked about 'a less attractive element . . . lurking just under the surface . . . there is a bit of him that I and a lot of others will never understand'. In fact in that championship-winning season Wilkinson named Cantona as a starter on only six occasions, though he came on as a substitute in another nine matches, weighing in with three vital goals. The following season Leeds and Cantona struggled, despite an early hat trick in a thrilling Charity Shield against Liverpool. It was to be the beginning of Cantona's romance with Wembley. After Leeds' elimination from Europe, Cantona's love affair with the Yorkshire side began to cool. He found himself on the bench more often than not and gradually the old restless feelings began to creep back. His unhappiness was becoming more evident by the day, and it was catching. What Leeds needed were players who in the words of McAllister could 'kick, bite and scratch to help us through a difficult season' – but, as McAllister adds, 'everyone knows that's not Eric's game'. Indeed, it wasn't. Cantona was a character who thrived on success, on encouragement, but when the chips were down he found it impossible to dig into his reserves to help others. As Leeds struggled, Cantona's state of mind deteriorated. According to one team-mate, he became more detached, more insular.

It was to be a casual telephone call between United chief executive Martin Edwards and his counterpart at Leeds, Bill Fotherby, that would bring Eric Cantona to Old Trafford. Ferguson was sitting talking to Edwards in his office, mulling over various possible signings. United needed a striker and had just had a £3.5 million bid for David Hirst rejected by Sheffield Wednesday. Who else could they go for?

'It's a pity we never got to know about Eric Cantona at Leeds,' mused the United manager. Ferguson had admired the Frenchman from a distance and could spot his un-doubted ability but had never reckoned him as a possible signing. Just then the phone rang; it was Fotherby. 'The timing was weird, absolutely uncanny,' admits Ferguson. Fotherby was making an inquiry on behalf of his manager Howard Wilkinson. He was interested in a defender and wondered what the chances were of signing Denis Irwin. Ferguson vigorously shook his head. Not at any price, he whispered.

Edwards and Fotherby got chatting. 'We're looking for a striker. I don't suppose there's any chance with Lee Chapman,' said Edwards cheekily. Fotherby gave him short shrift. Then Ferguson started gesturing and mouthing to Edwards: *Ask him about Cantona*, but Edwards couldn't understand what he was saying. Ferguson scribbled it down on a piece of paper. 'I hear Cantona's a bit unsettled,' Edwards suggested. 'I don't suppose there might be any business there.' Fotherby admitted that everything was not as it should be: there had been a dressing room bust-up. He would make an inquiry.

'We'd certainly be interested,' replied Edwards almost casually, 'although it would obviously depend on the price. And we'd want to do business as quickly as possible. If there's no chance we'd like to know early so that we can look elsewhere.'

Fotherby promised to talk to Howard Wilkinson as soon as possible and come back with an answer inside 24 hours.

Ferguson left Edwards to drive to Coventry, not feeling too hopeful. An hour later the car phone buzzed. It was Martin Edwards. Fotherby had already called back. 'We've got him,' said Edwards. Ferguson could barely believe his ears. 'How much do you think?' Edwards asked.

'Ooh, £1.6 million,' suggested Ferguson, making a stab in the dark.

'No,' replied Edwards, 'try again.' Ferguson had a few more stabs at a figure, each time going higher. 'No,' said Edwards. 'It's £1 million.'

The United manager was staggered. 'It's a steal,' he said. And so it was. By the end of the day a deal had been concluded. Cantona was on his way to Old Trafford.

There was much speculation on why Wilkinson sold the Elland Road hero so readily. In the pubs of Leeds much of it centred on gossip about a highly colourful love triangle, but it was all untrue. The real reason was far more pedestrian and mundane. It was simply to do with yet another substitution and a good old-fashioned row. Wilkinson, or Sergeant Bilko as he was known to the Elland Road staff, was a disciplinarian of the old brigade. When he named someone as a substitute they were expected to accept his decision. British football, after all, is not renowned for its democracy, unlike France and in particular Holland, where players' opinions weigh more. Wilkinson had simply tired of the rows and the Frenchman's sulking. He'd also noted how easily Cantona could be snuffed out of a game. Against Liverpool at Anfield, Ronnie Whelan had a dig at him after ten minutes and he was hardly seen after that. Wilkinson had also spotted Cantona's reluctance to take up unfamiliar positions when the going got tough. In a nutshell, Sergeant Bilko sized him up as an individualist, not a team player. And of course English football, or at least Wilkinson's game, is about teamwork and all too rarely about individualism. The blame for Leeds' failure in the European Cup was also laid at the door of the Frenchman, though by the fans rather than by Wilkinson.

Of course there was another side to it. A player with a reputation is always likely to be singled out. And just as Ronnie Whelan had a dig, so too did countless midfield toughies up and down the land. Needless to say, Cantona did not always shy away from them. It wasn't in his Gallic temperament to turn the other cheek. He was on too short a fuse and as everyone was to find out, the fuse sometimes burnt low.

What had been Wilkinson's problem was now Ferguson's. Eight moves in ten years was a worrying statistic. If Old Trafford had been a daunting prospect for Alex Ferguson that first morning back in November 1986, it was an equally frightening outlook for Eric Cantona precisely seven years later. Perhaps for the first time in his career, the Frenchman was at a club that was bigger than himself. At Old Trafford he was just one fine player among many. Here was a history he had never experienced before: Meredith, Roberts, Carey, the Babes, Munich, Law, Charlton and Best. Not to mention Busby. Cantona had at last found a natural home for his repertoire of talent. If only Shackleton had been able to find such a resting place.

Ferguson began to get the jitters. When he read the papers he wondered if he had really done the right thing. The back pages were all regurgitating Cantona's controversial past, and there was some new material: the Leeds players were also being quoted. The innuendos and stories were flying about, but Ferguson's doubts were short-lived.

Cantona took to his new home as if it had all been predestined. Doubts there may have been, but they never surfaced; or if they did it was in the privacy of his own mind. Outwardly, Cantona was his usual arrogant – call it confident if you wish – self. Not for him any look of bemusement or nervousness. His inner assurance saw to that. He stuck his chest out and held his head high. Even his new team-mates, pipped for the previous season's title at the final post by his former side, took to him and his abundant self-assurance. If they had doubts following their title upset, Cantona did not share them.

Just as his sulking could be catching, so too could his dedication. He worked at his training, always the first out *de bonne heure* and the last in, always putting in more effort than anyone else, always looking to perfect his game. In short Cantona had a professional attitude which had been ignored by the media and others. It was a side of him that neither his new team-mates nor Ferguson had known about, and it was just what United needed. Here was a man who could not only reproduce all the refinements of the game, but whose mood was infectious to those around him. As long as he was happy, United would prosper. The danger for Ferguson was if Cantona should become despondent, homesick, rejected. Then, as Wilkinson had discovered at Leeds, he would have a problem.

Cantona was a hit with the normally critical Stretford Enders from the start. The very fact that he had rejected champions Leeds to play for United was itself enough of a bonus, but when he displayed a range of skills and degree of arrogance rarely seen since Law and Best, he had no trouble in winning over his supporters. At Old Trafford they like nothing better than skill, a factor that has often compensated for a lack of points. Hang the victory, it's the style that matters. At Anfield, in contrast, winning matters more than anything.

Ferguson's immediate task was to keep Cantona happy. Arsenal manager George Graham, in an interview with the *Independent*, described Cantona as 'a cry baby who will let you down at the highest level'. Alex Ferguson found no such problems. Cantona's early displays could only draw the utmost praise from his manager. Ferguson quickly understood that Cantona was the kind of player who needed to have praise heaped on him. The more praise he received, the happier he was, and the better he responded. Astrologists would recognise him as a typical Gemini: one moment up, the next down. Ferguson may not have been a regular reader of the stars but he intuitively knew how to deal with his prize asset.

Cantona pulled on a United shirt for the first time in Lisbon for a friendly against Benfica to mark the majestic Eusebio's 50th birthday. He followed this with his league debut against Norwich at Old Trafford on 12 December and five months later was the proud owner of a league championship medal, one of the few players to have picked up title honours in consecutive seasons with different clubs. Ferguson couldn't help but think there was something of the talisman about his latest signing – but of course his 18 league goals also helped. The next season United secured both the league and the FA Cup.

Cantona's munificent contributions to United's triumphs were however to be sternly re-evaluated in January 1995. Against Crystal Palace at Selhurst Park, Cantona was involved in an 'incident' that was to lead the ITN *News at Ten* that evening and would fast become a *cause célèbre*. It was also to test his relationship with Alex Ferguson to the limit. After giving a bit of a kicking to the Palace defender Richard Shaw, Cantona was, quite properly, shown a red card. That was bad enough but worse was to follow. As Cantona made his way towards the players' tunnel, a torrent of abuse was aimed at him. In particular, one supporter was firing racist abuse faster than a loaded machine gun. Cantona, already incensed by his sending off, reacted with fury, lunging at his abuser in what was to become dubbed his famous kung fu kick.

An almighty commotion immediately erupted as players, police and fans started swapping punches in a general free-for-all. Ferguson watched in disbelief. Earlier he had stopped to sign an autograph close to that section but had turned away when he too was subjected to a shower of abuse. Back in the dressing room Cantona sat in silence. Ferguson was fuming. 'You've let the team down and you've let yourself down,' he told him. He got little response. Nobody seemed to be quite sure what had happened. Cantona remained tight-lipped; kit-man Norman Davies seemed to think something had been thrown, maybe a can. But nobody could be quite sure. In fact, it was not until Ferguson returned home and watched a video replay the following morning that he discovered precisely what had happened.

Before the United party rushed back to Manchester Ferguson had a quick meeting with the directors. With emotions running high and a pack of journalists on the prowl, they agreed that for the moment they should not get hysterical. The police also called Ferguson into a room but assured him that everything would be investigated thoroughly, in the cold light of day when tempers had cooled. 'We shall be interviewing everybody, including the players,' they insisted, adding that they had also had a complaint against Paul Ince who was alleged to have assaulted someone. It was the first Ferguson had heard of this – yet another problem. It had been a disastrous night, with United's 1–1 draw now fading into insignificance.

The players were out of their bath and on to the coach quicker than normal. As they made their way to the airport for their flight back to Manchester, not much was said. Most of the players sat in silence, peering out of their windows. There was little inclination for the usual games of cards.

Back home Ferguson's family were still up, waiting for him to return. Yet even though they had videoed the news for him and described it in detail, he could not bring himself to watch. That night he tossed and turned, unable to settle or get it off his mind. Eventually he rose early, went downstairs and turned on the video. He was horrified. 'I couldn't believe what I saw,' he later confessed. Ferguson had not realised – nor, it seemed, had anyone else in the United party – the full extent of Cantona's action. He had never seen anything quite like it before on a football pitch and it came as a shock. Cantona had simply leapt into the crowd and delivered a kung fu-style kick at a spectator.

There was speculation that Cantona had been appallingly abused, but this was no excuse. Players get abused every week in football, especially black players, and not just by spectators. Other players can also be abusive, trying to wind up their victims. Ferguson had seen players react to other players when they were abused, but this was the first case he knew of a player attacking a spectator because of what they had said. A few years earlier John Barnes had been the focus of some appalling racial abuse on Merseyside, with bananas being hurled on the pitch during a derby match against Everton. If anyone could be justified in attacking a spectator then it had to be Barnes, but he had never retaliated. You just didn't do it. Ferguson himself had played in enough Old Firm matches to know what abuse was like. In the frenetic, highly charged atmosphere of those religious confrontations, every player suffered verbal abuse from the moment they came out of the tunnel. He might have been hot-headed himself when he was young, but the idea of attacking a spectator never even occurred to him. It would have caused a riot. In the past year or so, United had been on the receiving end of some disgraceful abuse. Maybe it was to do with their success, maybe it was just old rivalries. He could understand the feelings between United and Liverpool – the abuse went both ways – but earlier in the season, he'd noticed how aggressive the fans at Elland Road had been. Sitting in the dugout, he himself had been the focus of much of their vitriol.

The abuse against United that season had indeed struck new heights. It had been gathering pace ever since United had won the title in 1993. United fans remembered their visit to homely Swindon the season after winning the title and being subjected to a torrent of abuse. They expected that kind of vitriol at Leeds and Liverpool but not at Swindon, for heaven's sake. Everywhere they went hostility was unleashed on them.

'I can't believe it,' he told his wife as he sat watching the video.

She wondered what he would do. 'You can't ignore it,' she counselled wisely, 'even if it means losing the championship.'

It was a grim dilemma but he had to agree. For once Ferguson would not be able to stand by one of his players, even if it was Eric Cantona. This time he had to put distance between himself and the Frenchman. Cantona had been in trouble already that season when he'd been sent off at Ibrox in a friendly against Rangers. Ferguson had supported him then and had always supported him in the past, but there came a point when excuses were no longer applicable. It led to suspension, and that caused problems for the team. The Frenchman was clearly in the wrong and neither Ferguson nor United could be seen to be condoning his behaviour. As the day wore on it became ever clearer that some kind of disciplinary action would need to be taken by the club. United could not abdicate responsibility.

A media rumpus had erupted. Old Trafford and The Cliff had been invaded by the press corps, adding to the handful of regular football writers they knew well. Now there was a new, unfamiliar pack. The cameras of ITN, the BBC, Granada, Sky, even French television, had all gathered threateningly, along with a crowd of newspaper journalists. The telephone rang incessantly. Training was almost impossible. Everyone, players and staff, just wanted to talk about the previous night's incident. They'd all watched it on television that morning as it was replayed over and over again. The front pages of the tabloids were full of it; so too were the quality broadsheets. It was the lead story of the day.

As the pressures mounted throughout the day, Ferguson's instinctive reaction was to suspend Cantona, but it was not that simple. The police had already opened inquiries, and the Football Association were involved as well as the PFA. The club would have to tread carefully. If they suspended a player, was that an admission of guilt, and how would they then prepare their submission for trial? But the signal from upstairs was that the FA clearly expected United to take unilateral action. The question really was how severe his punishment should be. The morning papers were already calling for a long ban – one even suggested that Cantona should be thrown out of the game altogether. United were in a no-win situation. No matter what ban they handed down, someone, somewhere, whether it was the papers or Lancaster Gate, would demand a stiffer sentence; and there was no knowing what sentence the courts would hand down. Finally, after a difficult meeting, Ferguson and the board agreed on a ban that would last to the end of the season. A ban ending any earlier would have looked mightily suspicious.

All Ferguson had to do now was to inform the player himself. Fortunately the Frenchman took it better than his team-mates. The players were angry, rightly protective of one of their number. Footballers may be arrogant and overpaid, yet they can be surprisingly supportive of one another when the chips are down. No doubt it's part of the breeding, attackers going back to help defenders and defenders going forward to strengthen the attack. Now the United players gave Ferguson, by his own admission, a hard time. They accused the club of overreacting, of failing to take the abuse of the terraces into account. Paul Ince, in particular, knew how racist and abusive an away crowd could be. But it was no good shouting at the manager. The decision had been made and that was that. Ferguson was uncomfortable. He could sympathise with them, even admire them for their support of Cantona, but he had enough political nous to know that it was not quite so easy or simple. There were other considerations to be taken into account, not least United's image to the outside world. The meeting broke up unhappily.

Of course the question that inevitably arose was: would this have happened in Sir Matt's day? And if it had, would he have shown Cantona the door? The answers were simple. Yes to the first question and no to the second. Sir Matt had more than his fair share of problems with George Best, repeatedly showing him a leniency that many another manager would never have tolerated. It was simply a case of accepting that highly talented individuals often come accompanied by a bagful of other problems, as demonstrated by Maradona, Paul Gascoigne, Rodney Marsh and Stan Bowles, among others. If you want individualism you sometimes have to pay the price. Throughout his managerial time at Old Trafford, Sir Matt never once showed Best the door. He was always understanding, fatherly and considerate. It was one of his successors, Tommy Docherty, who finally pointed Best in the direction of the exit door. Denis Law was another who gave Busby problems; often impetuous, temperamental and carefree, and regularly making that long walk to the tunnel. 'He never knew what to do with me. He would just shake his head,' jokes Law today. Ferguson got it spot on when he once suggested that 'not everyone can be like Bobby Charlton. Winners are winners and there are very few angels like Gary Lineker.'

The affair would rumble on for days. Not unexpectedly, United were accused of being too lenient. One paper even suggested that Cantona should have been sacked and immediately transferred to one of the Italian clubs always said to be hankering after his signature. Such a thought never occurred to United or Ferguson, yet they had taken a risk in supporting the Frenchman. If Cantona was to return from suspension and commit some similar misdemeanour, the press would, quite rightly, crucify Ferguson and the board. Ferguson had to feel sure that Cantona would not do the same thing again, that he could trust him and rely on his behaviour. It had to mark a turning point for Cantona. He had to stop playing the *enfant terrible* and become a responsible person. He would not be given any more chances. Even if he was simply shown the red card, the Football Association could be guaranteed to come down heavily on him, and as for the press . . . The only outcome then would be to sell him.

Cantona went off for a brief holiday to escape it all, but of course it wasn't the end of the situation. A week or so later the United man was reported to have threatened a photographer attempting to take a picture of him and his pregnant wife while they were sunbathing on some faraway beach. Fortunately, on this occasion most people seemed to sympathise with Cantona rather than with the British press and its harassing tactics, but there was still the matter of a court case and the Football Association's suspension.

Late in February the latter decided to ban Cantona until 1 October, a ban of almost nine months. The following month, on the day that Ferguson was being invested at Buckingham Palace with the CBE, Eric Cantona, a few miles away, was being sentenced to two weeks' imprisonment. It was a harsh sentence that left everyone at United shocked. The club appealed, and at the end of the month the sentence, not surprisingly, was reduced to a period of community service. It almost marked the end of a two-month period that had been a strain on everyone at Old Trafford, but especially on Cantona and Ferguson. The manager had had more than a few sleepless nights through the whole episode – and there was still one twist remaining in the tale.

Although United had stood by Cantona it was not always certain that their affections were reciprocated. Cantona had maintained a silence on his future, never committing himself to the club. Not unexpectedly, his emotions were still running high. He was still confused and uncertain. Did he want to remain in English football; would he be better off getting away from the media circus that had accompanied him for so long; should he go back home to France or even try a period in Italy? None of these questions had been tackled, but come April it was time to sort out a few answers and a new contract.

Ferguson and club officials met with the Frenchman and his advisers towards the end of April. They quickly established that, despite all, Cantona remained keen to stay at Old Trafford. But it was also apparent that terms for his new contract were going to be high. The club were left with two options: either to meet his demands or to sell him. Internazionale of Milan had already made an inquiry, tabling an offer of £4.5 million. It was not a particularly high sum of money in the inflationary world of transfer fees, but it was as much as they could probably expect for the Frenchman. No English club was going to make an offer, and transfer fees in Spain had plummeted in recent years.

It was a case of Italy or nowhere. That undoubtedly suited Cantona, as long as he knew he could sign a lucrative deal. United knew that they could take up Inter's offer at any point. The only problem was that if they sold Cantona they would have to find a suitable replacement. The names of Matt Le Tissier and Stan Collymore were high on Ferguson's list, but signing either of them would set the club back at least £7 million. Moreover, they would face stiff opposition from the likes of Liverpool, Everton and Newcastle. Getting their signature on a contract was by no means a foregone conclusion. United were also committed to constructing a new north stand which was certain to tie up cash in the forthcoming year. In effect it meant that money available for transfers was nowhere near as much as the newspapers suggested. It would be far easier to stand by Cantona and agree a new contract with him. It was a gamble but at least they knew what they were getting. Ferguson had little difficulty in persuading Martin Edwards to stick with Cantona, and a £1.5 million deal was quickly drawn up. Cantona was more than delighted to put his signature to it.

Ferguson drew a huge sigh of relief, and Cantona began his community service with enthusiasm, each week coaching schoolchildren in the Salford area. 'He was a shining example,' reported his probation officer, despite the enormous press attention that his earlier sessions drew. But there was to be a further hitch. Cantona was living in an hotel, and his wife had just had a baby. He was not happy. Then in August the Football Association interfered, suggesting that Cantona could not even play in any pre-season friendlies. Cantona and Ferguson were outraged. It seemed that Cantona was to be forever hounded by the authorities. The Frenchman sank into a deep depression.

His earlier decision to remain at Old Trafford was suddenly under reconsideration. His agent made contact with Inter Milan and the deal that seemed to have disappeared was quickly resurrected. Cantona was on his way to Paris. The likelihood was that he was about to conclude a deal with Internazionale. When Ferguson heard he immediately booked a flight to Paris and booked into the King George V Hotel. He was not alone. A pack of journalists were hot on his heels. Shortly after he arrived, Cantona's agent Jean-Jacques Bertrand turned up on his motorbike. The two of them sneaked out of the back door and with Ferguson on the back of the bike, they made for Cantona's favourite restaurant, owned by a close friend. His friend offered to close the restaurant for the evening and the four of them sat down to eat and chat. 'We've sorted out the problem,' Ferguson told Cantona. 'You can play in the friendlies as long as they are not "official".' The look on Cantona's face told everything.

In the absence of Cantona, United's season had come to a disastrous end. Pipped at the post by Blackburn in the final game of the season, they also lost out in the Cup final, going down 1–0 to Everton. Cantona's presence could have made such a difference. One kung fu kick, one irrational moment, had proved costly: two trophies, a place in the European Cup, and a great deal of money. But it was to the credit of both manager and player that they should draw strength from the predicament. Cantona returned with a vengeance and, in the final run-in of the following season, vindicated Ferguson's faith in him as he scored with alacrity, claiming the championship for United and then topping it off with a late goal in the Cup final to give United a second Double. Cantona had repaid his outstanding debt to Ferguson, the club and its supporters. Roald Dahl couldn't have conjured up a better script.

There is an old Spanish proverb that suggests that 'the blow that does not break you, makes you'. It was to prove uncannily accurate for both Alex Ferguson and Eric Cantona. The Frenchman's kung fu kick at Selhurst Park was to be his low point in English soccer but also a point from which he could grow. From that moment on he stopped acting the part of *enfant terrible* and began to assume a new responsibility. It was make or break for Cantona. Had Ferguson not stood by him, then he would almost certainly have quit Old Trafford for the San Siro. Quite what would have happened then is anyone's guess.

As for Ferguson, he was to be fully vindicated, his faith repaid with an heroic end-of-season goal-scoring spree and a delicious Cup final goal that secured a second Double. But it had been a nerve-wracking experience for him and not one that he would ever want to repeat. For some time it had been touch and go before the storm settled and Cantona justified the faith that his manager had placed in him. In the end it was much to do with mutual respect and a certain similarity of character. Ferguson himself was no virgin when it came to facing the authorities. There was a rebel streak in him too. As a player in Scotland he had been known to lash out and had been sent off six times. But at least he could understand Cantona, trade anger with him. The key, as Ferguson suggested to Cantona, was to focus your anger, not let it govern your actions. Anger needed to be constructively put to use, and not remain a negative influence.

'Eric knows he can depend on me,' says Ferguson. 'He knows I don't desert my players. They get it between the eyeballs generally if it's a criticism, but Eric knows that whatever happens it will be in the dressing room or in my office and that's the end of it. I don't bear grudges. I don't have time and it's not part of my management strategy.'

'Alex Ferguson is someone I can trust,' says Cantona on his *Eric The King* video. The feeling was mutual. That Ferguson could appreciate Cantona's dilemma said much for the man and his ability to understand his players. For Cantona he was prepared to abandon the policy of no superstars. That he should even take the trouble and patience when others had so swiftly shown Cantona the door spoke volumes for his respect for the Frenchman's talents. Cantona was crucial to United, the diamond in the crown, the one man whose footballing instincts were unmatched in the Premiership. He could turn a game with just one shimmy, one delicate touch, one back-heeled flick. He was worth the patience and Ferguson appreciated that.

Cantona had come to symbolise everything about United – arrogance, flair, enigma, the love-to-be-hated attitude. It was little wonder the fans took him to their hearts. He was the reincarnation of everything that United represented. That was what made him so special. He was the natural heir to Billy Meredith, George Best, Denis Law, Lou Macari and all the other Old Trafford favourites down the years who boasted the same sod-the-world-we're-United characteristic.

But there would still be the occasional heart-stopping moment when Cantona would give his manager apoplexy. There was the Charity Shield match at Wembley against Newcastle when Cantona shoved Philippe Albert to the ground in full view of a massive worldwide audience. As Cantona was ushered aside by the Liverpool-born referee, Ferguson feared the worst. For a moment his heart stopped, the headlines in the following morning's papers already beginning to flash before his eyes. But it was only a friendly and this time the referee was lenient, perhaps a little too understanding. Cantona escaped with a caution, a yellow card, and Ferguson returned to his seat, flashing a knowing glance in the direction of Brian Kidd. He was lucky, but Ferguson knew that in the heat of the Premiership he might not always be so lucky, might not always come across so generous a referee, especially playing away from home. How permanent Cantona's conversion would be was still anybody's guess.

As it turned out it was as permanent as anything in Cantona's life. A day after the 1997 Cup final he sprang the surprise of all surprises: he was retiring. He was five days off his 31st birthday and in a prepared statement said that he simply wanted to retire at his peak. It came without any warning and in typical Cantona style he was out of the country when the announcement was made, off on holiday, destination unknown. Ferguson was left to pick up the pieces.

Cantona had not enjoyed the best of seasons. At times he looked disinterested, short of puff, his mind elsewhere. Against Chelsea at Old Trafford, as United went down Cantona wandered about the centre circle ball-watching. He didn't seem to have the inclination or the will to battle. He had lost something. Perhaps he recognised it himself, or perhaps United's failure in Europe had underlined his own unfulfilled ambitions. He told Alex Ferguson on the Wednesday after the season had finished, just a few days before the official announcement. Ferguson tried to dissuade him, but once Cantona's mind is made up there is no changing it. The following day Cantona met with the chairman and after confirming that he was definitely going, arrangements were made for the announcement. The accountants must have groaned as they thought of lost opportunities and all that merchandise lying around with the man's name and picture on it. Maybe they would become collectors' items.

As Ferguson told the world's press, the despondency in his eyes was plain to see. The usual smile and laugh were gone. He acknowledged Cantona's massive contribution to United's success in the five years that he had been at Old Trafford. With Cantona in the side rather than sitting out the best part of a season suspended, they might well have done another Double. His influence had been extensive, not just on the field but off it as well, in helping to develop United's youngsters. Ferguson had lost his talisman and now he had the unenviable task of finding another. It wouldn't be easy.

CHAPTER TWENTY

The Double

The dark shadow that had been cast across Old Trafford by Busby for more than a quarter of a century had finally been lifted. The collective sigh of relief was clearly audible. The past was behind them.

And in a way Busby also was set free. He'd been an ill man for some time. The Munich disaster had left physical scars as well as mental ones. His wife had died and he himself, now 84, was being cared for in a local nursing home. In January 1994, just eight months after he had seen his beloved United celebrate the championship, he died. Manchester mourned. Busby would always be remembered, along with his teams which had brought so much honour, promise and anticipation. Probably no one would ever replace Busby or generate so much affection around Old Trafford, but in winning the league Ferguson had at least proved that somebody else could take the club to the top. Suddenly he was freed from the legacy of Busby. The only problem was how to follow up their league championship. The answer was the Double. It would be a fitting tribute to the Father of Old Trafford.

Ferguson might have achieved his immediate ambition, but it was no excuse for relaxing or thinking that United were suddenly omnipotent. You have to build on success, he told the board one evening. It's better to buy players when you are on top than when you are struggling. Although Ferguson had bought virtually an entire new team since his arrival, there was always room for improvement. Only Bryan Robson remained from the Ron Atkinson period, now 36, but as truculent and determined as ever. Robson had been a tremendous servant to the club over the years but he couldn't go on forever. Ferguson would need to find a replacement and groom him for the role of midfield general. Finding a replacement for Robson seemed a tricky proposition, but Ferguson already had his man in mind.

As soon as he saw Roy Keane playing for Nottingham Forest he had become an admirer. Keane showed all the characteristics of a Robson. He was fiercely competitive, not afraid to put himself about in the midfield and even managed to sneak regularly into the penalty area, where he was capable of grabbing goals. What's more, he was only 22 years old and was ready for a bigger stage than Forest. Other clubs showed interest, in particular Blackburn Rovers, but United always had the edge. Blackburn might have had resources but they were still in the process of building their side. Nevertheless, Keane still cost United a record fee of £3.75 million in July 1993. It wasn't the first time United and Blackburn had crossed swords in pursuit of a player that summer.

Throughout the previous season Ferguson had maintained a watchful eye on Alan Shearer, who was regularly hitting the target for the Saints. Southampton were still refusing to consider offers, but a £3.3 million bid by Blackburn Rovers in July suddenly had them re-thinking. Before the week was out Shearer was talking with Kenny Dalglish, the Blackburn manager. Ferguson moved swiftly, agreeing to match Blackburn's offer. Southampton accepted and left the decision to Shearer. The young striker came up to Old Trafford but left Ferguson in no doubt that he was not satisfied with the terms on offer.

Ferguson had deliberately constructed a rigid wages system at United that was built on appearance fees and win bonuses. Any player coming to the club was expected to fall into line with the system. If the system was to work there could be no exceptions; everyone had to operate within the range of pay scales. It was a touch of the old shop steward coming out in Ferguson. Blackburn, with all their wealth, were able to guarantee Shearer a far higher basic salary. And so Ferguson lost his man.

With Keane added to the squad, United began the 1993–94 season as favourites to lift the title again. The bookies wouldn't be wrong. Like greyhounds in their starting stalls, United could barely wait for the off. And once they were away it was to a flying start. They notched up five wins and a draw in their first six games and had shot to the top of the table. Much to the relief of the trailing pack, United lost their next game at Stamford Bridge, but it was a mere hiccup. International duty had left almost an entire squad jaded and jet-lagged after a batch of energy-sapping mid-week internationals. World Cup qualifier duty during the summer had also left a number of Ferguson's foreign imports feeling the long-term strain. A week's recuperation soon had them chewing at the leash again, and just to prove that they were not vulnerable, United pieced together eight consecutive wins to open up an 11-point lead over Norwich at the top of the table. There looked to be no stopping them – domestically, at least. In Europe the picture was somewhat different.

Winning the league title had given Ferguson another shot at the European Cup. It was the first time United had been in the competition since 1969, when they narrowly lost to AC Milan in the semi-final, defending the crown they had won the previous year. Indeed United had reached the semi-final stages on every occasion they had participated, but the 1993–94 season was to hold no such glamour. In the opening round United comfortably overcame the Hungarian champions Honved but in the next round faced a tricky tie with Galatasaray of Turkey. It really should not have presented major problems for United, especially after they'd taken a two-goal lead only 13 minutes after kicking off at Old Trafford, but then they relaxed and became careless. Galatasaray took advantage, equalising and then going ahead before Cantona snatched a desperate late equaliser.

After the game Ferguson was fuming, rounding on his players for letting a comfortable lead slip. They had become too casual, had stopped playing as a team, with one or two players, especially Giggs, intent on going for glory by hanging on to the ball far too long. They had not played for each other but for themselves. The players sat silently as Ferguson tore into them. The seeds of United's exit had been sown, and Ferguson sensed it.

In Turkey a fortnight later they needed to win or to come away with a 4–4 draw. Neither result looked possible. 'Welcome to Hell', read a banner to greet them at the airport in Istanbul. Their welcoming committee wasn't exactly over-friendly, although the tabloids back home were exaggerating slightly when they described it as a 'riot'.

In the end, it turned out as Ferguson feared, a goalless draw, and United were out of Europe. Moreover, Cantona was shown a red card in the final minute as a frustrated United probed for a late winner. Worse was to follow. As United made their way past shrieking, celebrating Turkish fans, they were attacked in the tunnel. Robson was struck by a policeman and as their coach later made its way to the airport a brick was hurled at a window. The glass shattered but fortunately the brick itself did not penetrate – otherwise Steve Bruce, sitting with his head against the window, might never have kicked a ball again.

In the dressing room after the match there was silence. Ferguson realised the enormity of what had happened. It wasn't just the losing of the game, or the loss in potential revenue, but the loss of valuable European experience. All he could say to reporters was that it was a 'shambles'. He would have plenty of time to reflect on the wisdom of leaving Mark Hughes out of the side, and there would be enough journalists ready to remind him. The whole episode left a bad taste. Nobody would want to return to Istanbul for some time. But there was some compensation: an early exit from Europe meant that they could concentrate on the domestic programme. Europe had been a rude awakening.

In their next game, at Maine Road, the after-effects were written all over their faces. They were nervous and hesitant, even a little sluggish. City swept into a two-goal lead. But after the interval United came back into their stride, slamming three goals past their rivals to win 3–2. Their astonishing run in the Premiership continued through the autumn and winter as they stretched their lead at the top of the table. At the end of November they were 14 points clear of Leeds United. They would not be defeated again until early March, when Chelsea came to Old Trafford, but there were enough draws and enough points dropped along the way to give their challengers some hope. However, rather than Leeds United seizing the opportunity, it was Blackburn Rovers who emerged as United's chief rivals, especially after snatching a draw at Old Trafford on Boxing Day. When in early April Blackburn inflicted a third defeat on them at Ewood Park, thanks to Alan Shearer, the man who had rejected United, the gap was suddenly narrowed to three points. After that performance Ferguson must have wondered if breaking the pay structure to sign Shearer might not have been worth consideration after all. Shearer was in a class of his own and perhaps that had to be acknowledged. After all, football was moving into a new and different financial era, and the pendulum of power was already swinging in the direction of players.

If United had a problem it was that they had become

sidetracked. Europe might have slipped off their agenda at an early stage but in domestic competitions they looked unbeatable. In the League Cup they brushed all opposition aside, reaching the final where they faced Aston Villa. In the early stages, Ferguson had looked to have his sights set on higher targets, opting to give some of his reserves a run-out. But even fitting reserves into the engine made little difference: it still kept running like a well-oiled machine. By that stage United were beginning to dream of a treble, and the prospect of achieving something that no other side had ever managed was beginning to whet the appetite. However, if there was one man who could suss United it was their former manager Ron Atkinson, now managing Villa. He'd done it once before as manager of Sheffield Wednesday, and now, in the final at Wembley, he would do it again.

The stakes were now so high that Ferguson reverted to his natural eleven, leaving the reserves who had served him so well in the earlier stages of the competition on the sidelines. In retrospect he regretted his decision. 'Once they got a sniff of Wembley . . . the regular lads . . . were desperate to be involved,' he told one journalist. But there were crucial players missing. Schmeichel had been sent off against Charlton in the FA Cup and was suspended. Les Sealey – good old Les Sealey – stepped into the fray yet again. Villa had them figured from the start, refusing to concede any space in the midfield while stifling the advances of Giggs and Kanchelskis. Villa went two goals up, but then Mark Hughes pulled one back with ten minutes remaining, and United threw everything forward in search of an equaliser. It was all or nothing. Of course this left them short at the back. Villa counter-attacked and Kanchelskis, racing back to help out, handled on the line. The Ukrainian was off and Saunders converted the resulting penalty. There wasn't much you could say. Ferguson acknowledged that he had been outfoxed by his predecessor.

Morale crashed around Old Trafford. Everywhere else there was rejoicing – United were not the most popular of clubs and their ill discipline was hardly winning them friends. But then, as Ferguson might have mused, there is little United can do to win friends.

Ferguson and his staff had to do a quick repair job on morale, deciding to impose a ban on any player talking to the press. He was angry at the way the press, and the tabloids in particular, were painting his players. The only solution was to stop giving them access. 'From now on you don't talk to the papers,' he told his players. 'I took the decision that none of the players should talk to the press until the Premiership was finished,' he later explained.

It didn't go down well with Fleet Street's football writers. 'It only made us more angry, more anti-United, more anti the whole United set-up with its commercialism and we're-bigger-than-God attitude,' remembered one top football scribe.

It was all part of the siege mentality; United were being attacked on all fronts. Ever since winning the title they had come under assault. The attacks came both on and off the field. On the field they had suffered with a succession of players being sent off. At times the players felt they were being provoked, that referees were more mindful of any United misdemeanours. Three players had been sent off in consecutive matches. Kanchelskis had been dismissed at Wembley in the League Cup final, Cantona had gone against Swindon where the crowd turned disturbingly nasty, and then at Highbury Cantona had again been sent off. Not surprisingly the press hounded them. They dubbed them 'bad boys' and seemed to revel in United's uncertainty. Cantona in particular was singled out – from being United's inspiration he was now the crazy Frenchman returning to his old evil ways.

In a way it all played into United's hands. The Mancs liked nothing better than being under attack, especially when it was southerners or authority doing the attacking. That had always been the United, the Manchester style. Opposing fans, opposing players, the tabloids, the Premiership – United and its fans would take them all on. Kitted out in their black shirts and black shorts they were ready to do battle with anyone. United fans will sneakingly tell you that of all their away kits the one they loved the most was the all-black one. And it was not for a good reason.

The siege mentality went back a long way, perhaps as far back as the days of Munich when the club and its fans had been forced to pull together to survive and overcome their tragedy. There was something of the Celtic nature running through Old Trafford. Ferguson could understand it and coming from Glasgow also knew how to manipulate it.

United may have been out of Europe but they were still riding high in the league and the FA Cup. After beating Oldham on Easter Monday they were three points ahead of their nearest rivals Blackburn Rovers. It might have been an unconvincing display but it was three points in the bag. Dion Dublin had returned to the side for a rare appearance and had scored the winner. A week later Dublin retained his place as United again faced Oldham, this time in the FA Cup semi-final, at Wembley.

United's progress towards Wembley had been steady rather than sweeping, though in fairness most of their games had been away from home. In the third round they had gone to Bramall Lane and beaten Sheffield United 1–0. Mark Hughes struck a memorable goal and then got sent off. He wouldn't be alone that season, as ill discipline became infectious at United. Then in the fourth round United travelled to Carrow Road and won 2–0. It was a game perhaps best remembered for a Cantona kick, missed by the referee but spotted by everyone on television. Fortunately the Frenchman got away with it.

The fifth round presented a tricky prospect, away to

Wimbledon. The Dons had a habit of upsetting most sides, though it had to be said that they had rarely upset United over the years. And 1994 was going to be no different. Three sweet goals from Irwin, Cantona and Ince settled the matter.

United were into the quarter-finals and for once came out of the FA's little black bag first of all. A home tie against Charlton Athletic. Not much chance of a Cup upset – though there might well have been when Peter Schmeichel dashed 30 yards out of his goal to upend Kim Grant's lone charge and was promptly sent off. Schmeichel's team-mates raged at him. They were now down to ten men and beginning to earn something of a reputation. But at least it seemed to shake United and roused the Old Trafford crowd out of their afternoon snooze. 'Ferguson didn't have to say anything to us in the dressing room at half-time,' reported Giggs, 'we were so fired up.' In the second half United tore into Charlton, their self-belief visibly returning, and went on to win 3–1.

And so to Wembley for the semi-final against friendly Oldham – surely another comfortable cruise into the final. But it was not to be. United were wretched. Dion Dublin acted as a lone front runner while Schmeichel and others whacked long balls in his direction. 'The belief had gone,' Ince explained afterwards. An Oldham goal was inevitable. Ferguson's shoulders were slumped, his dream of the Double turning into a nightmare. Then along came Hughes and with one mighty smack of the ball wiped the smiles off Oldham faces just as they were set to celebrate. Only two minutes were left on the clock. From that moment on everyone knew United's name was written all over the Cup, and probably the league championship as well. They were invincible.

The replay was a foregone conclusion. At Maine Road Kanchelskis almost single-handedly destroyed Oldham, even scoring one himself as United went on the rampage, winning 4–1. Ferguson applauded him off the field. There could be no stopping United now. But lo and behold, a week later at Selhurst Park they lost to Wimbledon. Fortunately Blackburn had lost earlier that day, so it hardly mattered.

Manchester City were next, but there were few fears. Ferguson welcomed his Frenchman back from suspension and Eric, fittingly, marked his return with a brace of goals. The season was now winding to a dramatic conclusion: four games remained and United sat on a three-point lead and a healthy goal difference. The title was in their hands. Ferguson remained confident but the same could not be said of most United supporters, who viewed their next fixture at Elland Road with some dread.

United/Leeds fixtures had not been known for their warmth in recent years, and the stealing of Cantona had hardly helped generate much affection. One thing was for sure: Leeds would be fired up for this game, determined to halt United's progress towards the title.

Ferguson called on them to give a professional performance. He didn't want anyone getting themselves sent off. It would be tense out there, he reminded them in the dressing room, and a sending off would only add to the pressure cooker atmosphere. They had to come out of this game unscathed and with three points. They must keep calm, keep their heads, play with intelligence. If they could win this they would be worthy champions.

It worked. They closed ranks, sweated for each other and came away with a 2–0 victory. It wasn't quite the title. Blackburn won at West Ham to keep their hopes faintly alive, but it was all down to United. As long as they kept winning, the title would be theirs. In fact they didn't need to. They won their next game at Ipswich and then sat back to watch as Blackburn went to Coventry. Rovers lost and United, without even playing, were champions again.

It wasn't as good as the first time, admitted Ferguson, but then you would not expect it to be. Maybe after the Cup final he would feel different. And so to Wembley, and the Double. Only three teams had done the Double this century – Tottenham, Arsenal and Liverpool. The Busby Babes had come close but had been robbed by the cruel charge of Peter McParland on goalkeeper Ray Wood. There were no substitutes in those days. Jackie Blanchflower had pulled on the goalkeeper's jersey and Wood, after a brief recuperation in the dressing room, returned dazed to hang about on the wing, a useless passenger. It was, everyone agreed, a tragedy that the Babes never achieved their rightful Double – but here was Ferguson's chance to make amends, and in the year that Busby himself had died.

United's record against Chelsea didn't exactly inspire confidence, beaten home and away by them, but to do it three times in a season was surely beyond the Stamford Bridge team. The Cup has a strange habit of reversing league results. It's usually the case that having lost in the league you then go and beat them in the Cup – and so it would be at Wembley. But it took a penalty and the cool resolve of Ferguson's Frenchman to break the deadlock. Chelsea, after enjoying so much pressure, had suddenly been turned. Then came a second penalty, and with as much composure as he had taken the first, Cantona planted his kick in precisely the same spot. It was just the beginning. United rattled in another two goals to give them a comprehensive-looking win, on paper at least. In reality it had been a lot closer. Cantona's two penalties had been the difference between the two sides. Once he had converted both, there was no coming back for Chelsea.

Ferguson had created a slice of history for himself. Busby might have won the European Cup but Ferguson had done the Double. He was about to become a legend himself. Yet somehow it had all been too easy. All along United were the front runners in the Premiership. They had lost only four games all season and had accrued a massive 92 points, eight more than Blackburn and 15 more than Newcastle in third spot. Only Blackburn had matched them in any way, though no one seriously expected that they would wrestle the title from United's grasp. Not this season, anyhow.

CHAPTER TWENTY-ONE

One More Goal

Old Trafford without Bryan Robson was like the *Beano* without Dennis the Menace. It seemed he'd always been there, but now he was gone. Robson had been mulling over his future with Ferguson for some time. He'd told the gaffer that he wanted to go into football management and that when the right opportunity came along he'd like to grab it. He'd achieved all he wanted at Old Trafford, seeing his club add the championship to their many other honours, and he had to be realistic: he was getting no younger and injuries were severely curtailing his appearances. Ferguson understood. When such an offer came up, he promised United would not stand in Robson's way. One or two overtures were reported but it wasn't until Middlesbrough, then in the First Division, made an approach that Robson was finally tempted. They wanted him as player-manager. It was a nostalgic return to his own north-east. But it left Old Trafford a little short on romance.

Others disappeared as well. Clayton Blackmore went off to join Captain Marvel at Ayresome Park, while Mike Phelan left on a free transfer. The only newcomer was David May, an elegant-looking full back signed from Blackburn Rovers for £1 million. It was something of a surprise signing. The only black mark on the pre-season matches was the sending off of Eric Cantona in a friendly against Rangers at Ibrox. 'It was the same old story,' wrote Ferguson. 'He was kicked, didn't receive justice from the referee, and took matters into his own hands.' Cantona might have been provoked but it was still no excuse. It meant that he could now be missing the opening European game against Galatasaray. At times the Frenchman could be a liability. It would get worse before it got any better.

The programme had barely kicked off when United's reputation for ill discipline surfaced yet again. This time the culprit was Paul Parker, dismissed in the opening fixture of the season against QPR. But at least United won and were off to a decent start. They stumbled against Nottingham Forest, only drawing, but then won their next two games, the first against a resurgent Tottenham boasting Jurgen Klinsmann up front, and the second against Wimbledon. Then came a dilemma for Ferguson as Coventry City faxed a £2 million offer for Dion Dublin. With European matches looming, Ferguson was reluctant to sell but recognised that £2 million was twice what United had paid for Dublin. He had to be realistic. It was a tempting bid and Dublin was desperate for regular first-team football, rather than a handful of European games. He agreed to sell.

United's first defeat of the season came against Leeds United at Elland Road. The one consolation was an encouraging performance from yet another Fergie fledgling, Nicky Butt, who came on as a substitute as United trailed by two goals. Butt was another in the long line of promising youngsters following in the footsteps of Ryan Giggs, through the youth team and reserve side to first-team football, in next to no time. Nor would Butt be the last; the conveyor belt was only just beginning to flow.

Next in line was a further test, Liverpool at Old Trafford, but United came through with flying colours, winning 2–0. After that it was the League Cup and all change. One of the difficulties of being in contention for every honour was that opportunities to field new young players were few and far between. Every game was crucial, with a temptation to field the best eleven rather than experiment or test out young-sters. It's only in competitions such as the League Cup or the early rounds of Europe where there is less pressure that the chance to blood a few teenagers is available. But by the 1990s even those early European rounds were not the foregone conclusion they had once been, which left the League Cup as almost the only chance to try out the kids. So, when United ran out at Port Vale, Ferguson had decided it was time to see just how capable his youngsters were. It was a very different-looking side from the one that had played Liverpool. Schmeichel, Bruce, Pallister, Kanchelskis, Ince, Giggs, Cantona, Sharpe and Hughes were all rested, and in came a crop of youngsters – Gary Walsh, Gary Neville, Keith Gillespie, David Beckham, Nicky Butt, Paul Scholes and Simon Davies. More than a few eyebrows were raised and there was even some criticism that Ferguson was short-changing the fans who were expecting a full-strength United. But nobody could complain. Ferguson was building for the future – and anyhow United won 2–1. The young-sters, especially Beckham, all acquitted themselves well. Perhaps he should have continued with them as United managed to lose their next league fixture, at Ipswich, though it was much against the run of play.

In the next round of the League Cup Ferguson kept faith with the kids, even adding Chris Casper and John O'Kane to the line-up. United won 2–0. But in the following league match they lost again, this time 1–0 at Sheffield Wednesday. The fixtures were piling up, with Europe adding to the chaos.

The old European Cup format had now disappeared, with a new league system introduced in its place. It may have meant higher revenue for the clubs but it also meant additional games. United however were off to a flying start, beating Gothenburg of Sweden 4–2 at Old Trafford, and drawing 0–0 in Turkey with Galatasaray in what could have been one of their trickiest games. Then at Old Trafford Barcelona were held to a 2–2 draw. United really ought to have won. Hughes had put them ahead but they had then missed a glorious opportunity to go two up. As it was, the dazzling Brazilian Romario equalised with a stunning goal. Barcelona added a second with Sharpe hitting an equaliser in the final minutes. United had been unlucky, but all was not lost. Providing they could get a result in Gothenburg and beat Galatasaray at Old Trafford they would be through to the quarter-finals.

In the league United kept plugging away, even winning 4–2 at Blackburn, against a side many predicted would be United's stiffest challengers. They would indeed, but at Ewood Park United put on a courageous performance, even though Blackburn were down to ten men after Berg had been sent off. United's next League Cup encounter against Newcastle posed a quandary for Ferguson. Should he continue playing the youngsters when they were facing one of the foremost sides in the country or should he revert to his normal, more experienced eleven? If he played the youngsters and they lost, he would be heavily criticised. But if he reneged on them, he was practically admitting that they were not good enough.

'What do you think?' he asked Cantona, half expecting the Frenchman to be ready to pull on a shirt again.

'I think you should stand by the youngsters,' Cantona replied surprisingly. 'They won the game at Port Vale.' He added that Scholes deserved to play instead of him.

Ferguson decided to compromise by playing an experienced back four but leaving the rest of the youngsters intact. It didn't work; United lost 2–0. But revenge came a few days later when Newcastle were the visitors to Old Trafford for a Premiership game. This time Kanchelskis, Cantona and Giggs were back. United won 2–0 in what Ferguson called one of their best performances of the season.

A few days later United suffered one of their worst defeats in years, going down 4–0 in Barcelona in front of 114,000, Barcelona's biggest gate in ten years. Before the game Ferguson had struggled with the problem of which of his foreigners to leave out. The new ruling was cruelly damaging to English clubs which had always flaunted numerous Scottish, Welsh and Irish players. Now those same players were to be classified as 'imports'. It meant that United's foreign contingent now included Denis Irwin, Mark Hughes, Ryan Giggs, Peter Schmeichel, Roy Keane, Eric Cantona and Andrei Kanchelskis. In the end, Ferguson decided to rest Schmeichel and let Walsh play instead. But Walsh could hardly be blamed for any of the goals. It was Romario who was the catalyst of Barcelona's victory as the Spanish side delivered a sharp lesson in the tactics of European football.

Ferguson came away despondent, knowing that United had fallen well short. They had not played possession football. It was a very different style of play, alien to English clubs. The British game had been created on winning back the ball when you lost it, but if you gave the ball away in Europe you simply did not get it back. Some of his players had also failed to deliver. In particular, Paul Ince had been prone to charging upfield when he should have adopted a more responsible attitude. Others were also to blame.

'You believe too much in your own publicity,' he was inclined to tell some of them. He knew that it could be a danger for young players to find themselves appearing in the tabloids. One headline, and sponsors were queuing up to hand over money for product endorsements, especially if they were United players. Every week it seemed one or more of them was splashed across the front covers of the flourishing football magazines, or even adorning the pages of *MIZZ* or *Just Seventeen*.

Ferguson too heeded the lessons, ordering his youth team

coaches to begin training the youngsters in possession football in their own half, and then learning how to release the long, quick, accurate pass that fires up an attack. He also decided to start curtailing some of the more bizarre and unnecessary off-pitch activities of his squad. Barcelona had brought them all down to earth.

After the disappointments of Europe it was back to the mundane rigours of the English league. Picking up spirits was not easy, but United managed it, winning 2–1 at Villa Park. Their next fixture was the local derby. United won 5–0, the club's best win over City in 100 years. Ferguson could have some sympathy for City manager Brian Horton, remembering that it was not so long ago that he had been on the wrong side of a five-goal hiding by their Manchester rivals. That had been one of Ferguson's lowest points at Old Trafford. He could understand how Horton must be feeling. A few weeks earlier he was feeling much the same himself. United had gone to Gothenburg and been beaten 3–1.

Ferguson was distraught. The Swedes had scored early on and from that moment United were chasing the game. They conjured up an equaliser midway through the second half but had then lost concentration with the Swedes replying almost immediately. Seven minutes later Gothenburg added a third. Even worse, Paul Ince was sent off. It was the same old problem, Ferguson told them. They had given the ball away and had then expected to win it back straight away. That wasn't the way of European football.

Two weeks later they beat Galatasaray 4–0 at Old Trafford, but it was too late. They were out of Europe. Gothenburg had topped the league with Barcelona and United level on points, but it was Barcelona, by virtue of their win over United, who were through to the next stage. United had scored more goals than anyone else. They had committed some inane errors and there was no escaping the fact that they had volumes to learn when it came to European football. On a more positive note, the learning process was underway, and the new league system in Europe did allow teams to continue playing and developing their tactics.

With defeat in Europe confirmed, United had to rely on winning the title if they were to have another crack at the Champions League. They were still going strong in the league until Nottingham Forest came to Old Trafford and won 2–1. Ferguson was impressed by Stan Collymore, the tall, much-talked-about Forest striker. United were still hunting for someone who could score 20 goals a season. Since Dion Dublin's injury and departure they had not had anyone who could be described as a conventional striker. Ferguson decided to put a call in to Frank Clark at Forest, but Clark was adamant that Collymore was staying put. There was no chance. Teddy Sheringham of Spurs was another possibility but Tottenham were looking for £5 million. Ferguson rejected that notion immediately. The only other candidates, he concluded, were Andy Cole and Les Ferdinand. He would keep a watchful eye on any development.

Early in the new year Ferguson concluded that they really needed new blood. Too many priceless points had been dropped. It was time for action. He tried Forest again but Clark was still insistent that Collymore was not for sale. Next he tried Queens Park Rangers and Les Ferdinand but again received no encouragement. Then out of the blue Newcastle manager Kevin Keegan called to inquire if Keith Gillespie might be available. Ferguson told him he wasn't but then, somewhat cheekily, asked about Andy Cole. To his amazement Keegan did not reject the thought out of hand as he had earlier that season. No more was said but there was plenty of food for thought.

By now word was out that United were in the hunt for a striker, with Collymore hotly tipped as the likely target.

The tabloids had talked to Frank Clark and there seemed a possibility that the Forest manager might sell. Ferguson tried to contact him but Clark was said to have gone home ill. Ferguson was all for setting up a deal for Collymore but decided to give Keegan a further call before making any official move for the Forest man. Again Keegan did not reject his suggestion. He promised to go away and give it some serious consideration. Later that day Keegan phoned back. Any deal, he insisted, would have to involve Keith Gillespie. Ferguson was in a quandary. 'I'll have to think about that one,' he told Keegan.

Ferguson went in search of Brian Kidd and pulled him into his office. 'What do you think?' he asked.

Kidd was all in favour. Gillespie was Irish and that didn't help with the European rules. Furthermore, he was not a regular in the first team – and anyhow they had Kanchelskis. Gillespie was dispensable, while adding Cole to the squad would be an enormous boost to the team and the supporters.

'Okay, let's go for it,' Ferguson decided, and made his way towards the chairman's office.

Keegan was happy to do a deal. 'But it'll cost you,' he told United.

'How much?' asked Ferguson.

'At least five million. That's the going price. Collymore, anyone, is going to cost you that much at the moment,' the Newcastle manager insisted.

Ferguson went away to discuss money with his chairman. They returned to make an offer of £5 million.

Keegan said no. Later that day it was upped to £5.5 million but again Newcastle turned them down. Finally Ferguson went to £6 million, plus Gillespie.

'That's fine,' agreed Keegan but then added annoyingly, 'You'll have to give me a little time as I'm in the market for someone.'

All Ferguson and Kidd could do was wait. Keegan, it

turned out, was in the market for Chris Armstrong of Crystal Palace but was receiving little encouragement from them.

It was a couple more days before Ferguson heard any more. He was lying on his bed in a hotel room in Sheffield prior to United's game at Bramall Lane when the phone rang. It was Keegan.

'It's a deal,' he said. 'Six million plus Gillespie. You can have him immediately.'

Ferguson was ecstatic.

'We're on our way now,' went on Keegan. 'Let's get it sorted quickly before anyone finds out.'

It almost took Ferguson's breath away. His major problem was to keep it all quiet. In the dressing rooms at Bramall Lane that evening he took Keith Gillespie aside and told him but didn't mention who he was being swapped for. Gillespie seemed happy enough at the prospect of going to Newcastle. The following day the deal was signed and sealed at Old Trafford. Andy Cole was now a United player.

When the news was finally announced it caused a sensation. Cole was the most menacing goal scorer in the division and had netted a bagful of goals for Newcastle. The Newcastle fans were stunned. How could Keegan sell their prize asset? they asked, as they gathered in their hordes outside St James's Park. At Old Trafford the United fans couldn't believe their luck. Nothing could stop them winning the title now, it seemed. One newspaper even suggested calling the season off and just handing the trophy over to Ferguson. It was that inevitable. But of course it never is, as Ferguson was about to discover.

As fate would have it United's next game was against Newcastle at St James's Park. However, the two managers agreed not to play their new signings. Ferguson even decided to leave Cole at home, knowing that he might get a hostile reception from some of the Newcastle fans, even though you could hardly blame him for the move. In the event the two sides drew one apiece, a reasonable outcome given the circumstances, but of more concern to United was a serious injury to Mark Hughes that would sideline him for some months.

It also came at a difficult time. Hughes was the obvious man for Cole to replace – so obvious that Joe Royle of Everton had already been on the phone inquiring after his availability. Ferguson was prepared to let him go. 'You know the situation,' he told Hughes. 'There will always be a place here for you, but I cannot guarantee you first-team football.' Hughes understood and had promised to think about it. A deal with Everton looked inevitable. Then came the injury.

As if that wasn't worrying enough, a few days later Ferguson was to become embroiled in the soccer sensation of the year when his favourite Frenchman decided to practise some specialist Far East kick-boxing on a spectator at Selhurst Park. It was to become known as *L'affaire Cantona* and would hog the front-page headlines for days, even weeks in some papers. In the end the distraction and the loss of their most inspirational player would cost them the championship.

Six-million-pound man Andy Cole eventually made his debut against Blackburn Rovers but didn't score his first goal for the club until a few weeks later as he fired the only goal of the match against Aston Villa at Old Trafford. His real moment of glory would come some weeks later when United trounced Ipswich 9–0 at Old Trafford. Cole hit five as United set a new Premiership record score. Sadly there were to be too few such moments of glory for Cole over the next year or so.

Since Cole's arrival, United had enjoyed a good spell, but then they came up against an Everton side at Goodison Park determined not to concede an inch. United lost 1–0 although they had created enough chances to win the game with ease. It was a major setback for United's championship hopes. Three weeks later they were back on Merseyside at fortress Anfield. This time they lost 2–0. It was, as Ferguson pointed out, 'Liverpool's cup final'; and they were up for it. 'You lost the title on Merseyside,' sang the Liverpool fans, and with some justification, although the full impact of Merseyside's influence on the final destination of the league and FA Cup had not yet been completed.

After the Liverpool defeat United remained unbeaten in the league for the remainder of the season, just eight more fixtures, but crucial points were dropped that ultimately cost them the title. Leeds United came to Old Trafford and sneaked away with a goalless draw. Then a fortnight later Chelsea did exactly the same. United had failed to score in their last three games at Old Trafford. It was almost unbelievable. They'd spent a small fortune on Andy Cole, but where were the goals? Just one goal and the title would have gone to United again and not to Blackburn. There had been too many lost opportunities. Perhaps United had simply become too bewildered, too distracted by too many competitions.

It wasn't just the league where United were challenging. They had had only a brief run in the League Cup before going out to Newcastle at St James's Park, but in the FA Cup they were going the whole distance. They had begun with a comfortable win at Bramall Lane against Sheffield United in early January. The dismissal of Sheffield's Charlie Hartfield was the turning point. The Yorkshire side never really recovered and as the game wore on United took control, although the goals did not appear until the final ten minutes. Cantona settled the match with a stunning strike, one of the best of the season, that gave United a 2–0 win.

In the next round United were given what looked a comparatively easy draw, against Second Division Wrexham, but when the Welsh side shot into the lead after less than

ten minutes it appeared as though there might be a major
upset on the cards. But Denis Irwin equalised eight minutes
later and United punctually slipped into gear, running out
5–2 winners.

That win put United into the fifth round and up against
the far tougher proposition of Leeds United at Old Trafford.
Yet it turned out to be one of United's best performances of
the season, with the game virtually over after just five
minutes. By then Bruce and McClair had given United a
two-goal advantage. After the interval Leeds readjusted
cleverly to pull one back but United kept their discipline
and even added to the scoreline to make it 3–1.

Next in line were Queens Park Rangers and, given
United's luck in a third home tie, you had to begin to
wonder if this wasn't going to be another Wembley year.
There was never much doubt about the outcome of the
game. United won 2–0 and were through to the semi-final,
where they managed to avoid Everton, finding themselves
instead facing Crystal Palace at Villa Park. Yet rather than
sweeping the London club aside, United huffed and puffed,
even granting Palace an early lead. Irwin equalised but then
in extra time Palace again went ahead. This time it was
Gary Pallister who saved them any embarrassment. If that
had been a dour affair, the replay turned out to be anything
but. Roy Keane was sent off, Giggs was injured, and a
showpiece semi-final replay turned into an ill-tempered
struggle of aggression and counter-aggression. United won
2–0, but the following morning there were yet more headlines for Ferguson to read about United's lack of discipline.
Still, at least they were into their second successive final.

The season was winding up to its dramatic conclusion.
After dropping so many unnecessary home points, United
suddenly increased the pressure on Blackburn by winning
their next three fixtures to leave the title on a knife edge.
Both sides had one remaining fixture. Blackburn were away
to Liverpool while United travelled to West Ham. Much

was made in the papers of Dalglish's return to his former club. Nobody could see Liverpool doing Ferguson any favours. Surely, suggested one or two pundits, Liverpool would not be putting too much effort into this one. But Ferguson was not going to be fooled by that kind of talk. Liverpool, he knew, were too professional to sit back and allow Blackburn to overrun them just to halt United's progress.

It was complicated at the top, but simple enough as far as United were concerned. They had to win if they were to retain the championship and even then would have to hope that Blackburn could manage no better than a draw. If Blackburn won there was nothing United could do. Ferguson decided to go for a five-man midfield to try and dominate the game, and left out Hughes. On the half hour, with United looking comfortably in control, West Ham scored a dramatic opening goal. Meanwhile over at Anfield Blackburn had taken the lead. The title looked to be heading for East Lancashire. Ferguson decided to bring on Hughes to add some muscle to United's challenge. Within six minutes it had worked as McClair hit an equaliser. Then came news that Liverpool had equalised. Suddenly United's championship hopes were alive again. They needed just one more goal. For fifteen minutes they bombarded West Ham's goal but time and again Ludek Miklosko was equal to the challenge.

Surely the ball must eventually go into the net – but no, every time it stayed out. Ferguson watched in horror, blood pressure mounting every time United swept into the penalty area. The tension in the dugout was near sizzling point. They screamed, they yelled, they played every ball. But even they could not help it into the net.

In the final minute news filtered through that Liverpool had taken the lead. In a way it didn't matter. The onus had been on United ever since Liverpool had struck their equaliser. Seconds after Liverpool scored their winner, the final whistle blew at Upton Park. The title was there to be won but United had failed. Just one more goal and they would have been champions again – it couldn't get much more frustrating.

Ferguson could not bring himself to watch the video. The experience had been too painful. No manager likes failure, but to come so close can often be harder. It was something Kevin Keegan would experience twelve months later and which would eventually lead to his resignation as Newcastle manager. Ferguson had been second before on two occasions. In his first full season in charge United had trailed Liverpool by nine points, but they could hardly grumble about that; they had been well and truly beaten to the title. And anyhow, Ferguson was still building. Then in 1992 they had been pipped to the post by Leeds. That had been agonising. At that stage Ferguson had still not won a title and had been six years in the job. It was one of his lowest moments.

At least in 1995 he could point to a couple of title successes as well as other trophies domestic and European. He had already proved himself. What's more, there was no time for moping, self-examination or inquests. They had a Cup final against Everton to prepare for in six days' time. The back-room staff's immediate task was to massage a few aching limbs and disappointed egos. That wasn't always the easiest of jobs, but most of the squad had already tasted success and were young enough to secure further honours. It would have been far more difficult to pick up a middle-of-table side.

Everton were always going to be a tough proposition. New manager Joe Royle had a reputation for robust, combative sides, and although United began as clear favourites, even Ferguson would have admitted a sneaking fancy for the Merseysiders. And he would have been right. Everton had an opportunity and scored; United had the bulk of play but failed to translate chances into goals.

Perhaps Sunday's disappointments at Upton Park had left their mark. Certainly United were not themselves, failing to show their usual swagger and self-belief. It was another case of 'one more goal', and United might have salvaged something from the match – but that had been the story of their season. A few more goals and they could have picked up a league and Cup double. It seemed astonishing to have splashed out so much on the country's top striker yet to fail to score enough goals. They had gone from double champions to double runners-up.

Ferguson was left wondering what might have been if Cantona had been available. His kung fu kick had brought adverse publicity and placed suffocating pressures on everyone at the club. 'I cannot recall being in the media spotlight so often,' he said. There was no doubt that they had missed the Frenchman's inspirational passing, his deft flicks, his uncanny shooting ability. Ferguson would not have liked to admit it, and perhaps it is a simplification, but it probably was Cantona's absence that made the difference. Certainly at Wembley he would have held the key that could have unlocked Everton's tight defence. A year later he was to show just how it was done.

As it was, it was disappointments all round: pipped to the title, beaten at Wembley and ignominiously dismissed from Europe. Perhaps the early dismissal from Europe was the most disappointing as it underlined the widening gulf between English and European clubs. Ferguson still had some work to do before United could match Europe's best.

Nonetheless, there were positive elements to be drawn from the season. A gaggle of youngsters had been given their chance, mainly in the Coca-Cola Cup, and had acquitted themselves with distinction. No fewer than eight made first-team debuts in one competition or another. 'I'll never know if a youngster is up to first-team football unless I give them a try,' argued Ferguson. It boded well for the future.

But as the season ended, even Ferguson could never have guessed how soon he was going to have to rely on them.

CHAPTER TWENTY-TWO

The Fergie Factor

When Kevin Keegan sensationally resigned as manager of Newcastle United early in 1997 there were many who pointed the finger at his amazing outburst with Alex Ferguson. Ferguson had guessed correctly that if you pricked Keegan he bled. It was the first clue that the Newcastle manager was feeling the stress of football management. It had been an unhappy incident as the 1995–96 season wound to its dramatic conclusion. Ferguson, no doubt tongue in cheek, wondered if Leeds would be giving their all as they faced Newcastle United in the final run-in. In retrospect they were thoughts perhaps best left to the darker recesses of the mind rather than being stated publicly.

Once Ferguson had made his remarks they drew a stinging response from Keegan. When asked about them live on Sky Television an angry Keegan let rip, retorting that Ferguson had suddenly gone down in his estimation and that any suggestion that Leeds might not play to the best of their ability was an insult to their players, their integrity and professionalism. Anyone who saw the Keegan response was left in no doubt as to his fury with Ferguson. Ferguson felt it better not to respond to his outburst, though there must have been some satisfaction in seeing his closest rival lashing out in such a frenzied state. A few weeks later Ferguson and Keegan appeared at Wembley on Cup final day, arm in arm, the jolliest of chums, their differences behind them.

It wasn't the first time Ferguson had drawn a sting from a rival manager. It was part of his style. Like most Glaswegians, Ferguson is well practised in winding up opponents. There can be few harder training grounds for life than the back streets of Govan, where wit, brawn and quick thinking are vital ingredients in the struggle for survival. Ferguson has come well equipped. He'll pick his target, have a go and then sit back waiting for the reaction. He did it with Keegan, Arsene Wenger, the Football Association, the Premiership, anything posing an immediate threat. It was all carefully calculated. He'll do it with players as well, especially the youngsters. If there's been a discipline problem he'll call them into his office and explode. Then as they walk out of the office, tail between their legs, he'll flash a glance at Brian Kidd and give a wink. He knows precisely what he is doing. But he will have chosen his subject carefully, knowing that a good rollicking doesn't work with everyone.

Players are called into his office for one of two reasons, either to be told they are playing well, or because they have misbehaved. If they are called in for bad behaviour he'll offer them two options. 'If you tell the truth you'll be docked one week's wages; if you lie you'll be docked two weeks'.' It usually works. Players own up, the fine is imposed and everybody gets on with their job. The joy of the system is that everybody knows precisely where they stand.

'I like my players,' he once told *Goal* magazine. 'I've got a good relationship with them without being too close.' Players don't just wander in or hang about for a natter. If they're called to the manager's office it's for a reason and not just to discuss the weather. But that doesn't mean to say that he's not approachable. Steve Bruce, the former United captain, testifies to Ferguson's concern about the welfare of his players. 'If a player had a problem he could go to Alex. He never had any difficulty with that side of the job. In fact it was one of his strengths. He dealt with a player's problems on a one-to-one basis. He protects his players to the hilt . . . and we respect him for it.'

Ferguson reckons the most difficult aspect of any manager's job is either in telling a youngster he will not make it or trying to keep an injured player's hopes raised before despair sets in. 'It's like when something goes wrong in your life and people tell you to keep your chin up, but no one's got an answer to your problem; no one tells you how to keep your chin up.

'Everybody can handle success, but not everybody can handle losing. That is part of the make-up of top management – or any successful person. They have to be able to thrive in any situation, especially a bad one, and know how to handle it well and then get over it.'

Ferguson likes to tell the story of how he successfully dealt with some tomfoolery at Aberdeen. Apparently he had received a call from one of the club's landladies telling him that she had had enough of some of her young lodgers. 'I want them out at the end of the season,' she told Ferguson. 'They were playing hide-and-seek last night.' It was as much as Ferguson could do to stop himself laughing.

'Are you certain?' he asked. They were, after all, 17 years old. Mrs Barker said she was, and Ferguson promised to sort it out. The next day he and Archie Knox confronted the lads one by one. But none of them was forthcoming. Eventually the last lad was wheeled in and given the most almighty roasting. He was the youngest. 'You'll be going back down the road if you don't tell us the truth,' threatened Ferguson, putting on a suitable display of steaming anger. Eventually the poor boy broke down and confessed their deadly deed. Yes, they had been messing and playing hide-

and-seek, he blubbered. The other three were then brought back in and given another taste of Ferguson's tongue.

'Okay, if you're going to act like children, then you'll be treated like children,' he began. 'I want you in here tomorrow morning having learnt the following nursery rhymes.' Each boy was then given a nursery rhyme to recite the next day.

It was a clever way to make a point without getting too hysterical. But it was enough to demonstrate that Ferguson expected the highest standards of behaviour from his players, even when they were off duty. However, there have been moments when, like most managers, he has simply lost his cool. He's shoved over tea urns, slammed more than a few doors and given one or two international stars a heavy time. Wherever he's gone he's arrived with a reputation as a bad-tempered, hard manager.

In April 1995 Ferguson brought young Simon Davies on against Chelsea at Old Trafford to try and give the team some much-needed width. Ferguson gave him careful instructions but the youngster did not heed them. United drew. Davies was singled out for criticism: he had not obeyed his manager's instructions, and Ferguson was furious. Two days later Davies asked for a transfer. Ferguson promptly agreed and told him that he could go at the end of the season. Davies didn't go, although his first-team appearances were to be limited from then on. During the 1996–97 season he was named only as a substitute. Ferguson is not a manager to be crossed. One dispute and you'll be shown the door. He rules with authority.

Most of the United players soon sussed him out, especially those who had been around a while. 'He frightened the younger players to death,' says Bryan Robson, 'but not so much us older ones.' Another of his players reckons that deep down he's just an old softy. Brian Kidd agrees. 'He's mellowed a little bit but he still wants to win.' His wife supports that view. 'He shouts a lot,' she says, but adds that 'his bark is worse than his bite'.

Nevertheless, her husband is a renowned disciplinarian. He demands exacting standards from his players off the field. He calls for good behaviour and smart dress. It's the old Bill Struth of Rangers coming out in him. When Struth governed at Ibrox after the war he ruled with a rod of iron. Players were not even allowed to go to the cinema or play tennis, and a three-piece suit was demanded for every public occasion involving the club. Struth's influence has permeated the corridors of Ibrox ever since, and in his own time at Rangers Ferguson picked up some of the habits. They weren't all bad, though sometimes they were perhaps a little excessive. One story had it that Struth once spotted one of his players standing with his hands in his pockets while talking to a friend. Struth marched up to the player, punched him in the ribs and told him sharply, 'Rangers players don't stand with their hands in their pockets.' Ferguson has never had to resort to such extremes – and with today's mega-rich footballers it would not cut much ice. Nevertheless he expects impeccable conduct.

If Ferguson has adopted something of the Rangers style of discipline, it has more likely come from Ibrox manager Scot Symon rather than Bill Struth. 'He was dominant with the team,' says Ferguson. 'Everything was based on discipline. He didn't have to say much, nor did he need to. He just had this overwhelming aura of authority.' It's much the same with Ferguson.

Even in these fashion-conscious times he expects his players to be dressed sensibly. Jeans are out. It was noticeable that United's dress for the 1996 FA Cup final was smart and conventional while Liverpool fannied about Wembley in white Armani suits. From the start it was obvious who was going to win. Similarly, you just had to compare the two sides in their pre-Wembley television interviews. There were the United youngsters, talking sensibly and dressed smartly, while the Liverpool players fooled about in their pop star gear. The Spice Boys, as they were later dubbed, might have been more fun for a night out, but the United lads looked the more professional and more interested in football.

Ferguson likes players with character, with spirit. He doesn't like moaners. He wants players who want to play for Manchester United, not mercenaries. He'll pay them well, yet gives the impression that he half expects them to be paying him for the privilege of playing for a great club. He was said to be furious and disappointed that money should have been the stumbling block when it came to Alan Shearer joining United. Ferguson finds it astonishing that anyone should turn down the opportunity to play for United, especially if the reason is money.

The one thing sure to irritate Ferguson is drink. When he arrived at United there was a serious drink problem which for some years gave him more headaches than any eight pints of bitter. Ferguson soon set the rules. He simply does not expect his players to indulge. He'll turn a blind eye to the odd pint on a Saturday night after the game but he will not tolerate mid-week drinking. Any player caught drinking will be hauled before him.

On one occasion he was said to have warned a clique of young players who had taken to drinking in a pub near The Cliff training ground. Some time later he spotted two of the clique downtown drinking in a bar as he drove past in his car. He is said to have stopped his car, wound down the window and simply told the lads that this was the last they would be seeing of him. They were out.

Although he doesn't object to the occasional drink, he is a convinced enemy of the lethal mixture of alcohol and football. He rates it one of the biggest problems at English clubs. 'If anyone can prove to me that drinking makes you play better, then I'll go along with it. But until then, no drink.' Olympic athletes don't train on pints of beer, so why should footballers? is his attitude.

Yet Ferguson himself is not averse to a glass or two of wine and is considered something of a wine buff. He knows his Burgundies from his Beaujolais and can often be spotted at wine-tasting evenings. He takes it seriously, buying fine wines and enjoying them. But apart from that and the odd glass of celebratory champagne, he hardly touches a drop.

Ferguson is a straight talker. There's no bullshit, no camouflaging of his opinions. If he likes a player, he'll stand by him, as he did with Cantona. Loyalty is important to him. But the player has to have the right attitude as well as the ability. 'You have to earn his respect,' says one insider. 'But once you've got that, you've also got his loyalty.' It's a two-way process. McGrath may have had the ability but he didn't have the attitude, and that was the end of him.

Yet Ferguson doesn't bear grudges. If a player has stepped out of line, he'll tell him straight, 'eyeball to eyeball' as he puts it. He doesn't have time for wearisome grudges that interfere with his management strategy or that waste endless hours in negotiations and cajoling. Once more, it's all down to a player's attitude, the ability to be mature and to get on with the job. Players can be temperamental as long as it doesn't cause friction either side of the dressing-room door.

Perhaps he's learnt from his own mistakes – six sendings-off in a fairly undistinguished football career of his own. 'You mustn't let things get you down,' he says. 'Perhaps that is why people with a temper are better suited to management than the more placid types. They can spark a reaction because losing means something to them.'

When he does genuinely lose his temper it can rebound on him. He's picked up impudent headlines, stinging responses and generally won little support for his claim, whatever that might be. He'll defend his players, his club, his cause, even when he's defending the indefensible. Sometimes Ferguson's loyalty is apt to exceed even *his* common sense. But in the dressing room they like that kind of thing – the gaffer defending them out there in the wicked world. It does wonders for team unity, everyone pulling together to fight off the enemy outside. Not for nothing has Ferguson encouraged the myth that everyone hates United. Over the years there have been calculated targets for his famed temper: the Old Firm, the Glasgow football mafia, Liverpool, the Premiership, and of course, the press. Now it's everyone who doesn't support United with the same passion as he does.

Fellow Govan lad Kenny Dalglish clashed swords with him on numerous occasions when he was manager with Liverpool. Their most notorious bust-up was not actually a bust-up at all. It came over Ferguson's decision as Scotland manager not to select Alan Hansen for the World Cup finals in Mexico. Dubious about taking Hansen, Ferguson had telephoned Dalglish to chat it over. 'I think I need someone who is more adaptable, who can play in two or three positions,' he said. Dalglish assured him that Hansen was well capable of playing almost anywhere at the back, even as a sweeper. Ferguson went away to reconsider but was soon back on the phone. 'I've decided not to take him.'

Dalglish did not agree with his judgement but accepted that, as manager of the Scotland squad, Ferguson had the right to decide who to take. It was his decision and his decision alone. Remarkably, a few days later, Dalglish himself was forced to pull out of Ferguson's squad for the finals. The press went to town, reading some hidden agenda into his decision to remain at home. The next morning the back pages were full of a major row, of Dalglish spitefully pulling out because his pal Hansen had been left out of the squad, but there was no truth whatsoever in the stories. The fact was that Dalglish had been advised to undergo an operation on a knee ligament. It was as simple as that. Although they had disagreed on the decision not to take Hansen to Mexico, there was no acrimony between the two men, just committed rivalry.

Dalglish also had a well-publicised clash with Ferguson after a key match at Anfield between Liverpool and United in 1988. The game had ended in a 3–3 draw after Liverpool had earlier been leading 3–1. United had also had a player sent off so that as the final whistle blew neither team – fans, players and managers – was particularly happy with the outcome. Ferguson was furious at some of the refereeing decisions and was heard to be screaming about never getting any favours at Anfield. Even when he later faced the press he was still ranting on about refereeing decisions and the reluctance to give anything at Anfield. As he left his meeting with the press, hotly pursued by a radio interviewer, he ran across Dalglish in the corridor. The Liverpool manager was carrying his six-week-old baby daughter in his arms. As the three bumped into each other Dalglish casually turned to the radio man and told him that he'd be better off talking to his baby daughter, as he would get more sense out of her than out of Ferguson. It was just Dalglish winding Ferguson up in typical Glasgow fashion, but on this occasion it was Ferguson who fell for it. He began ranting again. Dalglish continued on his way, just pausing to remind Ferguson to be careful, 'the baby's a bit young for that'.

Again the press made much of the dispute and soon conjured up a myth of an immense rift between the two men. It was never true. They may not have been the closest of friends, but there has always been respect between them. Ferguson even organised a team for Dalglish's Scottish testimonial and was responsible for awarding Dalglish his 100th international cap and making him captain for the occasion. 'I always enjoyed working with him at Scotland training; his coaching was excellent. We got on well during our time with Scotland,' says Dalglish, adding that 'Alex Ferguson is a great manager.'

Ferguson was equally warm in his attitude to Dalglish. After all, they were both from Govan and that had to count for something. When Blackburn pinched the title from United, he was quick to put aside any rivalry and add his congratulations. 'I just wanted to drop you a wee line,' he wrote to Dalglish at Blackburn, 'to congratulate you and your team on winning the Premier League championship, and I'm sure that the last few games got your pulse racing . . . I know they did mine.' He might well have added that the title had never really left Govan.

If anything, the brief differences of opinion between Ferguson and Keegan, and Ferguson and Dalglish, merely highlighted the stresses faced by any football manager, stress that can lead to rash words being uttered in the heat of the moment.

Now Ferguson has learnt to control his temper. Today, it's contrived, almost orchestrated. There might have been a time during his early managerial days when the cups went flying, but nowadays he's much cleverer. Pat Stanton, his assistant manager in those early days, remembers how Ferguson used to practise losing his temper and throw a few cups around. He soon discovered that it could be quite effective. The tale has probably become embellished with time, but it illustrates how Ferguson learnt to use his anger. He's almost turned it into an art form, ready to demonstrate when the moment is called for. Managers, he believes, can be better if they do occasionally lose their temper as it often 'triggers a reaction from players'. But it has to be restrained; you can't go using it all the time. If you do, it smacks of another tantrum, players become bored and it loses its impact. Alternatively, players can become genuinely frightened of you. Graeme Souness's famous outbursts at Anfield only added to the uncertainty. There was nothing contrived about them; it was Souness's blood pressure getting the better of him. In the end players became too frightened to play or express themselves naturally, always glancing towards the bench for assurance. Ferguson has learnt that managers have to tread a fine line. You cannot lose your temper with all players. Some need an arm around their shoulder with plenty of encouragement; bawl them out and you've destroyed them. Others will respond positively, a kick up the backside the very thing they need.

The most important aspect of management is not the training but man-management, the daily grind of motivating players, resolving their personal problems, knowing how to get the best out of them. Ferguson excels at it. In his long career he has probably faced most problems, from drink to marriage break-ups; from lack of motivation to an excess of ego. Ferguson knows how to handle them, knowing instinctively when to be firm with a player and when to ease up. It's a delicate balancing act.

'I know of nobody who is better at getting the best out of his players than Alex Ferguson,' says his former Aberdeen scout John Murphy. 'He could do it with the kids, the older players, and his staff. Everyone. You always did your best for him because he believed in you.' Even those in the outside business world such as Sir John Greenbury, chairman of Marks and Spencer, admire his managerial abilities. Greenbury rates him the best man-manager in Britain. 'He is a motivator of exceptional ability,' he claims.

In the past Ferguson has even called on the players' wives for help, regarding them as allies who can play a role in the success of their husbands and consequently of the club. Prior to Aberdeen's European Cup-Winners' Cup final against Real Madrid, he took the unusual step of bringing all the players' wives in to Pittodrie for a private chat. The players thought it bizarre, as would any other employer. But Ferguson gave it a chance. When he'd got them together he asked them to be understanding. These were difficult times for the players, he told them; they would be tense, nervous, anxious. The wives had to realise this and perhaps excuse behaviour that they would not normally have accepted. If they had any problems, they should try not to burden their husbands. He didn't want the players weighed low with worries. If necessary, the wives should come to him.

And it's not just those most closely involved with football. Ferguson's ability to make even the smallest person feel important is famed. He once invited a bunch of youngsters from his Govan boys' club down to Old Trafford to tour the place and meet the players. When Eric Cantona walked into the room there were broad grins and nudges among the lads. But Ferguson suddenly turned the tables. Instead of taking the boys over to Cantona and introducing him to them, he called the Frenchman over to the boys. 'Eric,' he shouted, 'come here. I'd like you to meet Jimmy, and . . .' They were being introduced to Cantona, not vice versa. 'He's never had any airs or graces, all the years I've known him,' says Malcolm Mackay of his first club Queen's Park.

He's not afraid to say hello to strangers and can make them feel as if they have known him for years. He draws strength from simply being with the fans. He's the sort of manager who tells his players that what they are doing is for the fans and that they should never forget that it is the fans who pay their wages. This line was probably more applicable in the sixties, but there is still a vestige of truth in it. Despite all the merchandising and television deals, it is still the fans who make a football club. Ferguson has been quick to grasp that. His remembering his promise to the Aberdeen fans after their team had won the European Cup-Winners' Cup, turning up at the quayside to shake each returning fan by the hand and thank them for travelling to Gothenburg to support their team, is just one example. It may have been a simple gesture but it was one that not too many football managers would have bothered making. It was the kind of thing Shankly used to do, stopping the coach as it neared some away ground and making the players get off to meet the fans. It was his way of saying 'Thanks for taking the trouble and spending the money to come and support us.'

Outside of 10 Downing Street, football management is perhaps the most stressful of all occupations. In recent years both Dalglish and Keegan have quit top clubs as the pressure became unbearable. Steve Coppell was also forced to leave Manchester City after just a few weeks in the job as he faced the realities of resurrecting City's season, while Johan Cruyff discovered that the combination of internal politics at Barcelona and the struggle for points was a match too taxing even for him.

Every football manager has more than his fair share of tasks – and Ferguson probably has more than most. A football manager's job these days is far more than simply picking 11 players and a handful of substitutes. The coaching aspect of the game is also just a small component of the manager's overall duties. In many clubs managers are content to leave the training in the hands of a well-qualified coach or a trusty number two, and are rarely spotted brewing up a sweat with the players on the training pitch. That has never been Ferguson's philosophy, although his many other commitments mean that he is frequently away from Old Trafford on other managerial duties. He has always put enormous trust in his number two and felt safe leaving them temporarily in charge.

Football management today is big business, with the average manager handling a multi-million-pound budget. Kevin Keegan spent a phenomenal £60 million in his time at Newcastle, Dalglish lashed out more than £30 million at Blackburn while Ferguson himself has spent something like £38 million at United. As transfer fees double almost every year, so the manager's budget shoots to dizzying heights. It's easy to get carried away, easy to get caught up into thinking that just one more extravagance in the transfer market will solve your problems. There are enough managers' corpses to prove that it's not quite so simple. Transfer deals are about pitching in at the right level, not some inflated price that puts a smile on another manager's face. But they are also about judgement of players. One only has to look at the millions United have spent on the likes of Peter Davenport, Ted McDougall and Garry Birtles to know that it is all too easy to get it wrong. Ferguson himself has made mistakes, with many of his early signings at both Aberdeen and Manchester United failing to justify the high prices he had splashed out on them. But the successes have far outweighed the failures. He likes nothing more than a spot of wheeling and dealing in the market, especially at the lower end, and coming up with a bargain. Despite this, Ferguson has never been afraid to spend money on players. He may not approve of escalating transfer fees, although he himself has certainly helped inflate prices with one or two of his acquisitions, but if he believes that a player will benefit his side, then he will recommend their signing without any hesitation.

Gary Pallister, Roy Keane and Andy Cole were all record signings that raised eyebrows in boardrooms up and down the land. But while other managers and their respective clubs have attracted adverse comment for their multi-million-pound activity in the transfer market, Alex Ferguson's own deals have gone largely without such comment.

What is outstanding about Ferguson's dealing in the transfer market is its success rate. Keegan, Souness and Dalglish found themselves not only buying expensively, but also selling at will. Not all their signings were successful. Many players were bought on a temporary basis, as their clubs struggled for promotion to the Premiership or to keep their championship dreams alive. Once there, players were discarded as not good enough and new signings brought in. Dalglish for instance sold £7 million worth of players, many of them his own signings. Keegan similarly sold millions of pounds' worth of players, including many he had signed, such as Andy Cole.

Ferguson's success rate with his signings has been

impressive north and south of the border. There were some failures at Aberdeen but he still came up trumps with Peter Weir and Frank McDougall. Certainly most of his acquisitions at Old Trafford have stood the test of time and few have been discarded with the speed with which other managers have dumped their 'failures'. Ironically, Ferguson picked up two of his rivals' cast-offs in David May and Andy Cole, both of whom went on to play starring roles in United's championship ambitions.

It was only in his early days that Ferguson made any signings that could be considered dubious. The principal question mark is probably against Danny Wallace, a £1.2 million signing from Southampton. But even then, it was not an obvious case of misjudgement on Ferguson's part. Just as Wallace was beginning to show some ability, he was unfortunately injured. It was the same with Neil Webb, his £1.5 million signing from Nottingham Forest, whose injury ruined his career. Apart from Wallace, there have been few failures at the top end of the market. Of course, many of his cheaper signings did not make it, but that is more understandable and excusable. They were deliberate gambles, often with young players, and mostly costing less than £100,000. Ralph Milne, for instance, although usually recognised as a Ferguson failure, cost only £170,000 when he was signed from Bristol City. It was the kind of mistake United and Ferguson could afford. Apart from that, Ferguson's track record compares with any manager in recent history and especially with most of his Old Trafford predecessors who lashed out millions on sub-standard goods.

When Ferguson played in Scottish football, wages were miserly, the subsequent fame and fortune of football still some time off. In a way, this modest early experience has been an advantage. Playing with and managing the likes of Queen's Park, Ayr United, East Stirlingshire and St Mirren helped keep his feet firmly planted on the ground. He was an ordinary journeyman, not even picking up much in the way of silverware or international caps. During his undistinguished career at Ibrox, Rangers always lagged behind Celtic in the race for honours. The only pressure was the ignominy, the humiliation of being second best in a city where football is the lifeblood. Ferguson was a mere mortal when he stepped into football management, no legend like Dalglish, Keegan and Cruyff, who all made the sudden and dramatic leap from superstar player to manager, and suffered as a consequence. The constant pressures they had endured as players and subsequently as managers took their toll. Ferguson simply struggled on, accepting the gradual increase in pressure by applying the lessons he was learning in his apprenticeship.

The lower divisions were a fine training ground for Ferguson, picking up a little experience here, a few lessons there, and always learning to live on a meagre budget, whether for the club or his own household. It was only when he arrived at Old Trafford that he suddenly discovered he had money to burn – but by then he was well equipped to handle the millions. He had been brought up in the Govan philosophy of 'look after the pennies and the pounds will look after themselves'.

Yet Ferguson can be a baffling contrast. One moment, he's the fan on the touchline, screaming at his players, tension etched across his brow; or sitting on the bench, biting his bottom lip with that famously pained expression on his face and giving his nervous cough. But then the next moment, he's having a hearty laugh back in the dressing room, glad-handing in the boardroom, or sniffing a delicate Bordeaux. He's a difficult man to pinpoint; he can't be categorised and simply slotted into some folder. He's far too complicated for that. You'd need a filing cabinet to do him justice.

In his time he's faced most predicaments, worked out

most problems. Now it's just a matter of putting those lessons to the test. If they don't work then it's back to the drawing board – or in his case back to the training pitch – find out why they didn't work first time round, then improvise and see if they work next time. It's almost making a science out of something that is clearly not a science, but it's much the same with any job. It requires thoughtful application.

But there is also something else: a resolve to succeed. Ferguson has little to show for his years as a player. He played for Scotland but they didn't even give him an international cap for it. Other managers boast European trophies, Golden Boots and international caps galore. With Ferguson there was nothing before, just a run-of-the-mill playing career. Management has been his career, his focus. He remains hungry for success, determined to add further trophies to those he has already won. This is his yardstick of success. The hunger never seems to have abated.

Although he is undoubtedly a disciplinarian, he loves the banter between players. He'll hang about the dressing room, just sitting there, soaking up the atmosphere, joining in the fun. He confesses that he misses that more than anything. As a manager you can't spend all your time with the players, can't get too close to them, and inevitably that means missing out on the jokes, the arguments, the mickey-taking. It's the kind of thing Glaswegians excel at, an essential aspect of their make-up. When he can, he'll join in and give as good as he takes.

It's all part of the boy in him. He oozes a youthful enthusiasm for the game. You can imagine him insisting that a training match go on until he ends up on the winning side. And then if he was to score the winning goal, nobody at Old Trafford would be allowed to forget it. Marcello Lippi, the Juventus coach, remembers once seeing a television clip of him dancing up and down on the touchline after United had scored. 'In that moment I caught a glimpse of what makes him tick,' said Lippi. 'Here was a man so passionate about the game and obsessed with winning. I am sure he passes on those characteristics to the team.'

He is not so passionate about the press. He trusts some reporters – mainly the Scots and the local lads – but the tabloids have given him problems over the years. He'll be charming, as helpful as he can be, but that doesn't mean to say he enjoys it. He's philosophical about it, recognising that the media are a necessary inconvenience. It's dealing with the press after games he hates most. It's a time for winding down, not an ideal time for a press conference when you might just say something you will regret. Above all he loathes the European half-time interview encouraged by UEFA. There are more important things to be done and said at half-time than wasting precious minutes in front of a camera, but unfortunately it's part of the job – a part that he finds adds to the pressures: 'Dealing with some of the characters who are in the media now is a real strain. They come with something in their minds, and that is what they want you to say.'

Alex Ferguson is a warm man, but anyone who imagines he's a soft touch should go to one of his post-match press conferences. It's not that he hates the press – well, not quite – just that he doesn't trust them one inch. It's the one aspect of being a manager that he loathes. It's doubtful – with the possible exceptions of Hugh McIlvanney and local journalist David Meek – if there is any member of the press he would consider a 'friend'.

It's been a bumpy road for him. Take this outburst, for instance. When United played Norwich in the FA Cup early in 1994, Eric Cantona was involved in a stamping incident that was missed by the referee but not by the television cameras. That evening on BBC Television's *Match of the Day*, pundit Jimmy Hill rightly took a close look at the incident. While acknowledging the skills and delight that Cantona had brought to English football, Hill stated that such behaviour was simply unacceptable.

Ferguson's response was vitriolic. 'If there's a prat going about in this world, he's the prat. I am not interested in Jimmy Hill. Four years ago he wrote us off in the warm-up, that's how much he knows about the game. The BBC are dying for us to lose. Everyone is from Liverpool with a Liverpool supporter's flag. They'll be here every time we lose, that mob – Barry, Bob, Hansen, the lot of them. Liverpool Supporters' Association.'

It was simplistic and unfair. Ferguson ought to have known better and his outburst only exacerbated the situation. Hill had a point and it was made in an honest and considered manner. The job of a journalist, after all, is to ask awkward questions, sometimes the kind of questions recipients don't want to answer. Ferguson is not the only prickly manager who doesn't take easily to challenging questions, but at the end of the day we are only talking football. It was the old paranoia returning, interestingly coupled with the bizarre belief that everyone was a closet Scouser – something that should have disappeared with United's championship triumph.

During the Double season of 1993–94 United were also the target of some stinging back-page comment about their ill discipline on the field. Six players had been sent off during the season, and with each game the commentators wondered at what stage a United player would be flashed another yellow or even red card. Ferguson did not like the media comment about ill discipline, yet the papers had a case. In their previous six seasons, United had had only five players sent off, a notable achievement, but suddenly their record had deteriorated to become one of the worst in the country. The presence of Cantona, of course, focused the media's attention on the question of ill discipline. It may well be that United were unfortunate with some red cards, but on the other hand, they could also count themselves lucky that there were not more.

It's really all a question of swings and roundabouts, but Ferguson's response was to protect his players and give the media short shrift for their comments. After the Coca-Cola Cup final and the dismissal of Kanchelskis, he was quick to point out that the famous Law, Best side had collected enough red cards to play whist. Rather than leave it at that, he took it a step further, deciding that none of his players would be allowed to talk to the press until the end of the season: 'The lads are coming up to me and complaining about this or that thing which is being written about them. About how certain journalists are putting their arm round them and treating them as mates one week, then the next writing stuff. We decided that we should allow no one to undermine our effort and determination. I will do the talking to the press and the players can concentrate on their football. The journalists can get whatever they need from me. As a club we can speak with one voice. My voice.'

That was fine, but of course it wasn't altogether success-ful. Stopping players from talking to the press is impossible – and even if players do remain silent, the papers will simply make up stories. Dealing with the press is as much an occupation for managers as coaching their players, and it is crucial. Football needs the coverage as much as the papers need the game. It's an uneasy, and at times an impossible relationship, but a necessary one nevertheless. In a way Ferguson should have been flattered. The more successful you are, the more the coverage.

In later seasons Ferguson would feel it necessary to protect his younger players. He had a point. Giggs and Beckham came in for considerable attention from the media and were not always capable of dealing with it. The pestering of George Best by prying hacks had given United a lesson they had thoroughly absorbed. But with players like Cantona you had to assume that they were capable of looking after themselves.

There were plenty of times when Ferguson's paranoia

about the press was entirely justified. He realised that reporters had to find stories, especially local reporters, and always went out of his way to feed them with a diet of team news, access to certain players, and transfer speculation. None of this prepared him for the headline in the *Manchester Evening News* at the start of the 1995–96 season which suggested that the fans wanted to get rid of him.

The story followed Ferguson's decision to sell Hughes, Ince and Kanchelskis. This had not gone down well with United fans, who enjoyed a special relationship with Hughes, realised the value of Ince and adored the scintillating skills of the little Ukrainian. Picking up on the bad vibes that were reverberating around the city, the *Manchester Evening News* set up a telephone hot line. Readers were invited to call in and cast their vote on the United manager, and there it was: 53 per cent thought he should resign.

In my view it was an appalling piece of journalism, the kind that gives journalists a bad name. It should have been obvious that a phone poll of that nature was susceptible to doctoring and highly unreliable. Who was to say, for instance, that the vast majority of votes against Ferguson had not been cast by Manchester City supporters? It was obvious, but apparently invisible to some on the paper.

Ferguson was furious. For years he had enjoyed an amicable, though occasionally tetchy, relationship with David Meek, the paper's veteran United spy. Meek was popular around Old Trafford and respected as a serious journalist. He had carefully built up his contacts and had his own column in the *United Review*. However, he had recently retired, and now the paper was running what I regard as little short of a scurrilous story.

The following morning the *Daily Star* picked it up and splashed it across their back page. Somehow it was to be expected with the *Star* – but not with the friendly local paper. The favours were over. The *Manchester Evening News* was going to get no more preferential treatment from

Ferguson. 'They never get anything that the rest don't get, they won't get anything special. I've done nine years of compromises with that paper and they stick the knife in you. And now they won't get any marking of their cards. They'll just get straightforward news as the rest do,' he said at the time.

You could hardly blame Ferguson for feeling angry and had to sympathise with his response. Yet he could also be cunning and, like some political spin doctor, was fairly adept at manipulating the press. When Cantona, for instance, was sent off during a pre-season friendly against Rangers at Ibrox, Ferguson deliberately decided to attack Rangers fans as a smokescreen to take the flak off his culprit. It worked: the Scottish papers homed in on his attack of Rangers fans rather than the sending off of the Frenchman.

Even in Scotland Ferguson had his moments with the press. The story was that he kept a log of how many times Glasgow-based journalists visited Pittodrie. Any journalist with a low attendance record usually found himself on the receiving end of some wisdom. Some might call it paranoia. Others call it keeping the balance.

The elite of Scottish commentators were known to receive a fusillade of verbal bullets. Archie Macpherson, one of the best-known of all Scottish football journalists, was once subjected to a tirade from an irate Ferguson in the main passageway at Easter Road. The attack came suddenly and without warning. Macpherson had said something about the Aberdeen goalkeeper – later he could barely remember what. The two men stormed down the corridors of Easter Road, the rage bouncing off the walls. It degenerated into 'quite lurid abuse', remembered Macpherson, 'as if we had forgotten what it was all about in the first place'. Up to that moment Macpherson had been personally friendly with Ferguson. They seemed to get on well together and Macpherson had been the first journalist on the pitch at Gothenburg, embracing the Dons manager as they celebrated Aberdeen's famous victory. Yet here they were, hurling abuse at each other in full earshot of dozens. It was not a pleasant scene, and one which Macpherson has long regretted, but it was a distinct indication of Ferguson's growing suspicion of the press, especially those journalists not afraid to speak their mind.

When he was at Pittodrie, Ferguson often felt wounded by the bigoted Glasgow media who continually underrated the success of Aberdeen. Aberdeen was provincial; the real heart of Scottish football lay in Glasgow, seemed to be their attitude. And yet at the end of the day Ferguson cares little about what the press say or think. Losing hurts him far more. All he expects is a fair write-up – honest, balanced and without prejudice.

Ferguson brings a voracious appetite to his job. His combative energy is undaunting, his application to detail famed. He even has an astonishing memory for matches and incidents. Bill Campbell, of Mainstream Publishing, remembers working with him. 'He had a photographic memory. He could recall matches, goals, even the time goals were scored and other such details,' he says. 'It was quite extraordinary. During a game he has 100 per cent concentration. I'm sure that kind of focusing helps him retain so much information about a game.'

Every morning Ferguson is up and out of the house before 7 a.m. to arrive at The Cliff training ground by 7.30 a.m. Often, even when there is no evening match, he is not back at his home until 9 p.m. It is this unfailing drive that has carried Aberdeen and United to such unlimited success over the past 20 years.

When he retires he'll probably move upstairs. He himself suggested that he might like a job, perhaps still with United, as director of football. It's easy to see him fitting into that role, although there is always the danger of repeating the Busby saga. What if the new manager failed, what if the fans had grown to expect too much success, what if the plc saw its profits falling? Under these circumstances, Ferguson might possibly be tempted back. It is undeniably true that the United success story has been built on the back of one man. All their commercial growth is due to the ability of the team. You can have the best commercial managers in the business but if your team is not winning trophies then your commercial fortune will come under increasing threat. It is impossible to imagine United having had anything like the commercial success of recent years without their on-field triumphs.

'I just get on with things,' Ferguson once explained to Hugh McIlvanney. 'There is no book about how to deal with the stresses of this job, no instruction manual. I believe it's mainly a matter of metabolism, of whether your personality has the mechanisms to cope. Some people are suited to banking or work in television. I think I'm equipped to do this.'

CHAPTER TWENTY-THREE

Kids Never Win Anything

It wasn't just the football pendulum that was swinging in the direction of Manchester. Suddenly economic prosperity and a thriving music scene were just as much the hallmarks of Manchester as the football. In the sixties, it was Liverpool with its daring music scene and its swaying, singing Kop that had captured the public imagination. The Beatles, the Cavern and Cilla would remain transfixed in the memory forever. But the poverty of the seventies and eighties had left Merseyside short on optimism. Only the football survived. Then with Heysel and Hillsborough and the subsequent resignation of their favourite son, Kenny Dalglish, even the football took a nose dive. The spotlight of popular culture shifted dramatically down the East Lancs road towards Manchester.

They have long been rival cities – Liverpool with its artistic temperament; Manchester, the home of free traders, with its entrepreneurial disposition. The politics of the eighties seemed to suit Mancunian characteristics far more than Scousers.

By the early nineties, the high unemployment that had dogged the area was losing its grip. Trafford Park, the home of United and once the industrial heartland of Manchester, had been destroyed by the Thatcherite economic policies of

the eighties – but at nearby Salford Quays a brash new
world of stylish high-rise office blocks was shooting up.
Everywhere there was building.

The city of Manchester was set to capitalise on the
fortunes of United. They even put in an audacious bid for
the Olympic Games. Downtown, trendy new bars were
sprouting everywhere to support the exhausting club scene
that had become the talk of the music world. The Hacienda
had taken over from the Cavern as the place to be seen.
Home to Oasis, Take That, the Smiths, Simply Red, M
People – Manchester was the capital of pop music, just as
Liverpool had been in the sixties. It hit the front cover of
Time magazine and was dubbed Madchester. The city's
universities had become the most popular in the country as
thousands flocked to fun city.

Once United had clinched their first title, there was little
doubt that Manchester was the place to be, the most
attractive and entertaining city in the UK. It now boasted a
new indoor arena for sporting and other events – the biggest
in Europe, capable of holding 20,000 spectators – as well as
the fastest indoor cycle track in the world. Work had also
begun on a new stadium to house the 2002 Commonwealth
Games. A new rapid tram link whisked fans from the city
centre and beyond to Old Trafford, where they built a new
stand to take the capacity of the ground up to 55,000. Manchester and United were booming.

The city played host to the European football championships and ended with a concert at Old Trafford. A swinging
Alex Ferguson appeared onstage to join in the madness.
Old Trafford, Mick Hucknall, Alex Ferguson; it all seemed
to gel.

By the mid-nineties there was little doubt which was the
richest club in the land. Indeed, United were even wealthier
than the mighty Rangers up in Scotland, as well as Arsenal,
Tottenham or Liverpool. The United replica shirt far outsold
those of their closest rivals. There were Ryan Giggs towels,

pillow cases, mugs, key rings, underpants. You name it and it was adorned with the badge of United, the gipsy locks of Ryan Giggs or the enigmatic stare of Eric Cantona. United even had the players with the looks to match their on-field skills. It made the merchandising all the easier. By 1997 the United merchandising arm was bringing in £30 million a year, as much as the takings at the gate.

Back in 1989 the unknown businessman Michael Knighton had nearly bought United for a knockdown £20 million. Five years earlier Robert Maxwell had come within a whisker of buying the club for considerably less. By 1997 United were reckoned to be worth more than £400 million. There may have been many factors involved in United's mushrooming fortunes, but it was essentially down to one man – Alex Ferguson. All the clever merchandising and all the foxy accountancy in the world would have been to little avail without success on the football field – and that was primarily the responsibility of Ferguson. There was little doubt that by 1997 Ferguson had succeeded Busby as the new father figure of Old Trafford.

Yet while Manchester had its attractions for most people, there were a few around Old Trafford who wanted to leave the city. Worse, they were just the players United needed to hang on to. Andrei Kanchelskis, Paul Ince and Mark Hughes were all set to walk away from the theatre of dreams.

The disappearance of Andrei Kanchelskis to Everton was partly self-inflicted. The Ukrainian never seemed to be satisfied. For at least a year before he departed there were faxes flying around suggesting that he was available for transfer. None of them originated from Old Trafford and United were as baffled as anyone as to why he should want to leave, but they had their suspicions that agents were at play. Ferguson grew weary, exasperated by him. Perhaps all he needed was a comforting arm around his shoulder, and Ferguson was always ready to oblige, but it seemed that no matter how many times he did it, there was always something else bothering the Ukrainian international. Perhaps it was simply something in his pysche. In the end Ferguson was resigned to losing him. Everton came in with a £4.5 million bid and the deal was quickly arranged and settled. Even then Ferguson was prepared, at the last minute, to give him another chance.

But there was no compromise. 'I've signed a five-year contract with Everton and that's binding,' Kanchelskis told Ferguson.

'Yes,' he replied, 'and last year you signed a five-year contract with us and that too was binding.' But it was pointless arguing. Kanchelskis had made up his mind and he was off, himself and his agent no doubt collecting a sizeable fee on the way.

Ferguson had to smile a year later when Fiorentina were reported to be on the brink of signing Kanchelskis with the Everton manager Joe Royle hopping mad at the suggestion. 'Kanchelskis is going nowhere,' fumed Royle. No doubt more agents were at it again. But by early 1997 Kanchelskis had left Goodison for Italy, his manager screaming at his couldn't-care-less attitude. Royle revealed that Kanchelskis had been talking with Fiorentina about a move since the summer. *Plus ça change*.

Yet Kanchelskis had proved a popular character at Old Trafford, always a favourite of the crowd with his cheeky tricks down the flanks. *Red Issue* called him 'irreplaceable'. He was an ace in the pack, a man as likely as any to win the game or set up a winning goal. In his short career at United he had scored 28 league goals and, as Ferguson well knew, had been the instigator of many more. He would be a loss to the club, but it was a loss they would have to cope with. There were plenty of possible replacements.

Of more concern was the loss of Paul Ince. Ince was a Trojan in midfield, a steely ball-winning Titan who could set up attacks, inflict damage and defend with venom. Every successful team needed a Paul Ince, and finding a deputy could prove difficult. The fans knew it as well. They had voted him the inaugural winner of the Sir Matt Busby Player of the Year award, such was the affection they had for him. Ferguson did not want to lose him, but Ince had always fancied a move to Italy before his career was ended and had inserted a clause in his contract that would allow him to leave the club if such an opportunity arose. He had now reached a stage in his career when the offers were likely to come in. If he didn't take them now, they would not want him in another twelve months. It was a case of now or never.

As soon as word leaked out that Ince was bound for Inter Milan, a campaign was launched by the fans aimed at pressing him to stay. Ferguson was being castigated by some as uncompromising and failing to see what a rich asset Ince was to the club.

The United fanzine couldn't figure out what was going on. On the one hand Ferguson had brought them plenty of glory, yet there still seemed to be supporters around Old Trafford who doubted his ability, reported one of their columnists, adding astutely that 'we'll probably only know how good it is when it's over'.

The fans staked out Ince's home, met with him and tried to persuade him against leaving. Ince claimed that he did not really wish to leave the club. But in fact the offer from Italy was too good to refuse. Ferguson was angry that Ince should be trying to pin the blame on him. 'I think that all the hullabaloo with Paul telling the fans "they're trying to sell me" doesn't wash too well now. I think people know the facts.' The affair soon died down and Ince was off.

In some respects Ferguson was probably not distressed at losing Ince. He was known as the Guv'nor in the dressing room. At first the nickname was a bit of a joke. Ince was a cockney with a wicked sense of fun and he relished the title, but after a while it began to grate. 'It got heavy,' says Ferguson. 'I didn't like it and it wasn't always appreciated in the dressing room. Paul got a bit carried away.'

The Mark Hughes affair was less complicated. Months earlier Hughes had been on the verge of a transfer to Everton. He had been in negotiations with United over a new contract but the two sides were unable to agree. He wanted a longer contract than United were prepared to give him, so no contract was signed. Consequently, he was a free agent. A deal with Everton was put together. United were reluctant to let him go but understood that he wanted first-team football and that at his age he probably would not get another tempting offer. But then, with Hughes set to sign for the Merseyside club on the Monday, he was injured on the Saturday and the deal was put on ice. So too was Hughes' leg, with a lengthy lay-off predicted. Everton lost interest.

But the word was out that Hughes was available. During the close season Chelsea made an inquiry. Hughes was interested, a deal was set up, and he duly signed. It was very uncomplicated – and an Old Trafford legend was gone.

Ferguson had lost three special players. He had not wanted any of them to leave, but in football, just as in life, nothing is permanent. What's more, Eric Cantona was still sidelined, banned until the beginning of October. The manager now had the task of finding suitable replacements.

In Roy Keane United already had the obvious replacement for Ince. Keane had never played in that role with United, but he was accustomed to it at Forest and Ferguson reckoned he was well capable of adjusting to the job of running the midfield engine. You only had to look at him play to know that he was a ball winner. However, only time would tell if he was really up to the job. Hughes had been nearing the end of his career and his injury had already forced Ferguson into finding a replacement as the season wound to its conclusion.

There was no ready-made replacement for Kanchelskis, yet the answer to Ferguson's dilemma was staring him in the face. Ever since the 1950s Manchester United had been recognised as a conveyor belt of young talent. The famed Busby Babes had established a new dimension in English football. With their youthful exuberance, United had taken the Football League by storm. Other clubs copied their attitude, though never with the same success. Chelsea, under Tommy Docherty, successfully blooded a coterie of exciting youngsters, as did Crystal Palace, and even Huddersfield Town in the days of Bill Shankly. But United seemed to have a monopoly on the talent, though of course that was never true. The United philosophy had always been to give youth its fling.

However, during the late seventies and early eighties the famed school of learning was a shadow of what it had been. Times had changed, new managers had concentrated on buying ready-made stars rather than nurturing them through years of patient grooming. Youth systems did not always work, with maybe only one youngster in a hundred finally making it into the big time. Mark Hughes and Norman Whiteside were the exceptions, rather than the rule.

By the 1980s, it was strapped-for-cash Manchester City who were concentrating on youth. Their school of excellence had become renowned throughout the land, producing a crop of young players that included Tommy Caton, Clive Wilson, Ian Brightwell, Dave Bennett, Andy Hinchcliffe and Paul Lake. Their youngsters reached the FA Youth Cup final in 1979 and 1980, and in 1985 actually beat United in the final. At Old Trafford they did not even look on in envy; they had other priorities, which seemed to be in the upper end of the transfer market. The famed youth policy of earlier years had been all but discarded.

But under Alex Ferguson, and in particular Brian Kidd, all that had changed. By the 1990s it was United who were winning the FA Youth Cup. Giggs, Lee Martin, Darren Ferguson, Gary Walsh, Nicky Butt, Paul Scholes and others had all been given a chance in the first team. Others were now knocking on the door, and as the big kick-off for the start of the 1995–96 season drew nearer, Ferguson decided to see what they could do. Straight into the line-up came the Neville brothers, Nicky Butt, Paul Scholes, with David Beckham and John O'Kane coming on as substitutes – none of them yet 21. United journeyed to Aston Villa for the first game, but within 40 minutes they were three goals down. Ferguson's new youth policy looked to be in tatters. As the game progressed they temporarily recovered but by the end of the afternoon had lost 3–1 and looked a pale imitation of the previous season's side. On BBC Television's *Match of the Day* Alan Hansen was damning. 'You'll win nothing with kids,' he told viewers. They were words that would come back to haunt him.

Hansen may have been premature in his assessment, and Ferguson was quick to have a go at him, but that evening his words seemed to ring true. United had been a shambles – too many new faces, too many apprentices. Hansen was remembering his Anfield days, when new faces were blooded at the rate of one a season. The Liverpool style was to buy in at the lower end of the market where it was cheap rather than to gamble on a costly youth system which did not guarantee success.

The fact is that during those early Ferguson years Ryan Giggs was the only youngster to emerge with any lasting ability. Of the 1985–86 Youth Cup finalist side only two players were to make the grade into the first team – Gary Walsh and Lee Martin.

Even Ferguson would have to admit that the United youth system was not always successful. For every first-team player it produced there were another dozen who failed to make the grade. And even those who did enjoy a first-team outing rarely went on to success. Of his first flush given their chance, only Lee Sharpe lasted the distance. Both Mark Robins and Lee Martin soon moved on. Martin played

85 games, and assured himself a spot in United's history with the winning FA Cup goal against Crystal Palace, but then early in 1994 he became surplus to requirements and was shipped off to Celtic.

Robins, a graduate of the Lilleshall School of Excellence, looked to be United's goal-scoring solution when he scored prolifically in his early games but then after just 29 games and with first-team opportunities looking slim he moved to Norwich. Russell Beardsmore was another Babe itching to explode into the first team. After a promising start he featured regularly in the squad, more often than not as a substitute, making 38 appearances in all. Eventually he was given a free transfer, joining Bournemouth.

Ferguson recognised that the vital years were between 16 and 19. Lads had to be given a chance then. Ignore them until they had turned 20 and they might have lost interest and ambition, but play them once or twice and you kept their ambition burning. It was in those years that other interests might emerge to sidetrack them – drink, women, fashion, clubs and so forth. Long-term injuries also during those years could destroy a boy's enthusiasm for the game. It was not just a question of talent but of endeavour, determination and application.

There was the case of Gary Twynham, a young lad who, for one reason or another, simply lost interest in the game. He'd had an ankle injury and been out for a short while, but when he was fit again he decided that he'd had enough. He wanted to go off to college. Ferguson tried to dissuade him and even went to see his parents. They agreed with Ferguson, but the lad had made up his mind and he was not going to be shifted. He didn't enjoy playing any more. Maybe he had simply played too much football in his short life.

For Ferguson, the key in assessing a young player is how much that player wants the ball. Is he always running into space, demanding a pass, or does he occasionally hide, looking for a rest, letting others do the work? 'They always have to be looking for the ball, wanting it and wanting to use it,' he says. 'That's the key to knowing whether a youngster will turn into a good professional.'

It wasn't long before Alan Hansen was being forced to eat humble pie. After the Villa debacle United rolled up their sleeves and battled through their next five games, with notable wins over Blackburn and Everton. They didn't always look convincing and most supporters, including Ferguson, guessed that this was going to be a season of transition, of blooding the youngsters so that they could gain experience. But there were positive signs. Young Paul Scholes was in devastating form, hitting six goals as United surged up the table to challenge early leaders Newcastle. Scholes was typical of the United youngsters. Born in Salford, he had made just a handful of appearances the previous season but was now considered a part of the first-team squad. Also coming in were the Neville brothers, Philip and Gary, as well as the fresh-faced David Beckham.

If United were making steady progress in the Premiership, the same could not be said of Europe and the Coca-Cola Cup. In the latter United were humiliated in their opening game by lowly York City, who came to Old Trafford and pulled off one of the biggest shocks in the history of the competition by winning 3–0. It was barely believable. But with a second leg still to play United at least had the opportunity to make amends. They partly did, winning 3–1, but it wasn't quite enough and so they were out of one domestic competition.

In Europe they fared little better. In the opening round of the UEFA Cup they were drawn against Rotor Volgograd. In the first leg in Russia they pulled off a creditable goalless draw and returned to Manchester optimistic that they would see off their Russian opponents with little difficulty. But it turned out rather differently. With United forced to attack, Volgograd simply sat back and waited their moment before hitting United on the counter. But for a last-minute headed goal from Peter Schmeichel, United's long record of never being beaten at Old Trafford in a European competition might have gone. In the end it finished 2–2, with the Russians' away goals edging them into the next round.

Ferguson was fuming. Yet again United had been humbled in Europe. The UEFA Cup may not have carried the glamour of the Champions' League, but it was a stern enough test and United had failed. It was perhaps understandable with so many inexperienced youngsters thrown into the furnace of European football, but it was disappointing nonetheless. Had the game been played a few months later, United might well have won and gone through to the next round. Everything was arriving just a little too quickly for Fergie's Fledglings.

United's season really began on 1 October when Eric Cantona, having served his long suspension after assaulting a Crystal Palace supporter, returned to the fray. And the team he faced was none other than Liverpool. Within minutes Cantona had marked his return by setting up Nicky Butt for United's first goal. Then, with Liverpool taking the lead, it was Cantona late in the second half who grabbed the opportunity to take a penalty and give United a draw. The afternoon had belonged to one man, Eric Cantona. The sigh of relief from Ferguson and his colleagues was almost audible.

After their opening defeat at Villa, United did not lose again until early November when they went down 1–0 at Highbury against Arsenal. That was followed by a couple of wins and three successive draws. Then in December United lost two successive fixtures, at Liverpool and at Leeds. At Anfield they were beaten 2–0, and at Elland Road a week later they lost 3–1 with Cole scoring a rare goal. Given the level of opposition, Ferguson could hardly complain at the results. They were tricky games, both clubs dedicated to beating United at almost any cost.

What he could complain about was the form of Andy Cole. The £6 million player had never really settled. The application was there, even the determination, but the goals were distinctly absent. Cole was dropped, injured, then reappeared, but still the goals failed to come. At the beginning of the season Ferguson had told the press that 'Andy will definitely get us 30 goals next season.'

There was much that was praiseworthy about Cole's game. He had learnt to drop back, to make dummy runs and pull players out of defence, but there were others who could do much the same job at Old Trafford. Cole had been signed for his ability to score goals and although United were still winning without them, doubts remained.

Former manager Wilf McGuinness put it down to the burden of being at Old Trafford. 'It's a big club and sometimes players coming here cannot live with that. Often the youngsters who have been here all their lives find it easier.' There was something in that. The United youngsters never froze when it came to turning out for the first team. Being at Old Trafford was simply part of their everyday life. They knew no different. Like royalty, they had been born to rule.

Ferguson remained loyal to Cole, saying nothing publicly, but there were plenty of others quick to voice their criticism. Ferguson responded by telling the press that Cole was worth every penny of his fee and that if he had to do it again, he would. In fact, he insisted, he was worth at least twice what he had paid for him. It was some vote of confidence, but if he did have so much confidence in him, you wondered why Cole spent so much time on the substitutes' bench. It wouldn't get much better the following year, either, although that was partly because his season was to be disrupted by a serious leg injury.

The league chase had been dominated by Newcastle, but as spring drew on, Kevin Keegan's exciting side began to feel the pace and the gap narrowed. Liverpool, who had been hanging on, just a breath away from the chief contenders, also faded. In early April they had beaten Newcastle 4–3 at Anfield in one of the most exciting games of the season, which was to put paid to Newcastle's dreams. But then the following week Liverpool lost at Coventry and waved goodbye to their own hopes.

Newcastle's bottle had gone – just as United had lost theirs in Ferguson's early years. The strain, the focus of the press, the expectations of supporters all took their toll. Even Keegan was feeling it, and shortly before the season ended he launched into an amazing outburst against Ferguson. In a way it didn't come as a surprise to Ferguson. He could understand the pressures Keegan was under, he could even identify with them. But he also recognised that Keegan had cracked and that gave Ferguson a certain self-satisfaction. There was only going to be one winner after that.

The only hiccup came at Southampton as United came temporarily unstuck, losing 3–1 at the Dell. They had played the first half in their infamous grey away kit. They never seemed to do particularly well in the grey kit and with some of the players complaining that it was difficult to pick out their men, Ferguson decided to switch kits for the second half. After the game Ferguson laid the blame on the kit. 'We'll not be wearing it again,' he said. It was a neat deflection. Instead of the papers talking about United's poor performance the next morning, the tabloids were instead full of jibes about United's grey away kit. Ferguson had cleverly taken the spotlight off his youngsters.

In the end it was comparatively easy for United. They simply kept on accumulating the points, losing just one of their last 16 games. Thirteen of those matches were won. Like a highly primed thoroughbred, they had carefully steeled themselves until the final straight. Once ahead they would not be budged.

United won the title at Middlesbrough. And they did it

convincingly, winning 3–0. Back at the BBC's *Match of the Day* studios Alan Hansen shrugged his shoulders, sheepishly regretting ever mentioning Ferguson's youngsters. On the terraces the United fans took to wearing a new T-shirt. Emblazoned on the front were the words 'Kids never win anything'. Ferguson also didn't miss the opportunity of having a dig at the former Liverpool man.

However, if there was any team United did not want to face at Wembley it was their old rivals Liverpool. The Merseysiders had beaten them once that season and gone away from Old Trafford with a well-deserved draw. Indeed it was United who could consider themselves lucky to get anything out of that game. Liverpool could always be counted on to give everything in a battle with United. Yet at Wembley on a warm early May afternoon the one thing that was oddly missing from both sides was passion. Perhaps the trouble was that too much pride was at stake, with neither team wanting to lose. United might well have scored twice in the opening minutes as Cole skipped behind the Liverpool defenders, but nothing came of it. The Liverpool defence looked in tatters, but as the opportunities came and disappeared, Liverpool began to sort themselves out. In the end the game became bogged down in the midfield. When Liverpool had the ball United found it difficult to get it off them and equally once United had won it back Liverpool could not prise it away.

There were few other opportunities until the dying moments when Eric Cantona, just outside the penalty area, volleyed in a David James clearance that astonishingly missed a mass of bodies and screwed into the net. It was the only moment of excitement since the first five minutes. But it was enough for United to claim their second Double, something no other club had ever done. As the final whistle went Ferguson was off the bench like a bullet, making straight for the hero of the hour, Eric Cantona. Little wonder they hugged one another.

The Frenchman had fully repaid his debt of the previous season when his suspension had cost United so much. It wasn't just his Cup final goal; it was also the crucial goals that came on five occasions in the closing games of the season to earn United 13 points out of a total of 15. And now at Wembley Cantona had scored the only United goal yet again. Football might be a team game but occasionally one man stands out above all others. Ferguson could be grateful for that chance telephone conversation with Leeds United all those years ago.

CHAPTER TWENTY-FOUR

In Search of the Holy Grail

On a warm Wednesday evening in late April 1997 Alex Ferguson walked dejectedly towards the tunnel at Old Trafford, tears almost visible in his eyes. United had just been beaten 1–0 by Borussia Dortmund and were out of the European Cup. It had been their biggest game in 30 years, the moment Ferguson had lived for. United had faced only a one-goal deficit. Ferguson was convinced they could overturn it, as were most of the 55,000 packed into Old Trafford. But it was not to be.

Earlier in the evening Manchester had partied; fans swapped shirts outside the Town Hall in St Peter's Square, flags fluttered colourfully in the crowd at Old Trafford, the old songs were aired and new chants seemed to herald a famous night. But the game had barely kicked off when United were a goal down and needing three goals if they were to go through to the final in Munich. It looked impossible. Yet United still set about their task as if they could achieve it; chance after chance was created. Opportunities fell to Cantona and Cole but nobody could squeeze the ball beyond the Borussia keeper. At the final whistle United had lost a third home game in Europe that season and been beaten five times in all. They might have missed their chances but they hardly deserved to be in the final. As

Ferguson walked towards the tunnel he knew that his search for club football's greatest prize would have to begin all over again the following season.

At Old Trafford Ferguson was following in a grand tradition. For Matt Busby the Holy Grail of football was never the league championship; it was always Europe. Busby was the first British manager to realise the importance of the new trophy when it was inaugurated in 1955. When he heard about the suggestion for the competition he rubbed his hands with glee at the prospect of challenging with the best for the title of European champions. Along with the rest of the nation he'd watched the old gold of Wolverhampton Wanderers take on the likes of Honved, Red Banner and Moscow Dynamo during a series of floodlit friendlies at Molineux during the early fifties. Billy Wright and company had done English football proud. But although those matches had a natural competitive edge they were still essentially friendly games. The European Cup promised to be different. It was make or break, good old-fashioned cup football, but with a difference. Games would be played both at home and away with goals counting. The eventual victors would rightfully claim the title Champions of Europe.

Chelsea had topped the league that season and were invited to participate in the new tournament. But when they applied to the Football League for permission, the League, in one of its most egregious decisions, denied them the opportunity. Chelsea chairman Joe Mears was asked to reconsider 'in the best interests of the League competition'. Mears did and Chelsea withdrew. The Scots were not so reticent, encouraging Hibernian to enter. They did so and even reached the semi-finals, before losing to the French champions Rheims.

Busby was not going to be fobbed off as easily as Chelsea. When United won the title the following season he promptly encouraged the club to accept an invitation to play in the tournament. As expected the Football League applied pressure, but Busby's mind, and as it proved, his heart also, was set on Europe. By then Busby dominated Old Trafford. His word was law, the board merely rubber-stamping his demands. The Football League never stood a chance of persuading United to stand aside.

And so, in September 1956, United made the short hop across the Channel to Belgium to play RSC Anderlecht. United won 2–0, then in the second leg trounced the Belgian champions 10–0 in a memorable contest, though 'contest' is hardly the word to describe the events that night. By the end of the evening the Anderlecht manager was calling United 'the greatest side he had ever seen'.

United's excursions into Europe that season were to live in the memory. If there had been any doubters about the value of continental competition, United were to quickly dispel their anxieties. Borussia Dortmund were on the receiving end next, with more than 75,000 turning up to watch the first leg, played oddly enough at Maine Road. They might have hankered for European football at Old Trafford but someone forgot to think about erecting flood-lights. However, Maine Road proved a lucky hunting ground. They won 3–2 and then drew goalless in Germany.

Then, again at Maine Road, in the quarter-finals United came back from a 5–3 defeat in Bilbao to overwhelm the Spanish champions 3–0 in one of the most stirring European games ever witnessed on English soil. Another 70,000 watched. As if that wasn't enough, a total of 200,000 were to watch the semi-final confrontation between champions Real Madrid and United. By then Old Trafford had switched on its own floodlights.

Real had been the first European champions, a side stashed thick with gems such as the Argentinian striker Alfredo Di Stefano, Spanish winger Francisco Gento, another Argentinian Hector Rial and the Frenchman

Raymond Kopa, who had battled for Rheims against Real in the previous year's final, plus half a dozen others capped at international level. It was as glittering a side as English football had ever encountered. In an historic contest in Madrid's Bernabeu stadium United went down 3–1 in front of 135,000. There was no coming back from that deficit. United managed a draw at Old Trafford and went out 5–3 on aggregate. But a dream had been born.

Busby was learning all the time, absorbing the lessons of continental football. The next season his young side were again in the competition, sweeping all before them as they raced, once more, towards the semi-final. But then, returning from Belgrade, where a 3–3 draw with Red Star had put them into the last four, came the disaster at Munich. Busby's dream appeared to have died on the runway with so many of his players. In the semi-final, the team's mixture of desperately young players and a few older hands was no match against AC Milan. Despite a 2–1 win at Old Trafford, they went down 4–0 in Milan.

For ten years Busby's dream of being the first English club to crack Europe was forced to take a back seat as United concentrated on rebuilding and simply winning the league championship. Then in 1965 came their opportunity as United won the league championship and the following autumn set off on their European travels. In the quarter-finals they powered their way past Portuguese champions Benfica, beating them 5–1 in Lisbon, to set up a semi-final against Partizan Belgrade. It looked a mere formality but in Belgrade they went down 2–0 and were left with an impossible mountain to climb. Busby's dream had evaporated yet again.

Two seasons later however they were back, this time determined to fulfil Busby's ambition. And in Law, Best and Charlton, United boasted three players who could rank with any in the world. They did not let their manager down. In the semi-finals they took on Real Madrid, the side who had thwarted the Busby Babes' assault on the Cup ten years earlier. This time United were not to be outgunned as they narrowly edged past the undisputed masters of European football. Then on a balmy May evening, appropriately at Wembley, United faced Benfica in the final of the European Cup; and, even without the ebullient Denis Law, were more than a match for the Portuguese. The nation wept along with the rest of the United team at Busby's joy.

The following season, United were almost there again, storming through to the semi-finals to face AC Milan. It was their fifth appearance in the tournament and their fifth semi-final. But unlike the previous season it was to end in disappointment, with a 2–0 defeat in Italy proving too much to retrieve, even at a packed Old Trafford. And that was to be the end of United's flirtation with the European Cup. Of course there were other competitions. They regularly featured in the UEFA Cup but never progressed far, although they did reach the semi-finals in 1965 when it was known as the Inter-Cities Fairs Cup. They also featured in the European Cup-Winners' Cup, reaching yet another semi-final in 1984 when they lost to Juventus. But that was the sum of their success until Alex Ferguson arrived in 1986 and began the quest for the Holy Grail once more.

It was to be some years before he could put his methods to the test. In May 1985 39 football fans, most of them Italian, had been killed in a riot at the Heysel stadium, precipitated by Liverpool supporters. During the European Cup final between Liverpool and Juventus, Liverpool fans sharing the infamous sector Z with Juventus supporters had smashed through the flimsy barrier that separated them and had forced the Juventus fans to retreat across the terrace. In the crush at the far side a wall toppled and most of the fans were suffocated as they spilled over it. It was an horrific tragedy that brought shame on British football and in particular on Liverpool Football Club. Millions watched in horror as live television pictures were transmitted around the world. The result was a five-year ban on English football clubs participating in Europe. Alex Ferguson arrived at Old Trafford just one year into the ban.

The ban was eventually lifted in 1990, just as United clinched the FA Cup, making them eligible for the European Cup-Winners' Cup, the one European trophy Ferguson had already won with Aberdeen. In many ways the ban was of no great consequence to United. They would only have been eligible in one season, 1988–89, after having finished as runners-up in the league. That would have given them a shot at the UEFA Cup, but in other seasons they were way out of contention for any of the European places. Their FA Cup final victory over Crystal Palace was sweetness itself, allowing them a return to Europe and the Cup-Winners' Cup. Moreover, the focus of English clubs in Europe was almost totally on United, as league champions Liverpool were forced to sit out a further season.

Europe had become as much an obsession with Ferguson as it had with Busby. The Champions' Cup was now undoubtedly more difficult than it had ever been. For a start, there were more clubs participating. Sides had learnt the complex strategies of home and away legs, and there was far more travel involved, often to distant venues in eastern Europe, where the quality of sides was an unknown factor. Clubs had also become more tactically and technically aware, while the domestic programme was more pressured than ever.

Ferguson had built up his own leather-bound filofax of European experience. At Aberdeen he had lifted the Cup-Winners' Cup in a display that had the footballing establishment in Glasgow looking on in disdainful envy. The following season they had reached the semi-finals of the same competition and had beaten the European champions Hamburg to lift the Super Cup. Then in Ferguson's final season at Pittodrie they had reached the quarter-finals of the Champions' Cup. Ferguson had enjoyed eight seasons of uninterrupted European football at Aberdeen.

Yet deep down he knew that Aberdeen could never match the likes of Milan, Ajax or Liverpool. They might be capable of lifting one of the lesser European trophies, but they could never rival the grand European clubs whose resources, support and finance far exceeded the wildest ambitions of Aberdeen. Aberdeen was a homespun club and would always remain so. To win the European Cup in the eighties and nineties you had to be among football's elite. That was one reason why Ferguson headed for Old Trafford. United had the resources, the history, the stadium and the ambition to become one of Europe's great club sides again.

'Winning the Double again was obviously a massive achievement, but I don't think the team or the manager will get real appreciation until we've done well in Europe,' says Peter Schmeichel, adding that 'until we can be mentioned in the same breath as Real Madrid, Ajax and Milan I don't think he'll rest'. This sums up Ferguson's ambitions.

United kicked off the 1996–97 season with a cadre of new foreign names among their ranks. Although Ferguson had every confidence in his youngsters after they had won the Double, he feared not only that they might be overawed by a European adventure but also that they did not have the vast experience necessary to cope with the added pressure. More players with European credentials were needed. And so, to supplement his pack of hungry teenagers, a breathtaking coterie of international stars were recruited. The most exciting appeared to be Karel Poborsky, the Czech Republic international who had caught the eye during the European Championships. A terrifyingly pacey winger, Poborsky had been brought in to give some extra zest and width to the midfield. In the Czech Republic they called him the 'express train'. Poborsky, a £3.5 million buy from Slavia Prague, soon teamed up with another thrilling winger and one of the famous surnames in European football, Jordi Cruyff. The young Cruyff was a £1 million signing from the Spanish club Barcelona. Another arrival was the goalkeeper Van der Gouw, followed by the Norwegian defender Ronny Johnsen, signed from Besiktas for £1.2 million. But the man who would prove to be the most rewarding of all the new recruits was Ole Gunnar Solskjaer, a 23-year-old Norwegian from Molde signed for just £1.5 million. He would turn out to be the bargain of the season. With his boyish looks and fresh features Solskjaer appeared more suited to being the ball boy than a hardy goal-scoring centre forward. Yet his contribution throughout the season was second to none.

It was an expensive summer that must have left one or two of Fergie's Fledglings wondering if they really fitted into the manager's plans as they saw their positions being usurped by costly continentals. Months earlier they had been good enough to clinch the league and Cup Double. Now it seemed they were being discarded in favour of the new boys. Paul Scholes, for one, was briefly left out in the cold while out-of-favour Lee Sharpe was transferred to Leeds United for £4 million to help balance the books. By the beginning of the new season there had been a substantial turnover in the United staff as Ferguson planned his assault on Europe.

'I will always remain the hungriest person at Old Trafford,' said Ferguson. 'If I allow that to slip, then the club has no chance. That's why I won't get carried away by having won the Double for the second time. Sir Matt won the European Cup for Manchester United and it's an honour to be spoken about in the same breath as him, but we have a vast improvement to make if we are to achieve anything in this season's competition.'

United kicked off their programme in stirring form, slamming championship runners-up Newcastle United 4–0 at Wembley in the Charity Shield. Poborsky, Cruyff and

Johnsen marched straight into the line-up with the others sitting it out on the bench. United looked invincible and in their first league encounter reproduced much the same as they smashed three goals past Wimbledon. But then suspicions began to emerge. First they drew at Old Trafford with Everton, miraculously pulling two goals back after trailing 2–0 at half-time. Next they could only draw with Blackburn Rovers and Derby County. They had six points out of a possible twelve. Too many new players, too many differing styles seemed to be the problem. Ferguson could have done with a few more weeks of preparation.

As ever, the European games were upon him just weeks into the season. It didn't begin well. United could hardly have been set a more forbidding task – away to European champions Juventus. What's more, they made the trek to Italy minus the uncompromising Roy Keane, out injured. Juventus themselves bragged a plethora of new stars, and with only one competitive game behind them faced much the same problem as their opponents. But it was United with Cruyff, Poborsky and Johnsen in the starting line-up who looked more like strangers than the new-look Juventus. Ferguson had also opted to play Cantona up front with Poborsky and Cruyff wide. It was doomed to failure, with neither of the wide men capable of making any progress down the flanks. United soon fell a goal behind. At half-time Ferguson was forced to admit his tactical error and introduced Brian McClair at the expense of Ryan Giggs. Cantona dropped back and United began to find and hold the ball. But they were never in the same class as Juventus and in the end were lucky to escape with only a one-goal defeat. United's Frenchman had been outshone by Juve's collection of Frenchmen. Throughout the 90 minutes they had failed to create one clear-cut chance. It had not been a bright dawning, and although, equally, it had not been a disaster, it left United needing to win their next game – against Rapid Vienna at Old Trafford – if they were to have any prospect of qualifying for the quarter-finals.

Rapid Vienna were duly dispatched 2–0 in a performance brimming with confidence and invention. A few weeks later, in an impressive performance in Istanbul against Fenerbahce, United came away with a similar scoreline. In the opening 20 minutes it had looked as if there might be a very different outcome as the Turks carved holes in the United defence, but eventually they ran out of steam and United regathered their wits and gradually took control. Second-half goals from Beckham and Cantona gave them a 2–0 win. They looked to have booked their passage into the quarter-finals. It was Cantona's most convincing display yet in Europe, with United's overall performance silencing the critics.

Yet a fortnight later, with Ferguson supposedly celebrating his ten years at Old Trafford, United came disastrously unstuck against the Turkish champions at Old Trafford. It was United's first defeat in 40 years of European football at Old Trafford – records are made to be broken. United had failed to take their chances and by the end of the evening had lost their proud record, beaten 1–0, and seen their claims to progress impeded. Their defeat came on the back end of one of their poorest ever runs in the league, which had seen them concede five goals at Newcastle and then six the following week at Southampton. The jitters had well and truly set in.

The 5–0 defeat at St James's Park might have been rich retribution for Newcastle after their hammering in the Charity Shield but it was hardly deserved. The gulf between the two sides was never that colossal. All Ferguson could do was shrug his shoulders and hope that it was a one-off. But then a week later came a second calamity as United travelled to the south coast to face Graeme Souness's Southampton. They lost 6–3. Eleven goals had flashed past Schmeichel in a week.

Even though they had suffered their worst ever defeats

under Ferguson, they had not played so poorly. Newcastle's 5–0 win flattered the north-east side, while at the Dell they had managed three in a fight back and might have had more. All the luck had gone Southampton's way that day. Then again, they should never have lost against Fenerbahce. Schmeichel had been caught off his line with a scooped shot from outside the area while United had rattled the post and created enough opportunities to have won the match convincingly. But that is the way luck is. Sometimes it works in your favour; at other times it is a cruel companion. United's fortunes were sure to change and there were enough good players at Old Trafford to make sure that they did.

Ferguson had had his say with the United players immediately after the Southampton match, blasting them for their lack of concentration at the back. Publicly he suggested that United had been desperately unlucky. They had lost Pallister early on with an injury, Butt also had been injured and Keane had been sent off. For much of the match they had played with ten men and a changing formation. They had still scored three goals and made a match of it. Although they had leaked six goals, he did not feel unduly concerned. On other occasions they would play worse and win.

The papers had a field day. Words such as 'humiliated', 'farce', 'tired and tetchy' jumped out from the back pages. 'Eleven goals conceded in two Premiership matches provides a clear message of decline in England's dominant footballing force,' wrote the *Guardian*. A week later United entertained Chelsea at Old Trafford, expecting to put the record straight. In a performance that suggested their minds were elsewhere they lost 2–1. Three consecutive defeats. Now there was genuine talk of crisis. Ferguson had faced bleaker times at Old Trafford. Back in the winter months of 1989 his very future had been in doubt. There was no question of that this time, even though the bookmakers had been up to some nonsense by slashing the odds on his still being at the helm come the end of the season. There was never any prospect of that. But there was undoubtedly a problem to be resolved, and what it really boiled down to was injuries. Roy Keane, the stoker in United's engine room, had missed games through injury as well as suspension. Gary Pallister was also far from full fitness and in the end would be admitted to hospital for a cartilage operation. Giggs was injured too, and would be in and out of the side all season. The new imports also had not bedded in well. Poborsky was starting to produce the occasional electrifying run but Jordi Cruyff was still struggling to find a role. Of the other new signings, only the Norwegians looked the part. In particular Ole Gunnar Solskjaer was proving a genuine threat up front, while his compatriot Ronny Johnsen had also settled well into the heart of the United defence. As the going became tougher and the pressure increased, Steve Bruce's calming presence was being missed after his departure at the end of the previous season.

There was a more worrying problem. Eric Cantona was going through his leanest spell yet at Old Trafford, a shadow of the player who had brought so much pomp to the club with his immaculate displays towards the end of the previous season. He seemed out of sorts, a little overweight, and showing none of the instinctive positioning of old. For much of the season Cantona's sparkle would be absent. He seemed tired, at times almost uninterested.

On occasion Ferguson also seemed tired, especially with the press. Throughout the campaign his old paranoia would surface time and again. In October, after their two heavy defeats, Ferguson obligingly faced the press to discuss United's impending European clash with Fenerbahce. He was in no mood to talk about domestic affairs, his only interest was Europe. The press, not unnaturally, were more concerned with the Premiership than the mere formality of defeating the Turkish champions. Ferguson immediately reacted angrily and began to man the barricades.

'Is it a relief to get the show back on the road after the last two games?' asked one journalist innocently.

'Why are you talking about that?' rapped Ferguson. 'Why do you think that should be on my agenda?'

'Do you put it down as an aberration?' asked someone else.

'I'm not discussing it. Why should I?' the United manager replied.

Someone tried a different tack. 'Alex, you've obviously dismissed the last few results. Do you think it will be preying on your players' minds at all or are they just as . . .'

Before he could finish his sentence, Ferguson descended like a ton of bricks. 'Let me stop you there right now. I'm not discussing anything that has happened before. Right? You've heard me saying that twice. It's not on my agenda. You can talk about it – you'll do plenty of talking about it – I don't see why I should.'

Ferguson is just as adept at staging a rage as he is at genuinely throwing one. In this instance it may simply have been staged, but it did ruffle a few feathers and make everyone feel uncomfortable.

Ferguson had planned a comfortable passage into the quarter-finals of the Champions' League so that they could concentrate on the domestic game. Instead United faced the prospect of needing vital points from the visit of Juventus and a tricky away game in Vienna. They were still in second place in their European league but the Turks were now breathing down their necks. Suddenly United's dreams of Europe were evaporating. It was far from ideal.

The next European visitors were Juventus. This was the test of progress. Just how much had United learned? Not too much, it seemed at first, as Juventus strode into an early lead through Alessandro Del Piero. But as the game wore on United began to reshape and re-emerge. In the second half they were undoubtedly the better side as they repeatedly put the Italians under intense pressure. Keane, forced into an emergency centre back role, was a marvel, while Ryan Giggs, picking up the ball with uncommon frequency, was creating havoc with his diagonal runs. Time and again United came close, with Cantona burning the paintwork with a rising drive in the last few minutes, but the goal failed to materialise and United had lost a second European game at Old Trafford.

A place in the quarter-finals was now in the balance. No matter how well United did in their final game in Austria against Rapid Vienna, their destiny was no longer in their hands – it was also a question of whether Fenerbahce could beat Juventus in Turin. It was Giggs who set the pace as he ran at the ragged Rapid defence before passing to Cantona, who returned the ball for the Welsh international to pick his spot. Beckham laid on the second for Cantona. Juventus meanwhile defeated the Turks.

United were through to the quarter-finals where they faced the much-fancied Porto. The Portuguese side had won five and drawn one of their six matches, compared to United who had lost three. They had even beaten Milan in Milan. For once United started as underdogs. But on a night that was high on adrenaline and oozing with Old Trafford excitement, United took the Portuguese champions apart. The papers called it one of their greatest ever performances. Somehow they always seemed to do particularly well against Portuguese sides. They rattled in four goals and could well have had more, but their emphatic victory possibly camouflaged the fact that Porto were nowhere near as clinical as their earlier form had suggested. They were going through a bad patch, having recently lost ground in their domestic championship, beaten at home for the first time in years. At Old Trafford they looked slow, vulnerable and lacking up front. United simply overran them. Their

330

four goals were more than enough to take them through to the semi-finals.

In Portugal a fortnight later they drew 0–0 without ever playing above themselves and were into the semi-finals where they faced the German champions Borussia Dortmund. From having limped home from Turin, United were now into the last four of the competition. Their European learning curve had been taking an upward turn since November and against the Germans they looked impressive enough to at least have earned a draw. But it wasn't the best of performances, chances were missed and what luck that was on offer went to Dortmund who sneaked a vital goal as Tretschok's 74th-minute shot took a mean deflection off Pallister. But it was only one goal and Ferguson insisted that his players could perform far better than they had in Dortmund. If the Old Trafford crowd got behind them, they could pull it back, he told the papers.

Old Trafford was buzzing in anticipation: 'This is the most important game in decades,' Ferguson told them. The fans responded. The well-worn banners flew again, the songs echoed around the ground and everyone waited in nervous expectation of a famous United victory. But the two sides had barely shaken off their pre-match nerves when Dortmund struck with an eighth-minute goal that left United with an almost impossible task. Their plans lay in tatters. And yet they still managed to muster enough character to create a flood of chances to defeat the Germans. But bad luck and bad finishing denied them. United had lost their fifth game in Europe that season, each by a single goal. Old Trafford was the theatre of broken dreams.

From the start of the 1996–97 season none of the big clubs seemed able to set the pace. It had been Wimbledon who had seemed the most resourceful, though it was inevitable that come the season's climax they would run out of steam. Newcastle had started well but immediately after

Christmas manager Kevin Keegan resigned as they slipped yet again. Arsenal, after a shaky start, did not begin to look championship material until after the New Year. It was really left to United and Liverpool, but neither club seemed to have the key to breaking away.

After losing to Newcastle, Southampton and Chelsea, United's autumnal blues had barely improved. They had also been knocked out of the Coca-Cola Cup at Leicester. In a nine-game spell in October and November they had lost six fixtures and managed only two wins.

Over the winter things improved and they had a spirited run. By early spring they had leapfrogged Liverpool and Arsenal to take over at the top of the table. But if United were making giant strides in the league, there would be no Double for them this season. In the FA Cup they eventually came unstuck in the fourth round when they were drawn at home to Wimbledon. With the south London side also challenging at the top of the Premiership it was always going to be a difficult tie, but at least United had home advantage. All looked to be going to plan with United a goal ahead, until the Dons fired a dramatic equaliser in the last minute of the game. Suddenly the odds were stacking up against United, and although they entertained Wimbledon for a Premiership game a few days later that they would win, taking them to the top of the table, the trip to Selhurst Park proved to be too much of an ordeal. Wimbledon won 1–0 and any dream of the Double was gone. It was United's first defeat in the FA Cup outside of Wembley in four years. It had been a remarkable Cup run – one of the finest in the history of the competition – which had taken them to three finals and brought them two FA Cups.

Back in the league United's progress continued un-impeded. Despite the occasional hiccup, they climbed steadily to the top. They thrashed Sunderland 5–0 just before Christmas and the following week put four past

Nottingham Forest, and then began their run-in with a crucial 2–1 win at Highbury.

It could hardly have been better stage-managed: United versus Liverpool in an end-of-season title-decider. On a chilly Saturday morning at Anfield, with the sea breezes whipping in off the Mersey, England's two most successful sides met to contest the Premiership title. It was a game Liverpool simply had to win if they were to stay in the race, although United, with a game in hand, could just about afford to lose. For much of the season the fight for the title had been between them, with Arsenal and Newcastle always lurking in the background. Yet time and again as United slipped in the race, Liverpool had failed to take advantage. On at least six occasions United had handed their rivals the opportunity either to climb over them or to put some space between themselves and their rivals, but on each occasion Liverpool had blown their chance. They seemed to lack the edge that Ferguson had so astutely cultivated in United.

United shot into the lead, with Gary Pallister sneaking into the area to rise above everyone and power home a corner. John Barnes soon equalised at the other end, but it wasn't long before United were ahead again, with an identical goal from Pallister. In the second half Andy Cole scrambled in a third after David James had pathetically fumbled at the ball. United were home and dry without hardly breaking sweat.

Despite all the pre-match hype and tension on that April Saturday morning, it could hardly have been easier. The passion usually reserved for these intense occasions simply didn't seem to be there. Ferguson could scarcely believe it. Had United ever confronted such a lacklustre Liverpool? he wondered after the game. It had been much the same at Wembley in the Cup final the previous year, but here they were at Anfield, and the commitment was still lacking. It had all been too easy.

It was the moment that all the old paranoia about Liverpool was swept away. Finally, they had clambered over the psychological barrier they had faced for so many years. The old enemy had been supplanted. What had once been United's problem was now Liverpool's.

'Fergie, Fergie, give us a wave,' sang the United supporters packed into the Anfield Road end. Ferguson looked towards them and punched a fist into the air. Like them, he knew it was all over. United were going to win the championship.

Of the new signings it was Solskjaer who was proving the most effective. Jordi Cruyff was a disappointment, making only a handful of appearances. Poborsky looked a brighter prospect but again failed to establish himself as a first-team regular. Solskjaer, on the other hand, was always available, eventually scoring 18 league goals in 33 appearances. Time and again he found the net at crucial moments. But perhaps the most thrilling of all the United stars was David Beckham, another product of the club's youth system. Although he had played in previous seasons, the 1996–97 campaign saw him blossoming as a major star at Old Trafford, with all the hallmarks of a young Bobby Charlton. By the end of the season he had not only gained a championship medal, but had also collected England caps and the PFA's Young Player of the Year award.

There were a few more stumbles on the way. Against Leicester, with just three games remaining, United briefly came unstuck. Within 20 minutes Leicester were two goals ahead. United had missed opportunities themselves, but then on the stroke of half-time, just as Leicester rattled the bar at one end and almost went three ahead, United promptly soared downfield and made it 2–1. A few minutes on the other side of the interval Solskjaer added his second to give United a draw. And it was the boyish Norwegian who saved United's skin a few days later as they faced Middlesbrough in the savage rain at Old Trafford. At one stage United were 2–0 behind, then 3–1 adrift, but Solskjaer struck to eventually earn them a draw. The significance of their win over Liverpool began to take on monumental proportions. United were four points ahead with two to play. But when Liverpool travelled to Wimbledon and lost on the same evening as Newcastle could only manage a draw at West Ham, the race was over. United were champions for the fourth time in five years without having kicked a ball. Ferguson had not even watched the game on television. 'Why put yourself through so much torment?' he asked. Instead he enjoyed a quiet glass of champagne at the home of one of the directors. It was the Fergie way.

Ferguson has brought his Red Army at Old Trafford a bundle of honours – four championships, two FA Cups, two Doubles, the European Cup-Winners' Cup and the League Cup. And, but for a handful of goals, we would be talking five championships and a third Double. Add to that his honours north of the border and you are talking about one of the most successful managers ever in the British game.

It had been a strange season. During the late summer there had even been a few doubts about Ferguson's own future at Old Trafford. The idea of retirement had first been mooted by Martin Edwards shortly after Ferguson's first championship with United. Edwards mused aloud that Ferguson might want to retire at 55. At the time he was 51 years old and nothing was further from his thoughts. Edwards almost certainly intended nothing by his innocent inquiry but it took Ferguson aback. He'd never considered retirement, but the suggestion set his mind working overtime.

'It's amazing how that casual comment created an agenda,' he told Peter Ball of *The Times*. 'All of a sudden, from feeling a fit 50-year-old, people are suddenly pigeon-holing you as if you are about to fall off your perch.' Ferguson began to reflect on his future. Fifty-five wasn't that long off. At best he had only three or four years ahead of him at Old Trafford. From the comparative security of having won the league, he was plunged into uncertainty and insecurity. 'Maybe they want me to move on,' he thought. If Edwards had realised the impact of his innocent question, he would no doubt have curbed his tongue. But what was said was said, and it didn't help when Ferguson came to renegotiate his contract in the summer of 1996.

For all his successes, Ferguson had never been the best-paid manager in the land, but it had never worried him unduly. Winning trophies was far more important than money in the bank. But with United now a limited company and a business that had to be run in a commercial and professional manner, it seemed the time to make a stand and demand a salary that truly reflected his position within the game. In effect Ferguson held all the cards. United could not afford to let him go and they could well afford to improve his salary. If he was to retire at 55, then he knew that this could be his final contract. It was his last chance. Yet when it came to negotiating the new contract there was a surprising reluctance to reflect his success with an improved pay packet.

'We had come to a deadlock between what I felt I was worth and what they felt I was worth,' Ferguson later told *The Times*. The talks dragged on.

Ferguson had not anticipated any hitches, yet here they were, haggling over money. His pay was well behind that of the players, particularly Eric Cantona. It seemed illogical that the club would pay almost any amount of money to guarantee the Frenchman's presence at Old Trafford but would hesitate over much smaller amounts of money when it came to the manager. Ferguson had always done his utmost to guarantee that his players were as well paid as any in the Premiership but had neglected to look after his own prospects. It was time to dig in his heels. But it was a risk. 'At that point you say to yourself, if they don't think you're worth what you want, you may have to leave . . . You don't want to, but because it's your last contract, you've got to make sure you're paid what you're worth.' It was the old shop steward resurfacing in Ferguson. 'My determination to make sure I was level with the players and other managers was important.'

The battle lines were drawn. Then the news of a deadlock filtered through to the papers. It was Ferguson's ace. It didn't look good for United to be seen to be quibbling with their manager over a few thousand pounds. The richest club in the country, the most successful in the Premiership, and here they were risking the chance of losing their manager. The fans were soon asking questions. If United weren't prepared to pay his asking salary, there was certainly more than one club in Britain ready to meet it – and that was to say nothing of half a dozen clubs on the continent who would have cherished his presence, and probably doubled his salary in the process. United quickly settled before any chairmen had the chance to reach for their phones. Ferguson was tied to them until he was 60. Everyone heaved a sigh of relief, but United had probably come closer to losing Ferguson than ever before.

And so United celebrated in fitting style with West Ham United as the visitors to Old Trafford. They could have partied at the previous home match but the authorities – or the television companies – had decided that it had to be the final game, being transmitted live, of course. Captain Cantona was handed the monumental Premiership trophy – yet again – and the team performed another lap of honour.

At the time nobody, maybe even Cantona himself, knew that this would be the Frenchman's farewell performance. Precisely one week later Alex Ferguson and Martin Edwards announced to an astonished press gathered at Old Trafford that Eric Cantona had retired. At 30 years of age he had played his final game for United and was no longer a part of the Old Trafford set-up. He wasn't even there that afternoon. He had gone off on holiday and wouldn't be seen around Manchester any more. That was it – he was gone, before you could even say 'Ooh-ahh-Cantona'.

It was a sad moment for Ferguson and everyone associated with United. Cantona had brought undoubted success to the club, even though he might have brought one or two problems in the process. Ferguson now had the difficulty of finding a replacement, though finding anyone with the mystique, popularity and marketing potential of a Cantona was almost an impossible task. In the end, he turned to Teddy Sheringham, signing him from Spurs for £3.5 million. Sheringham had established a great reputation as a deep-lying forward, a similar role to the departed Frenchman.

Twelve months earlier Cantona had been instrumental in United's league and Cup double, scoring crucial goals at crucial moments. Ferguson couldn't help but reflect that a year is a long time in football.

CHAPTER TWENTY-FIVE

Life Without Eric

Never count your chickens. Not that Alex Ferguson ever would, but long before the clocks went forward he must have reckoned the league title was sewn up for a third successive year. By late February United were streets ahead of the rest of the field when it came to points in the bag and quality on the field. It looked a foregone conclusion. What's more, with United comfortably easing themselves into the quarter-finals of the Champions' League, Ferguson must have fancied his chances in that competition as well. United had played with such overwhelming style during the early part of the season that few gave anyone a chance of catching them in the league. The eventual champions Arsenal trailed them by 11 points. The bookies had stopped taking bets and had already installed United as favourites to inherit Borussia Dortmund's crown as European champions. But, as Jimmy Greaves once famously remarked, 'It's a funny old game.'

Life without Eric had not been anywhere near as onerous as everyone had anticipated. New signing Teddy Sheringham had slipped into the Frenchman's boots with consummate ease and although Roy Keane was absent with a long-term injury, United's youngsters seemed to be growing ever more confident with age and experience. But as the season wore on and Sheringham's ageing legs tired, so Cantona's influence, or lack of it, began to tell. Eric wasn't just a footballing genius, he was also United's talisman. Everywhere he'd been in England he'd brought success. He'd won a title in his first season at Leeds and then the following year had broken Old Trafford's 26-year drought of championship honours. And, before he shocked everyone with his surprise departure, he'd helped United to a further three titles and a couple of FA Cups. He'd even notched that delightful winner at Wembley to clinch a unique second Double.

His leaving had come as a shock, too soon to set in motion the job of unearthing a worthy successor. It was a case of finding an immediate replacement and that meant dipping expensively into the transfer market. Sheringham was hardly the obvious choice and even after Cantona's departure few would have linked his name with United. Liverpool were rumoured to be in for him but were balking at the asking price of £5 million. Even Ferguson, despite the vast fortune at his disposal, hesitated at spending that much on a man of 31. But when he made an initial inquiry he discovered that Sheringham was desperate to come to Old Trafford, so desperate that Tottenham were prepared to drop their fee to around £3.5 million.

Sheringham wanted silverware, not money. It was worth a try. Jürgen Klinsmann had once claimed that the Spurs man was the best partner he'd ever had. What United needed was a man to play alongside Andy Cole or Ole Gunnar Solskjaer, a goalmaker rather than a goalscorer. Sheringham may not have been in the same class as Cantona but he'd scored plenty of goals in his career – one in every other game at Spurs – as well as assisting some of the game's best. At £3.5 million Sheringham might turn out to be the bargain of the year.

United's season had begun so well. Cole was finally firing on all cylinders, netting 16 goals by Christmas. Giggs was back to his best, reproducing those darting diagonal runs that wreaked so much havoc, Sheringham was also performing with boyish enthusiasm while Beckham was ready to shoot at any opportunity. The only disappointment was the injury to Roy Keane which ruled him out for the entire campaign. But at first, even his absence was hardly felt.

United kicked off the season at Sheringham's old stomping ground, White Hart Lane, where they notched up their first victory. They went on to win five of their opening six fixtures, drawing the other, and leapt straight to the top of the table. They did not lose until their ninth league fixture, when Leeds United got the better of them at Elland Road. A month later they slammed seven goals past Barnsley and followed that with another six at Old Trafford against Sheffield Wednesday. Cole was on the rampage, scoring five in those two games alone and then a hat trick days later against Feyenoord. Then in November came a repeat of the previous season's scoreline at Anfield, as United saw off their closest rivals 3–1. They looked invincible and by Christmas were outstripping the rest of the field, playing some of the most delightful football seen by an English club since the days when Liverpool ruled. United had absorbed the lessons of Europe, seemingly able to slip up a gear at will or similarly drop a gear once they had control.

It was pretty much the same in Europe. After the crushing disappointments of the previous season when Borussia Dortmund had destroyed their European dreams at the penultimate hurdle, Ferguson was even more determined to find European gold. They began their European crusade in Slovakia where they clinically disposed of FC Kosice. Then came the plum tie with the visit of Italian champions Juventus to Old Trafford. It was United's chance to avenge the previous season's disasters against the Italians. But with only one minute gone Juve were a goal ahead when Alessandro del Piero slipped the offside trap. By half time

United had pulled one back but then in the second half the match turned on the dismissal of Frenchman Didier Deschamps. Within two minutes Scholes had put United in front. Then in the final seconds Giggs dashing down the left announced his return to top form with a third United goal.

Next in line were Feyenoord and, although the Dutch side were hardly rated, United struggled to take advantage of their apparent superiority at Old Trafford. Scholes again opened the scoring in the first half but a second goal did not come until well after half time when Sheringham was brought down in the area. Irwin comfortably converted the penalty. In the return leg it was Andy Cole who almost single-handedly destroyed the Dutch side with a thrilling hat trick that virtually secured United a place in the quarter-finals. It was a comforting feeling for Ferguson to know that United had almost completed the first part of their mission. Meanwhile they were half a dozen points ahead of the pack in the Premiership. Three more goals against Kosice at Old Trafford, their fifth consecutive European win, and United had booked their spot – the only side in the entire Champions' League with a 100 per cent record.

All that remained was a trip to Turin to face Juventus, whose qualification for the quarter-finals depended on their beating United. United ought to have maintained the momentum but it had slipped and they lost 1–0. It made no difference to United's European fortunes but it was sufficient to resurrect Juve's dismal start to their season. After that, the Italians never looked back. For United it marked a watershed; they were never able to regain the same momentum. But next in line for United were the French champions Monaco.

United were confident, so were their fans and, after a goalless draw in Monaco, they had every reason to believe that they would be into the semi-finals, just one step away from their ultimate goal. Ferguson seemed every bit as

certain as most people. All that had worried him was the
state of the pitch at the Stade Louis II. 'Too many teams
have gone to Monaco with attack in mind and suffered as a
consequence,' he had argued, convinced that, 'if we could
come out of the game in Monte Carlo unscathed then it
would give us a marvellous chance of completing the
mission at Old Trafford.'

But any neutral observer could spot that Monaco were a
highly technical side, well capable of turning the match at
Old Trafford. The slickness of their passing and the sharp-
ness of their attack were more than in evidence in Monte
Carlo. Tactics have changed since the days when United
last picked up the European Cup. In those days a draw
away from home was a good result. Then at home you could
concentrate on attacking. But as Liverpool had demonstrated in the 1980s, it was often easier to win away from
home, catching the opposition on the break as they pushed
forward. But in the 1990s, under the mini-league system
that ruled in the earlier stages of the European Cup, a draw
away from home was a point gained. Had United still been
in that league, then they could have been well satisfied. But
now they were into the knockout stages and that required
different tactics.

At Old Trafford, United surged forward and the gaps at
the back were there to be exploited. It took only five minutes
for Monaco's David Trezeguet to suss it out and suddenly
United were in a different game, needing two goals instead
of one. The more they went in search of those two goals, the
more vulnerable they became to a vicious counter-attack.
And so it was. United managed an equaliser but could not
find the vital second goal. In the end they were lucky not to
lose. Ferguson could point to the absence of four of his
stars – Keane, Schmeichel, Pallister and Giggs. But equally
Monaco had key players missing, especially in the first leg.
The dream was over for another year.

The FA Cup also proved a disappointment. Again it had

all begun so encouragingly with a glorious 5–3 thrashing of Chelsea at Stamford Bridge. At one stage United had led 5–0 but had then taken their foot off the pedal and almost came to a standstill, with Chelsea seizing the opportunity to pull three goals back. The next round brought another five goals as Walsall were summarily dumped out of the Cup. Ferguson's luck seemed to be in again as United were drawn at home to Barnsley, the side propping up the Premiership. Few doubted that United would slam another bagful of goals past them. But it rarely happens that way. Plucky Barnsley held United to a 1–1 draw and, as Ferguson later admitted, with a bit more luck the Yorkshire side might have finished the job off at Old Trafford. Instead they had it all to do again at Oakwell ten days later. Barnsley played well enough to end any United hopes of another Wembley appearance.

The writing was on the wall although few at the time spotted it. Instead, it seemed that United's dismissal might be a blessing in disguise, giving them the time and space to concentrate on the Premiership and the Champions' League. But it didn't work like that. United seemed to have lost the plot. They'd already been beaten twice in the league since the beginning of January. And after the Barnsley humiliation came further defeats, at Sheffield Wednesday and more importantly at home against Arsenal. March was a disaster with only one victory in the whole month. Slowly their lead was being whittled away. Liverpool always looked best placed to take advantage but typically, the Merseysiders seemed always to match United's hiccups just as they had the previous season. Instead it was Arsenal, so far behind at Christmas that everyone had written them off, who were gradually making up ground. Then in April came a couple of draws that were finally to rob United of the title. First Liverpool came to Old Trafford and even though the visitors were reduced to ten men following Michael Owen's dismissal, United failed to take advantage.

A week later Newcastle also comfortably held Ferguson's side to a draw at Old Trafford. Meanwhile Arsenal, against all the odds, just kept on winning.

And so United ended the season with only the Charity Shield, claimed back in the heat of August, to show for all their undoubted talent. None of the big prizes had come their way. It was back to normal; a case of no Cantona, no trophies. Arsenal had even gone on to complete the Double, beating Newcastle in the FA Cup final to match United's famous double Double achievement. But at least United had finished in the runners-up spot in the Premiership which allowed them another crack at the Champions' League. To have lost out on that really would have been a disaster for Ferguson.

But where to lay the blame? It would be easy to point to a catalogue of injuries. Most importantly, Roy Keane had been absent for almost the entire season. Giggs also had been out of action at crucial moments, as well as Schmeichel and Gary Pallister in the final weeks of the campaign. But then all teams have their injury problems. If anything, complacency seemed to have set in. Cole had stopped scoring, managing only five since the end of January, and Sheringham was coming in for some rough comments from the Old Trafford crowd. David Beckham had also lost his edge, at times seemingly more concerned with his star status, while Giggs had his problems as well. The Spice Boys tag was beginning to look more suited to United than to Liverpool. Perhaps the hunger for victory was not quite as sharp as it was at Highbury.

There was no denying that the season had left a few question marks. Cole had failed to maintain the momentum of the first half of the campaign when he was scoring with so much ease. Similarly, Sheringham had chipped in with ten goals before the New Year but after that had managed only four. United had simply stopped scoring goals between January and mid-April. There had been an apparent curious lack of drive. And although they had conceded fewer goals than any club in the Premiership, their defence at times looked vulnerable, particularly when caught on the counter-attack. Ferguson knew that the United style of throwing midfielders and wing backs into attack left them susceptible, particularly in Europe, where technically skilled forwards could take advantage. That was precisely what had let them down against Monaco. Improvements needed to be made in both areas.

Pallister was also getting old. In the summer of 1998 he reached the grand age of 33 and some of the pace of former years was slipping away. The moment looked right for him to leave United. Steve Bruce had moved on in 1996 and, although replacements had been bought in the shape of Henning Berg and Ronny Johnsen, neither yet had quite his presence or command. Ferguson had been trailing players throughout the season but nothing had come of any of his inquiries. Wherever he asked the 'Not for Sale' notice shot up. Even the United millions could not tempt. As Ferguson knew, there was no point in buying any player just for the sake of it; they had to be the right person. And so the search and the enquiries went on.

Back in 1988 United had hesitated at paying out £1 million for Gary Pallister. At the time it seemed an excessive amount of money for a defender. But a year later, United were reluctantly dipping even deeper into their pocket, lashing out £2.4 million for the Middlesbrough man. Now nine years on, with Pallister 33 years old, Ferguson was having to stump up almost five times that much to find a replacement. Such was the astonishing rate of inflation in European football. Who would have dreamed that defenders would one day command such fees? But there it was. Football was a marketplace and Ferguson was having to match others in the race for signatures. In hindsight Pallister looked a bargain.

The man finally given the task of stepping into Pallister's

size eleven boots was Jaap Stam, the PSV Eindhoven defender who cost United a world record fee for a defender of £10.75 million. A number of clubs, including Liverpool, had been tracking the Dutch international all season, but most had balked at the asking price. Ferguson held no such reservations. If that was the going rate, then so be it. United had the money, and the plc, once reluctant to release too much of their reserve, were now opening the treasure pot for rebuilding. It was Ferguson's to spend.

Before the summer was out he promised further recruits. United inquired about the Argentinian striker Batistuta but Fiorentina insisted that he was staying put and anyhow a host of Italian clubs were already at the front of the queue. He later put in a £5 million bid for Marc-Vivien Foe of Lens but the French club wanted £8 million, which was too high. By the end of the World Cup, the search was still going on.

For Ferguson there were personal successes. He signed a rumoured £1 million deal to write his autobiography, enlisting his old friend Hugh McIlvanney as ghost writer, while his horse Queensland Star romped home winner in the Lily Agnes Stakes at Chester. It was two wins out of two for the colt, setting up a day out at Royal Ascot. It seemed that everything under Ferguson's charge had the winning touch. Even his shares prospered as he discovered another clever way of making money. It was a different world to the shipyards and engineering factories that had shaped Ferguson's background and where money was at a premium. But Ferguson was beginning to get used to his new world. Govan and Remington's must have seemed a long time ago.

At 56 years of age, you began to wonder if Ferguson might soon think about calling it a day. The dark moods which once overwhelmed him, even at the very notion of defeat, are now gone. The moments, like in his early days at Old Trafford, when success seemed to elude him are long in the past. In place of those fearsome emotions is a more relaxed, jovial man. It's only at times, such as the defeat by Monaco, that he is once again plunged to the very depths of despair. He may have mellowed but he still remains ambitious. That one trophy still eludes him and one suspects that until it has taken its place in the cabinet alongside all the other silverware, he will not fully relax.

He's still capable of the odd bit of psychological warfare. At one point in the season Arsenal manager Arsène Wenger was his target. But this time he found a match. Wenger was not interested in his opinions. And at the end of the season there were plenty around north London ready to remind him that he had once asked what this man coming from a Japanese club could know about football.

Brian Kidd, as loyal as ever, remained at his side, learning all the time and becoming increasingly ready to take command. Perhaps one more season. The quest for European gold still haunts Ferguson but you can't help but think that if United do succeed in Europe, he might then stand down and hand over to his number two, maybe moving upstairs or to some other advisory role with the club. Similarly, if they fail, could Ferguson take another year of frustration and agony? Whichever, the next twelve months could be critical for Alex Ferguson.

CHAPTER TWENTY-SIX

Ahcumfigovin

On the wall of Alex Ferguson's office there is a simple framed sign. It reads: 'Ahcumfigovin'. For the uninitiated in the Glasgow vernacular, it means simply 'I come from Govan'. Alex Ferguson has never tried to hide his background nor ever been ashamed of it. On the contrary, he has always been proud of his roots, always the first to boast that he comes from Govan. 'I come from Govan first,' he insists, 'Glasgow second, and Scotland third.'

Even today, though he lives in one of the more wealthy Manchester suburbs, he regularly returns north, playing a not inconsiderable role in the Govan Initiative, a scheme aimed at regenerating an area of the city that has been almost decimated by the closure of its shipyards, factories and workshops. Over the years Ferguson has helped raise more than £150,000 for the restoration of Harmony Row, the Govan Football Club he once played for, the club that has bred so much footballing talent in the city.

The Initiative's chief executive Ron Culley calls Alex 'a man among men'. Over the years he's had many dealings with the United manager. 'He cares genuinely,' he says, 'and always phones to find out how things are.'

Ferguson's good deeds don't just extend to inner Glasgow. Every year United receive a stream of requests for charity games. 'Most are from genuinely good deserving causes,' says Ferguson, 'but obviously we can't send a team to all of them.' With a team full of multi-million-pound players, a tight schedule, daily pressure and the need for a large, fit squad, United, like most clubs, are reluctant to take on too many friendlies. Nevertheless, Ferguson has never turned down a genuine good cause. When the famous amateur club Bishop Auckland reminded United 38 years on that they still owed them the promise of a friendly game, Ferguson was quick to respond. Immediately after the Munich disaster, Bishop Auckland had loaned Warren Bradley, Derek Lewin and Bob Hardisty to United to help them out of their difficulty. The Bishops did not want anything in return but simply mentioned that someday United might like to come north and play them. It was a debt that was forgotten, until in 1996 the Bishops hit a financial crisis. Someone remembered the debt and called United. Ferguson was more than delighted to take a team north.

Charity matches, testimonials – Ferguson has an admirable record for supporting just causes. You'll see him down the YMCA in Manchester unveiling a plaque to the Busby Babes or visiting sick children in a hospital. But more often than not you'll spot him driving back north to Govan to lend a hand to some charity or other. 'He's a socialist and not just by name,' claims his old friend Jimmy Reid, the former trade union leader.

Ferguson's socialism is embedded in him. He is not some recent ideological convert to the cause. His Govan roots have dictated his politics from the year dot. In an interview in 1996 for *New Labour, New Britain*, the magazine of the Labour Party, he explained that 'I've got the same pals I grew up with. I've got the same attitudes I've always had. I'm a feet-on-the-ground type of person . . . a product of my background.'

Ferguson does not pretend to know the secret of his

success. But he has few doubts that his background and the lessons it provided has been a vital ingredient. Its influence was pervasive. 'I know deep down that it has got to be the naturally hard-working background I come from,' he told one journalist. 'I am proud and happy to say that I had wonderful parents who worked hard and passed on to me the value of that ethic. There was not a lot of money flying about in our home but my background was not poor, because you never considered yourself to be poor.'

Reid, the former leader of the Upper Clyde Shipbuilders shop stewards' committee, reckons Ferguson's trade union background was crucial. 'Trade unionism was an integral part of the community, and not just the working community. It could provide an enriching experience for a young person and provide them with so many important early lessons about the nature of labour. It was where his leadership qualities began to emerge,' he insists. 'That was where he learnt so many of his skills in man-management.'

Men like Ferguson will always regret the loss of a culture that was rich in its hospitality and experience. Football is the community at play, and Ferguson's understanding of the community is second to none. The thousands who once stood on the terraces each Saturday had a camaraderie of their own. They came from the same back-to-back terraced houses, walked through the same muddled streets each Saturday afternoon, squeezed into the same shoebox football stadiums in our towns and cities. And on the terraces they cheered shoulder to shoulder with their neighbours, friends and relatives. They had much in common: nine-to-five jobs in the shipyards, mills, pits and engineering factories; the same kind of holidays; the same consumer goods; the same limited ambitions. It was all about family.

Ferguson would identify with that concept of community. His generation will be the last to have known such societies. He understands their value and has taken on board the lessons they offer – loyalty, honesty, protection. His apparent paranoia about Glasgow football, Merseyside, the United haters, is simply about throwing up a wall between them and us, and inviting those on the inside to stick together. They detest us; we are a community; we must protect one another. That sense of community is absent from today's plush all-seater stadiums, but then it has also largely disappeared from today's world. The communities of old have been broken up, spilling on to new out-of-town housing estates. Traditional jobs have been replaced, either by unemployment or by short-term contracts and service industries. The mighty shipyards have all but disappeared, the pits been sealed, the heavy engineering for which Scotland was famed long gone.

Ferguson has never been afraid to flaunt his politics. He's Labour through and through, though as he emphasises 'not a party member'. But he'll write for the party's magazine and at the 1996 Labour Party conference he was more than happy to take a day off and join Tony Blair in Blackpool for a photo opportunity as the pair of them jollied with some local schoolchildren. It was no stunt for Ferguson – though of the two men, it was Ferguson who was more in demand for autographs. Manchester Withington's Labour MP Keith Bradley has also found him more than helpful when it came to doing the odd favour. 'He has always been interested in supporting Labour,' he says. 'Being associated with the party and its politics is clearly important to him.' During the miners' strike he was said to have donated money to the miners.

One reporter once had the temerity to suggest to him that, like Margaret Thatcher, he only needed a few hours' sleep. 'Don't compare me with *that* woman,' he retorted. Ferguson doesn't just talk Labour, he is Labour, though how much of it rubs off on his players is a matter of conjecture and no doubt a matter of concern to him as well. But all you can do is set an example.

Cliff Butler, editor of the Manchester United programme, recalls being on a trip to Glasgow with the team. 'We were on the team bus and as we went past the Fairfields shipyard, Ferguson pointed it out to the players, telling them that was where his father once worked. He then asked if any of them would like to go in and have a cup of tea in the yard's canteen.' His suggestion was greeted with little enthusiasm by the players. Only Cliff Butler fancied it. Ferguson shrugged his shoulders and the coach drove on. It was a different world to the youngsters, way beyond their understanding.

During the 1997 general election campaign that swept Tony Blair into Downing Street, Ferguson was spotted at Blair's side as he campaigned in Glasgow. He must also have been the first football manager to feature in a Labour Party manifesto. Football-loving Blair liked nothing better than having someone with Ferguson's credibility on board. The *Sunday Times* reported that he had also been 'giving some tips on staying ahead of the game' to Blair's press secretary Alastair Campbell. It was said that when Labour wobbled over privatisation Ferguson told Campbell that 'nobody gives a damn about this stuff. Keep going on the things that matter – jobs, schools, hospitals, crime.' More significantly, he was reckoned to have told Labour that 'teams work on mutual respect and loyalty. You can argue all you want in private, but you stick together in public.' Certainly you could hear him saying that. It was, after all, a fundamental tenet of Ferguson's religion that you stick together in adversity.

If in the week before the 1997 general election you had asked him which gift he would prefer – a Labour election victory or United winning the title – he might have had to think about it for a few moments.

There's a bit of the Bill Shankly about him: clinging to his roots, preaching socialism, decency and respect, a man who has captured the minds and hearts of the people. It's the old Protestant work ethic. Ferguson may lack the charisma and the street credibility of a Shankly, who lived all his Liverpool days in the same semi-detached house, always ready to make a cup of tea and have a natter with anyone who turned up on the doorstep. But in his own way, he has the same set of clean-cut values. If he isn't in the same league as a Busby, Stein or Shankly, he's certainly not far behind. Maybe it's not possible to make the comparison: football is different today, with its multi-million-pound transfers and open cheque books.

Busby, Shankly and Stein were the last of a tradition, men reared in the hardest of times, men whose backbone had been born out of poverty. As players they had never earned much more than the average working man and even as managers never received their just rewards. For men like them, money was never the priority. They had a job and they carried it out to the best of their abilities. Ferguson has many of their attributes.

There's something of the Stein in him. He has his bullishness, his temper, his self-belief and sense of urgency. The Big Man might have perfected his temper, ready to spring it on some unsuspecting soul – often a journalist, though he was just as likely to rage at players, linesmen and referees – yet at press conferences Stein could be as taciturn as anyone, one answer bringing a shroud of silence to proceedings. You trod carefully in Stein's company.

Ferguson also has elements of Busby about him. United is his family, Old Trafford his home, the players his sons, the staff his pals. Like Busby, he's obliging to the point of being overgenerous. Nor has he been afraid to put his trust in youth. He also boasts Busby's application to detail, his tactical awareness, and sense of vision. Today, Ferguson is as much the father figure at Old Trafford as Busby once was.

He shares the same passion for the game as these men, along with their honesty and discipline. And like them he too has bucked the religious fanaticism of the West of Scotland. 'He is one of the only men I've known who has transcended the Rangers–Celtic rivalry,' says Ron Culley. That in itself is a remarkable achievement in a city where football is sometimes influenced more by religion than by the usual criteria of quality or geography. Jimmy Reid backs that up: 'He's looked askance at religion. All that bigotry seems to have passed him by.'

Queen's Park director Malcolm Mackay, who has known Ferguson all his footballing career, remembers him as a totally honest lad even when he was 16 and had just joined the club. 'There was no bullshit about him,' he says, 'even in a slightly snobby club like Queen's Park.' At a time when under-the-table payments threatened to plunge the game into disrepute, not once was Ferguson's name linked with any questionable dealings. 'He's as clean as a pipsqueak,' says one insider. 'Nobody has ever had to keep a quiet eye on him and his dealings. We know he can be trusted.' That hasn't always been the case in the past at Old Trafford.

He is almost totally without ego, insists Ron Culley, chief executive of the Govan Initiative, 'and genuinely seems more proud of the attainments of his own family than his personal career'.

Busby, Stein, Shankly. Add to that list Alex Ferguson; men whose lives have been linked by football and shaped by adversity. 'There's no doubt that Alex is the natural successor to these men,' insists Govan-born Jimmy Reid, a lifelong friend of Ferguson's. 'They were all products of heavy engineering with a latent confidence in their own collective abilities. They gain that confidence in sheer numbers. They know that collectively they are strong. It's part of the trade union, socialist conviction where strength in numbers can overcome all adversity. They were men who have espoused the principles and benefits of collectivism.'

Busby, Stein and Shankly were members of a pre-war generation where money and ambition were limited. All three would doubtless have found the modern game an enigma. It was enough of a dilemma for them in the sixties. Someone once told Shankly of a First Division player who had a house with a tennis court. 'A tennis court!' he fumed. 'And the man hasnae even won an international cap!' Busby coped as well as any of them with the trappings of the emerging modern game, though even he had his problems with the wayward Best. They'd still all be winners, but would they enjoy their football as much?

Ferguson is not just the successor to these men, he is also the natural link, a bridge between the old values and the modern game. He may have moved on, but there is little doubting that his heart and his values remain in Govan. He still espouses all those traditions and principles. And if you analyse his style of management it is peppered with those same values – discipline, loyalty, hard work, compassion.

He doesn't always like what he sees at Old Trafford. Executive boxes, a megastore selling costly replica kits, swanky dining areas and the daily glance at the share price are not what Ferguson grew up on. This is not his brand of football. But he's big enough to accept that this is what the modern game is about. It's sink or swim, and he will always swim. Ferguson wants what is best for his club, his players and, above all, his supporters. If going down the avenue of big business is what is needed then he will encourage that. But it wasn't always so. Not so many years ago he called the Premier League 'a piece of nonsense'.

'The agreement with Sky,' he argued, 'sells supporters right down the river and hits hardest at the most vulnerable part of society, the old people. Pensioners and thousands of old people who can ill afford it must now buy a satellite dish to see top football on television ... Sky are putting a lot of money into football but it is the fans who are paying the price.' He'd probably regret those remarks today, slightly ashamed to be reminded of them, but at the time that was how he felt. Perhaps not everything in the Premiership has been so bad.

Dalglish, on the other hand, represents the modern game. He may have been raised in Govan but the shipyards that he could once see from his bedroom window soon became a distant blur. Unlike Ferguson, the former Celtic man never served his time in heavy engineering, never experienced life under the maximum wage. By the age of 26 Dalglish had left Scotland behind. He is at ease with the Premiership, its agents, sponsorship deals and commercial contracts. None of this is an anathema to him.

More than any club in the land, United generate a highly emotional response. You either love them or hate them. There is no in-between. It has been so for many years, though their glamorous aura and the sympathy that Munich generated used to contrast sharply with the dull, workaday football they produced. Before Ferguson, some of the sniping about United might have been justified. They hadn't won much silverware in two decades, while other, less glamorous clubs had collected more trophies than United could have dreamt of. In recent years attitudes have been hardened by United's phenomenal success. They have the most glamorous stars and the classiest stage on which to perform, with an army of well-wishers. It's little wonder they give rise to so much envy. And their manager's abrasiveness has only sharpened up the critics.

Yet Ferguson, with his breathtaking energy, has also set the record straight. In his eleven seasons at Old Trafford he has won four league titles, three FA Cups, two Doubles and the European Cup-Winners' Cup. United are no longer a big club with a debatable reputation. Today, they deserve to be envied. They've done it all. And mostly thanks to one man.

Football is Ferguson's community, and whichever club he belongs to is the focus of that community. As a community they'll pull together, fighting off hardship, pitting their wits against the opposition, and striving to protect one another. There's a distinct similarity with old-fashioned Labour and the best protectionist ideals of trade unionism. It's what unions were originally formed for, to protect their community. And it's also what communities like Govan, Salford and the Yorkshire mining villages built their spirit on. You could take the man out of Govan but you cannot take Govan out of the man.

Alex Ferguson

Born Glasgow, 31 December 1941

PLAYING CAREER
Queen's Park: Summer 1958 to summer 1960
St Johnstone: Summer 1960 to June 1964
Dunfermline: June 1964 to summer 1967
Rangers: Summer 1967 to October 1969
Falkirk: October 1969 to September 1973
Ayr United: September 1973 to July 1974

MANAGERIAL CAREER
East Stirlingshire: July 1974 to October 1974
St Mirren: October 1974 to summer 1978
Aberdeen: Summer 1978 to November 1986
Scotland: November 1985 to summer 1986
Manchester United: November 1986 to present

MANAGERIAL RECORD
St Mirren
1975–76	4th Scottish Division One
1976–77	1st Scottish Division One
1977–78	8th Scottish Premiership

Aberdeen

1978–79	4th Scottish Premiership/Runners-up Scottish League Cup
1979–80	1st Scottish Premiership/Runners-up Scottish League Cup
1980–81	2nd Scottish Premiership
1981–82	2nd Scottish Premiership/Scottish FA Cup winners
1982–83	3rd Scottish Premiership/Scottish FA Cup winners/European Cup-Winners' Cup winners
1983–84	1st Scottish Premiership/Scottish FA Cup winners
1984–85	1st Scottish Premiership
1985–86	4th Scottish Premiership/Scottish League Cup winners/Scottish FA Cup winners

Manchester United

1986–87	11th Division One
1987–88	2nd Division One
1988–89	11th Division One
1989–90	13th Division One/FA Cup winners
1990–91	6th Division One/European Cup-Winners' Cup winners/League Cup runners-up
1991–92	2nd Division One/League Cup winners/ European Super Cup winners
1992–93	1st Premiership/Manager of the Year
1993–94	1st Premiership/FA Cup winners/League Cup runners-up/Manager of the Year
1994–95	2nd Premiership/FA Cup runners-up
1995–96	1st Premiership/FA Cup winners/ Manager of the Year
1996–97	1st Premiership/Manager of the Year
1997–98	2nd Premiership

OTHER HONOURS
Scotland Schoolboy international, Scotland Youth international, Scotland amateur international, Scotland senior international
Freedom of the City of Glasgow
CBE
OBE

Index

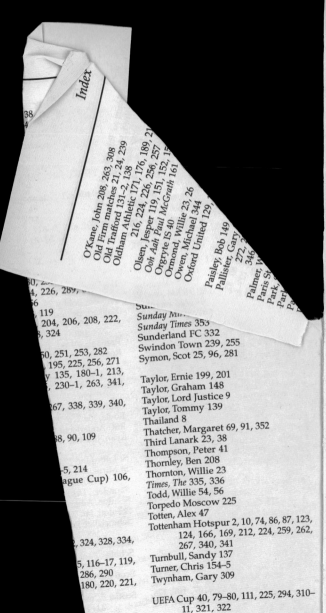

The Red Army Years
Manchester United in the 1970s

RICHARD KURT AND
CHRIS NICKEAS

'A sheer bloody joy' *Total Football*

The Red Army Years is an in-your-face, blood-and-guts look at Manchester United's most turbulent decade, written from the single most important viewpoint – that of the fans. It takes you back to the Old Trafford battlefield of the 1970s, as well as on to the pitch, into the stands and behind the scenes, and brings together for the first time all the ingredients of this 'golden age'.

- The football: from deathly atrociousness to historic brilliance and back again

- The personalities: Best, Docherty, Macari et al, with their myriad scandals, feuds and heroic deeds

- The Red Army: testimony of the veterans themselves, most of whom have never talked openly before

Raw and unvarnished, *The Red Army Years* is an indispensable guide to the beginnings of the modern United. It can be funny, brutal, sad and uplifting – just like United's sides in the 1970s.

'It works a treat. The narrative is lively and opinionated' *FourFourTwo*

NON-FICTION / SPORT 0 7472 5633 0

ATHERS
The Authorised Biography of
Michael Atherton

DAVID NORRIE

'A detailed and perceptive account of Atherton's life'
Michael Parkinson, *Daily Telegraph*

'The ups and downs of Atherton's career . . . make
fascinating reading' *Wisden Cricket Monthly*

Even before his Test debut in 1989, Michael Atherton
was being viewed as a future captain of England. His
natural ability, calm demeanour and knowledge of the
game marked him out as the man destined to take on
the toughest job in English sport.

Those predicting great things for him were quickly
proved right, but it has not always been a smooth ride.
There were ball-tampering allegations, reports of a rift
with the chairman of selectors, Ray Illingworth, and
the constant pressure of trying to succeed in the media
spotlight. Atherton – now England's longest-serving
captain – talks candidly about his role and explains
why, when everyone expected him to quit after
England's 1997 Ashes defeat, he decided to stay and
lead the tour to the West Indies.

NON-FICTION / BIOGRAPHY 0 7472 5446 X